A
PRIESTLY
PEOPLE

BAPTISMAL PRIESTHOOD
AND PRIESTLY MINISTRY

JEAN-PIERRE TORRELL, OP

Foreword by Msgr. Kevin W. Irwin

Paulist Press
New York / Mahwah, NJ

All unattributed translations of primary source texts are by Peter Heinegg.

Cover photo credit: Scala / Art Resource, Inc.
Cover design by Cynthia Dunne, www.bluefarmdesign.com
Book design by Lynn Else

Library of Congress Cataloging-in-Publication Data

Torrell, Jean-Pierre.
   [Peuple sacerdotal. English]
   A priestly people : baptismal priesthood and priestly ministry / Jean-Pierre Torrell, OP ; foreword by Msgr. Kevin W. Irwin ; [translated by Peter Heinegg].
   pages cm
   Includes bibliographical references (pages   )
   ISBN 978-0-8091-4815-8 (alk. paper)
   1. Priesthood—Catholic Church. 2. Pastoral theology—Catholic Church. 3. Priesthood, Universal. I. Title.
   BX1913.T6713 2013
   262'.142—dc23

                            2012042403

ISBN: 978-0-8091-4815-8 (Paperback)

Published by Paulist Press
997 Macarthur Boulevard
Mahwah, New Jersey 07430

www.paulistpress.com

Printed and bound in the
United States of America

CONTENTS

CONTENTS

Contents

PREFACE

Anyone who sets out to write on a given subject has to begin by obtaining documentation. Novelists dedicate months and sometimes more to reflecting and to collecting the material that they need to construct a believable story. Nobody finds this process surprising. I myself have spent years collecting the long bibliography I used in order to write this book. But at the last minute, just to complete the list of what I had already gathered, I thought of turning to the Internet and a well-known search engine to check whether I had missed anything recent. I was astounded. When I typed in "theology of the priesthood," I got 140,000 results in a fifth of a second. The most recent information had been put online an hour before. Even if this mass of work contained many repeats, it at least shows how interested a lot of people are in the topic. As always with this kind of research, you find things that are good and some not so good: from the last speech by the pope to the most subtle questions, from serious theological contributions to spiritual reflections on various levels, from high-quality exegetical and patristic research to pastoral considerations closer to everyday life....

Obviously I did not read it all, but I read enough to realize that my own contribution would not be useless. The most valuable studies among those just mentioned were most often too specialized to reach a very wide public. Others that were more broadly interesting were, despite their value, too short to support sustained reflection. I have tried to address these two points in this book, which aims both to profit from the most thorough research and to place it in the general context without which it cannot be entirely meaningful. This context obviously has to be a theology of the Church. But we must be clear about this. When my title says "a priestly people," I am not thinking of the ecclesiastical institutions or arrangements with which the Church is often confused, but of a fundamental fact linked to our Christian life, starting from baptism. Christian existence is once and for all an existence in the Church, where everyone is equal by the grace of baptism, and yet not everyone has the same role. My desire to fathom this basic truth is at the root of this book; and understanding what that truth means should be the main benefit to be derived from reading it.

To that end, the first thing we need to do is make the theological point about the two aspects of my subtitle: *baptismal priesthood* and *priestly ministry*. In fact, this subject has undergone an enormous renewal since the mid-twentieth century; but the really new contribution of the Second Vatican Council was accompanied by just as much radical questioning and misunderstanding. It is not easy to get a clear picture here, but we have to recall that it has often been that way in the history of the councils. Their teaching is, to be sure, the point of arrival of a previous movement, as well as the point of departure toward new horizons. But for all that, the councils do not abandon the basic truths that the Christian community has always lived by, and Vatican II is no exception. Paradoxically, by the way, what was most novel about it was also what was most traditional: its wish to hold on to both ends of the chain as to the sacrament of holy orders and its relationship with the priesthood of the baptized has turned out to be a potentially subversive topic—as is the way with the Gospel, of course, but nonetheless subversive with regard to all sorts of preconceived ideas. So it is no cause for wonder that people nostalgic for the old days were as much put off as those who thought there was nothing more here than a transition to a sort of modernity closer to the expectations of our time.

That is why the other objective of this book is to help readers situate themselves in the Church—whatever their place, as men or women, laypersons, married, unmarried, priests or nuns—with respect to what is being called the crisis of Christian identity and of the Catholic priesthood. Many causes have been assigned to this crisis that we are experiencing: psychological (loss of faith or appetite for altruistic service, but that does not affect only Catholics); sociological (the disappearance of Christian social structures and the dwindling prestige of the priesthood, but teachers and doctors have not fared much better); general questioning of authority; a cultural or civilizational crisis; and who knows what else.

All of that has surely played a part, but when it comes to the specific issue of the priesthood, there is another, rarely mentioned cause that may well be the deepest of all: the enhanced valuation of the priesthood of the faithful, which has led certain individuals to take themselves for what they were not, and which has undermined for many postconciliar priests the summary certitudes that they had been indoctrinated with as to the superiority of their state. Other causes linked to that one have completed the work of deconstruction. This particular crisis is in the process of being overcome, but we have already entered into a new crisis, and it is more than likely that it will not be the last. So it is urgent for all of us to get a clear view of things to affirm ourselves in our own identity—equally removed from extreme positions or even simply from the hardening and contracting that never fail to emerge in a time of difficulties. Hence, it is important to join the Council in holding on to two basic realities at once: baptismal priesthood and priestly ministry go together, and neither can be sacrificed for the sake of the other.

To honor these intentions and to answer the questions they imply, it is essential to return to the sources, both in the New Testament and the Fathers of the Church. We must never lose sight of the fact that such a return to the sources has always been the sine qua non for all real renewal in the Church of Christ. If there is one conviction that animates this book, that is it. Unsurprisingly, there will be many references to the New Testament and to the origins of the Church as a source of solutions for problems that may seem very remote from those of our epoch. In other words, what does the Scripture read in the Church teach us about the priestly quality of the people of God and the various manifestations of the priesthood? This return to the foundational doctrines of our faith, read as honestly as possible, is a necessary step if we want to move beyond a narrow theology. We have to rebuild, not just patch.

To conclude this Preface, I need to say a few things about my method of writing. This book was part of a theology course meant for future priests, for teachers of religious studies, and for catechists—for professionals, one might say. So there are traces here of the many different authors that I researched who could be pointed out explicitly, should the need arise, to a trained audience, which itself by definition might be called upon to transmit it to others in their turn. But I did not want to highlight that research now. Experts will recognize various influences here and there, and I readily confess my debt to them. Still, I prefer to avoid too many references and learned footnotes at the risk of needlessly frightening away well-intentioned readers who do not necessarily have the same sort of specialized interests. So my annotations will be limited to the bare minimum. I have opted for the simplest and sparest of styles for a direct and sometimes even didactic expository tone, in hopes that this pedagogical clarity will make reading the book easy rather than uncomfortable, and that educated Christians will find here what is right for them in order to make their faith deeper and more reflective.

* * *

It is my pleasant duty to thank Marie-Anne Compare, who computerized the first draft of this book—for which she deserves not a little credit—and Denise Bouthillier, who read the final draft of the manuscript. All my gratitude to both of them.

FOREWORD

Two texts are on my mind as I reflect on how best to introduce this important book. The first is from *The Roman Missal,* the First Preface for Sundays in Ordinary Time, based on the text from 1 Peter 2:9, in which we acclaim Christ as Lord and then pray:

> For through his Paschal Mystery,
> he accomplished the marvelous deed,
> by which he has freed us from the yoke of sin and death,
> summoning us to the glory of being now called
> a chosen race, a royal priesthood,
> a holy nation, a people for your own possession,
> to proclaim everywhere your mighty works,
> for you have called us out of darkness
> into your own wonderful light.

This text is remarkable for its succinct summary of what Christ did for us and for who we are as the baptized, his chosen ones, destined for holiness because he called us out of the darkness of sin into his unsurpassing light. Throughout this insightful and reflective book, Father Torrell continually puts into proper relationship who the baptized and ministerial priests are and are destined to be. He reminds us again and again that we together are ministers of what Christ has accomplished and that our baptism and ordination place demands on us to witness to who he is, to what he accomplished, and to who we are in and through him. This book is about how holy people live as holy people whose witness before the world is nothing less than life-giving for us and for those we serve. It is the ministry of ministers that matters, and ministers have their identity from Christ, the sole Mediator of salvation.

The second text on my mind is from the Dogmatic Constitution on the Church (*Lumen Gentium*) from the Second Vatican Council. In paragraph 10 it states:

> Though they differ from one another in essence and not only in degree, the common priesthood of the faithful and the ministerial or hierarchical priesthood are nonetheless interrelated: each of them in its own special way is a participation in the one priesthood of Christ. The ministerial priest, by the sacred power he enjoys, teaches and rules the priestly people; acting in the person of Christ, he makes present the Eucharistic sacrifice, and offers it to God in the name of all the people. But the faithful, in virtue of their royal priesthood, join in the offering of the Eucharist. They likewise exercise that priesthood in receiving the sacraments, in prayer and thanksgiving, in the witness of a holy life, and by self-denial and active charity.[1]

This text has been much debated and discussed for the way it lays out three priesthoods: that of Christ, of the baptized, and of the ordained. In trying to get this equation right, some have asked whether the baptized or the ordained are "higher" than the other. In point of fact, the late Cardinal Avery Dulles stated in *The Priestly Life* that, with regard to the teaching of Vatican II on the ordained priesthood, "If anything, the common priesthood is more exalted, for the ministers are ordained for the sake of service toward the whole people of God."[2] My own sense is that to ask which is "higher" than the other is to ask the wrong question. My reading of Father Torrell is that he also would like to avoid asking who is "higher" or "lower." Consistently, through this carefully reasoned book based on a judicious selection of and reflection on a wealth of Church sources, he will invite readers to reflect on the reality and meaning of their own priesthood, baptismal and ministerial, with profound respect for the other. Father Torrell consistently amasses data, synthesizes it, and offers new ways of reflecting on what are monuments of the Catholic theological and magisterial tradition.

This is a book of insight and integration. Its note references are comparatively few for a work of its breadth. The continued use of key sources within the text invites readers to research and reflect on the original sources themselves and to appropriate them in an integrated and integral way. Father Torrell's wise use of these rich sources reflects his own immersion in and devotion to them. At a time when even theology is not immune to politicization and ideology, Father Torrell provides a roadmap that avoids any characterization or a priori critiquing or reprimand. Quite the contrary, what is offered here is profoundly respectful of a multiplicity of sources and approaches to what is admittedly a delicate topic.

This book fills a gap by being an excellent textbook for courses on ministry, both ordained and lay. It also fills a gap by being both a theologically rich *and* accessible *tour de force* offering of treatises, theological opinions, and magisterial teachings. The astute reader will pause more than once on each and every page to reflect on what is said and to allow it to take deep root in his or her heart.

It is often said that the Dominican vocation is to contemplate and to pass on to others the fruit of their contemplation—*Contemplare et contemplata aliis tradere.* We are indebted to this master Dominican teacher for doing just that in this modest yet extraordinarily profound book.

Msgr. Kevin W. Irwin
Catholic University of America

INTRODUCTION

The best way to explain the purpose of this book might be to indicate some notions of what its title involves. No doubt, talking about the Church as a "priestly people" will not strike everyone as something to be taken for granted. For many individuals, it may even be an enigmatic expression. It seems to me, however, that we must first justify the priestly quality of the whole people of the Church before we can have a chance of getting a clear picture of the different problems mentioned in the Preface: What do we mean when we speak of a priestly people?

A PRIESTLY PEOPLE

A Royal Priesthood

A passage from the First Letter of Peter marks our point of departure. The author, who is speaking to newly baptized persons, says this to them: "But you are a chosen race, a *royal priesthood* [in Greek, *basileion hierateuma*; *basileion* is translated as "royal," from *basileus*, "king"], a holy nation, God's own people, in order that you may proclaim the mighty acts of him who called you out of darkness into his marvelous light. 'Once you were not a people, / but now you are God's people'" (1 Pet 2:9–10). Exegetes have long stressed that these few words come directly from an Old Testament verse in which God himself reveals to Moses the destiny he has in mind for the people he has chosen: "You shall be for me a *priestly kingdom* [*mamlèket kohanim* in Hebrew] and a holy nation" (Exod 19:6).

Pardon me for these references to Greek and Hebrew. I will try not to use them excessively, but citing them is the only way to

1

draw attention to the nuances in the original texts. For example, just by reading the translation of the passages, one can see that there is a difference between the two verses; the Hebrew is translated literally as a "kingdom of priests," but the First Letter of Peter makes use, not of the Hebrew text, but of the Greek version of the Old Testament known as the Septuagint, which freely adapted the original and replaced the plural word *priests* (*hiereis*) with a collective singular (*hierateuma*). That word is found nowhere outside the Bible and appears to have been created by the translators from Alexandria in Egypt (where the Hebrew Bible was translated into Greek around the middle of the second century BCE). There is nothing extraordinary about this, and all translators have learned that any translation that aims to be more than an incomprehensible word-for-word "trot" often has to leave literalism behind to provide a better rendition of the author's thought. Translators are expected to have a double fidelity: to the original, but also to the communicative function of language. Whether in writing or speaking, one seeks to be understood. But since the expression from Exodus has been picked up in the most literal fashion twice by the Book of Revelation (1:6 and 5:10: *basileian, hiereis* = "a royalty of priests," according to the Jerusalem Bible; "a kingdom of priests," according to the translation of the Ecumenical Bible), we can well imagine that *hierateuma* has a particular significance that we need to try to discover.

Even though it is unknown outside the Bible, the word *hierateuma* can be easily understood by comparison with similar collective singular words that are commonly encountered. We are familiar, for example, with *bouleuma*, a group of senators; *techniteuma*, a guild of artisans; *politeuma*, a body of citizens. Without going into too much detail, we can sum up the findings of researchers by recalling that words such as these have a triple connotation: (1) They apply to persons (2) who are not considered individually, but insofar as they form a group, and (3) this group is characterized by a specific function. So we can conclude that, like other words formed the same way, *hierateuma* has a meaning that is at once "personal," "communitarian," and "functional." This communitarian feature is what *hierateuma* adds or, rather, spells out, whereas the earlier Hebrew use did not expressly contain it. I say "spells out" and "expressly," because this collective sense is already present in the earlier context, which speaks of "kingdom" and "nation."

First

We can gather from this analysis that a first meaning of *hierateuma* is that of a "priestly organism." Even if the way they put it sometimes differs slightly, the majority of exegetes hold on to this implication and try to render it by translating the word as "a royal priestly *assembly*," or "a holy *community* of priests," or "the priestly *community* of the king," or "a sacred priestly *body*." The advantage of these translations ("assembly," "community," "body") is that they clearly spell out the collective meaning of *hierateuma*. The disadvantage is that they add an extra word. So I will keep the phrase *royal priesthood* from the Jerusalem Bible, but we must not forget the collective sense of the word *priesthood*. And one question remains: How and why is this organism *priestly*? I will come back to that later, but at this point we must still add a second meaning of *hierateuma* to the first one.

2nd

The second sense of *hierateuma* is found in the First Letter of Peter a few verses earlier: "Like living stones, let yourselves be built into a spiritual house, to be a *holy priesthood* [*hierateuma hagion*], to offer spiritual sacrifices acceptable to God through Jesus Christ" (1 Pet 2:5). The nuance introduced by this novel use of the word is the *exercise* of that priesthood or, if I may use the expression, of that *priestly functioning*. Here, once again, the comparison to a word with the same structure is enlightening: as before, *bouleuma* has the possible meaning of the senators as a group, but also the senators while in session. In both cases, the meaning is collective, but the second underlines the concrete exercise of the senatorial function by the group of senators. The same is true of *hierateuma*, which applies equally to the concrete exercise of the priestly community's office. The end of the verse specifies what this lived exercise consists in: *offering spiritual sacrifices*. Some scholars see an analogous use of *hierateuma* to designate the carrying out of the priestly function in 2 Maccabees 2:17, where we see the people that have received from God "the inheritance…and the kingship and the priesthood and the consecration."

Hence, we can see Sacred Scripture as the foundation for the double sense of the word; the Church is a *basileion hiera-*

teuma—a royal, priestly organism whose specific function is to offer spiritual sacrifices.

The Cultic Dimension of the *Ekklesia*

This manner of understanding the Church as a royal priesthood has other scriptural connections besides the correspondence between the verse from Exodus (19:6) and those from 1 Peter (2:5, 9) that we have just read. Along the same line of continuity between the two states of the People of God under the Old and the New Covenants, we need to recall the cultic sense of the word *ekklesia* ("church"). In the Hellenistic world, the word *ekklesia* referred to an assembly of the people as a political force deliberating on the city's affairs. But it is different in the Bible. In the Greek of the Septuagint, the word designates an assembly summoned for a religious celebration. In that context, *ekklesia* is used as the translation of the Hebrew term *qahal*, which appears especially in Deuteronomy. Scholars like to stress the liturgical flavor of the term: *qahal* is the name taken by the People of God marching toward the promised land when they gather to worship God. The word is used notably to designate the assembly at Mount Horeb during which God gives his people the Tablets of the Law with their "ten words" (Deut 4:10) about the conditions of purity required to participate in the "assembly [*qahal*] of the Lord." It is used yet again in reference to "the assembly of Israel" (Deut 31:30) gathered on the steppes of the Moab to hear Moses' last sermon. The term will still be applied to the assemblies of the people even after they have arrived in the promised land, for example, at the dedication of Solomon's Temple (1 Kgs 8; 2 Chr 6–7), and again at its purification during the restoration of Hezekiah (2 Chr 29–30).

Those are just some uses of the word *qahal*, among others. Other cases can easily be found under the word *church* in biblical dictionaries (for example, *The New Interpreter's Dictionary of the Bible*, 5 vol., ed. Katharine Doob Sakenfeld, Abingdon Press, 2009). A careful reading of these passages shows that *qahal* is distinguished by four regular elements: (1) the *convocation* by God and the actual *gathering* of the Israelites who have been convoked;

(2) the *presence* of God within his assembled people; (3) the *proclamation* of the Law or the Word amid the faithful gathered together; and (4) the *sacrifice* during the course of which the Covenant between God and his people is concluded or renewed. It is striking to note how these four elements recur in the New Testament Church: (1) Once again it is God who *calls and gathers* his own, and (2) who *remains in their midst* (3) even if the Word is no longer that of the Law but of the *Gospel,* and (4) even if the sacrifice no longer involves unreasoning beasts but Christ, who is commemorated in the *eucharistic celebration.* There is both an incontestable deepening of the concept here, and real continuity as well.

This continuity becomes still more striking if we recall that the only time the word *ekklesia* is placed in Jesus' mouth (see Matt 18:17), it is probably translating the Aramaic *qehala,* which clearly comes from the same root as *qahal.* With the exception of Acts and the Pauline Letters, there is only one other use of *ekklesia* in the Gospel. There is no need just now to emphasize further the different ways in which the potential modes of this cultic assembly unfold; but it is already evident that this liturgical character of the Church is in profound harmony with its designation as a priestly organism. The Church is the people assembled by God to worship him. This is an eminently priestly occupation, even if we still have to define the manner in which this cult is carried out and if we must take care not to limit it to the interior of a church built of stones.

The Principal Manifestations of the Church

The foregoing discussion should help us understand a statement from Vatican II that might surprise us if we had run into it without preparation. The Constitution on the Sacred Liturgy declares:

> They [all the faithful] must be convinced that the *pre-eminent manifestation of the Church* consists in the full active participation of all God's holy people in these liturgical celebrations, especially in the same Eucharist, in a single prayer, at one altar, at which there presides

the bishop surrounded by his college of priests and by his ministers. (41; italics added)

The opening part of the Constitution explains what the liturgy means for a Christian. In fact, it is in the liturgy and especially in the celebration of the Eucharist that the work of our redemption is carried out:

> [The liturgy] is the outstanding means whereby the faithful may express in their lives, and manifest to others, the mystery of Christ and *the real nature of the true Church*. It is of the essence of the Church that she be both human and divine, visible and yet invisibly equipped, eager to act and yet intent on contemplation, present in this world and yet not at home in it; and she is all these things in such wise that in her the human is directed and subordinated to the divine, the visible likewise to the invisible, action to contemplation, and this present world to that city yet to come, which we seek. (2; italics added)

Reading these lines, we get a better sense of why the eucharistic celebration is the principal manifestation of the Church. The reasons that they offer are, to be sure, of a profoundly theological nature; but in truth, all these features will have caught the eye of any attentive observer of the liturgy anyway. One can also readily recognize in them the principal characteristics of the *qahal*. All the faithful gathered in celebration have the same fundamental quality in common; here, they are part of a *baptismal community*. They have come together around one and the same object that they share and that is sacramentally present in their midst, Jesus Christ. Hence, this is a *eucharistic community*. In this assembly, not everyone has the same role. We see clearly that one person presides, the bishop surrounded by his presbyterium (college of priests) and various ministers, whereas the community of the faithful participates in a different manner. So it is a *differentiated community*. And so, without prejudging the way in which we understand the term, let us call it a *hierarchical*

6

community. Continuing the list of qualities that present themselves to the observer, we discover that the various parts played by the different members of this assembly correspond closely to the description that St. Paul gives of the Church by comparing it to the human body (1 Cor 12:12–30; Rom 12:4–8)—that is, a body has a head and different members that do not all have the same function. The liturgical community manifests the Church as the *Body of Christ.* The individual who presides over the eucharistic assembly thus plays in its midst the role of Christ as Head. Christ is the one through whom the gift of the Father makes its way to us; this is a *descending* mediation, of which the ministers are no more than the instruments. Christ is also the one through whom the prayer of everyone present is gathered into a unity to be presented to the Father; for example, at the end of the Collect and the Canon, the faithful answer *Amen.* This is *ascending* mediation.

For all these reasons—and the list is by no means complete—we have the right to say that the liturgical assembly is the *sacramental manifestation* of the Church at its most profound level. To be complete, we can add this point concerning the relationship of the Church to the world: The fact of going to the liturgical assembly symbolizes that the citizens of the world who are the faithful recognize themselves to be members of another City as well, which they have set out to find, as their fathers in the faith did (Heb 11). In the same way, the dispersal of the assembly at the end of the celebration is the sacramental expression, constantly renewed until the end of time, of Jesus' sending his disciples to bring to others the good news that they themselves have received.

So what we have here is a very rich vision of things whose possibilities we have not exhausted. By placing ourselves from the outset at the focal point of the eucharistic celebration, where the Church reveals itself to us, we can approach the baptismal priesthood and the priestly ministry in a properly ecclesial way, as they should be—that is, in their relation to Christ, on whom they both depend, but also in their relation to the Church, outside of which they have no meaning. The sacrament of holy orders will then appear to us as a "doubly relative" reality: relative to Christ as Head, whose work of dispensing grace it prolongs sacramentally, but also relative to Christ in his members, that is, to the baptismal community in whose service Christ chose to place himself. This vision is at once as simple and grand as it is easy to grasp. What is left for us to do is follow its implications to the limit.

QUESTIONS OF WORDS, QUESTIONS OF THINGS

Anyone who wants to probe more deeply into the expression *royal priesthood* (*basileion hierateuma*) has to begin by asking how the New Testament uses the priestly vocabulary. This is not an easy process, but fortunately for us, we can benefit from the results of the research done by the many scholars who have preceded us.

Priestly Language in the New Testament

We can discount the uses of "priestly language" as it applies to Israelite priests or the priests of pagan religions, and instead limit our investigation to its use in a Christian context (that is, its application to Jesus or to his disciples). In so doing, we find only five different terms, and they are used relatively infrequently: (1) "priest" (*hiereus* in Greek), used seven times in the Letter to the Hebrews, and three times in the Book of Revelation; (2) "high priest" (*archiereus*), used ten times in the Letter to the Hebrews; (3) "priesthood" (*hierosyne*), which expresses the dignity of a man who is a priest—used only once, in Hebrews 7:24, in relation to the "eternal priesthood" of Jesus; (4) "priesthood" (*hierateuma*), which means, as we now know, "priestly organism or functioning"—used in 1 Peter 2:5, 9; and (5) "accomplish a sacred action" (*hierourgein*), which actually does not belong to the current priestly vocabulary, and which may not even apply to a priestly activity, but we find it used in Romans 15:16.

Although these statistics do not make exciting reading, they enable us to draw some notable conclusions. The language of priesthood is never used by the Gospels or in the Acts of the Apostles. It appears only once in Paul, but in a sense that has yet to be verified (*hierourgein*). Only the Letter to the Hebrews applies to Christ himself the titles of priest and high priest (*hiereus* and *archiereus*), and also attributes to him the dignity of priesthood (*hierosyne*). First Peter recognizes in baptized Christians, taken as a collectivity, the quality of a priestly system (*hierateuma*); likewise, the Book of Revelation attributes to believers as a whole the title of priest (*hiereis*). And now a "negative finding," but one no less important: This specific vocabulary of priesthood is never actually used to describe those whom today we call "priests." In fact, the word *priest* comes not from *hiereus*, but from *presbuteros*, which means "elder." As we will see below, priests are given various different names.

Ministerial Language in the New Testament

So that readers will make no judgments about the relative importance of the terms used to designate ministers (= servants) in the New Testament, for the moment I will cite them in alphabetical order and limit myself to one or two references in each case. Readers who would like a more complete list can consult a concordance or biblical dictionary. These are the terms we find:

Apostolos: **apostle, emissary.** This word is less well known than people think, so it may be useful to recall that Christians used it to translate a Hebrew term that designated a very active institution in its original Jewish milieu, namely, the *schaliach*. By calling someone a *schaliach*, one might be delegating to him all one's own authority as a plenipotentiary. The *schaliach* could act not only in the name of the person who had sent him, but literally in his place. A man's *schaliach* was like another self for that man; this was a dictum of Jewish law. Jesus applies that concept to himself, and it constitutes the background of the mission that he entrusts to his own emissaries: "Whoever welcomes you welcomes me, and whoever welcomes me welcomes the one who sent me" (Matt 10:40). As we know, similar statements are often encountered in the three Synoptic Gospels, as well as in John. For our purposes, one need only remember that when he is appointing his apostles as his *schelihim*, Jesus is delegating to them his full authority, and he confirms in advance what they will do in his name: "All authority in heaven and on earth has been given to me. Go therefore…" (Matt 28:18–20). It is important to recall this, because this is what guarantees the validity of what the Church will do after the death of the Twelve. Later on, the term *apostolos* will undergo a kind of banalization, but when applied to the Twelve or to St. Paul, it recovers something altogether special: Some of the apostles' prerogatives could be passed on, but not all.

Diakonos: **servant, deacon**, but not entirely in our present-day sense. This word designates the ministers of the Church in the most general sense. It is often employed by St. Paul for all the traveling ministers (see, for example, Rom 16:1; 1 Cor 3:6; 6:4; and so forth).

Didaskalos: **teacher**. This term is rarely used by itself and sometimes with reservations, prompted by the memory of Jesus' command, "Nor are you to be called instructors, for you have one instructor [*didaskalos*], the Messiah" (Matt 23:10); and in a similar vein, the Letter of James: "Not many of you should become teachers (*didaskaloi*), my brothers and sisters" (Jas 3:1). And yet, the term is not in the least pejorative when used in the triplet "apostles, prophets, teachers" (1 Cor 12:28).

Episkopos: **bishop, overseer, inspector**. A word we will return to at some length, it is used three times by itself (Acts 20:28; 1 Tim 3:2; Titus 1:7), and once in combination with *diakonos* (Phil 1:1: *episkopoi kai diakonoi*).

Evangelistes: **evangelist**. This word is found in various places (Acts 21:8; 1 Tim 4:5). It is a title that seems to apply to the apostles' collaborators who move out from a town in which they have become established to evangelize the surrounding territory (for example, when Philip is sent to Caesarea, and Timothy to Ephesus); we also find the expression "evangelists and pastors" (Eph 4:11).

Hegoumenos: **hegumen, head, guide**. The word occurs three times in the plural in the Letter to the Hebrews (13:7, 17, 24; see Acts 15:22). It seems to have been a term of ministry, especially in Rome (which may have been the source of the Letter to the Hebrews).

Poimen: **shepherd, pastor**; applied to ministers. The word appears only once in the New Testament (Eph 4:11) in the expression "evangelists and pastors," referring to those who hold the place of the "apostles, prophets, and teachers" in the postapostolic generation. By contrast, the title is applied to Christ himself several times (Matt 26:31; Mark 14:27; John 10:11, 14, 16; Heb 23:20; 1 Pet 2:25). Still, it must be noted that the verb "to feed" or "to take out to graze" (*poimainein*), which designates the office of pastor, is used for the function entrusted to the ministers: John 21:16 ("Feed my sheep," Christ says to Peter); Acts 20:28 (the bishops of Ephesus are also pastors); 1 Corinthians 9:7 (comparison of the apostle's work to that of the keeper of the flock); 1 Peter 5:2 (the elders must feed the flock entrusted to them). We will need to recall this association between "feeding" and various other terms referring to the ministers; when one wants to define the task of the Christian minister most simply and completely, one says that he feeds his flock. However, it is also interesting to note in passing the limitations of an approach that is too tightly bound up with vocabulary; the concepts, the ideas, can be there without the words that usually designate them and that we would spontaneously expect to see.

Presbuteros: **elder**. Often used in the plural, but also in the singular (for example, in 1 Pet 5:1; 2 John 1; 3 John 1), this word is perhaps the one most commonly used to refer to Christian ministers. It is also the source of our own word *priest*, but one has to be careful not to translate it that way, because in reality what our "priest" corresponds to is the *hiereus* (*sacerdos* in Latin). I will need to return to this title and the function of the *presbuteroi* to try to explain their relationship to the *episkopoi*. For now it is enough to say that "elder" was the usual name given to the heads of the Jewish-Christian communities; the title won the day because it was based on the Old Testament and Jewish tradition.

Proïstamenos: **president, person put in charge**. This is the term by which Paul and the Pastoral Epistles express the activity

11

of the head of the assembly, which falls to the elders in charge of the local Church; it includes a number of functions (1 Thess 5:12; Rom 12:8; 1 Tim 3:4–5, 12; 5:17). We will need to return to this word also to define the nature of the president's activity in the Jewish assemblies of New Testament times. This is something Christians are seldom aware of, but it is nonetheless real: The advent of the new People of God took place in a very progressive manner; and although the Christian faith completely changed in relation to the Jewish faith, many of the Jewish institutions were kept, especially in the domain of the liturgy.

Prophetes: **prophet**. This last term to be mentioned is used often enough in the triad of "apostles, prophets, and teachers" (see, for example, 1 Cor 12:28; Acts 13:1). According to some experts, it may come from the vocabulary used in Antioch during the very first Christian generation (between 30 and 50 CE). We also find the binary combination "apostles and prophets" (Eph 2:20; 3:5; Rev 18:20) in expressions suggesting that their activity already belonged to the past. As for the plain term *prophets*, the word is mentioned rather frequently by Matthew (7:22; 10:41; 13:57; 23:34), by Luke in the Acts of the Apostles (4:36; 11:27; 15:32; 21:10), and by Paul, who applies himself to regulating their activity (1 Cor 14:29, 32, 37). We also find the word in the *Didache*, a text written at the same time as the Gospels, in its rules for distinguishing between true and false prophets in the first Christian communities (*Didache* 10:7; 11:7–11). The prophetic ministry seems to be an essentially itinerant one, but the prophets can also decide to settle down in the community, and the *Didache* foresees this development (13:1, 3–6). Except for the *Shepherd of Hermas*, where the prophets seem already stabilized and subject to the authority of the elders (*Shepherd*, Mandate 11.7.12, 15–16), prophets are not found in the other writings of the Apostolic Fathers, that is, the first Christian authors after the New Testament, for example, Clement of Rome, Ignatius of Antioch, and others belonging to the early second century.

The Questions That Arise

The words in the two preceding lists of both the priestly and the ministerial vocabulary of the New Testament are different, to be sure; but there is one point on which our two lists agree: *The priestly vocabulary is never used for Christian ministers.* This is not an a priori postulate, but an unquestionable conclusion reached after all relevant terms have been exhaustively reviewed. This double inquiry and the fact that the second one confirms the data of the first are going to raise some questions, of which the following are just a few:

Why is this vocabulary never used? Although this question is the first to arise, it must be answered last of all, because we must begin by seeking out the reasons that explain this situation. In fact, various convergent reasons can be cited, but they remain in the realm of probability, because no New Testament author or writer from the first Christian generation has offered any explanation for this silence.

Does this silence force us to conclude that Christian ministers never exercised any priestly function? That is the conclusion that the Protestant tradition has drawn from these texts, extending the title of priest to all the faithful and refusing to admit that ministers have a new and different claim to it. Nowadays some Catholic authors are not far from sharing these views. Very early on, however, from the end of the second century, Christian documents did not hesitate to employ this priestly language for the ministers, and we must keep this in mind.

This leads to yet more questions: *Was the "sacerdotalization" of the Christian ministry, which took place very early in the Catholic Church, a legitimate process? Can we justify it theologically on the strength of New Testament texts? And since we cannot supply "proofs" in the strict sense of the term that this evolution was legitimate, can we give a likely historical account of it?* The link between these questions is clear: The Tradition of the faith cannot be reduced to its written documents, but we should not be too quick to maintain that we can dispense with them.

Assuming, then, that a certain priestly quality of the ministers has been acknowledged, *how can we articulate this quality in*

13

connection with the authentic priesthood of the faithful in Christ? Putting it in modern terms, this is the question of the relationship between baptismal priesthood and priestly ministry. Obviously, the relationship between the two must be understood according to the model that already governs relations between the faithful and the hierarchy in the People of God. But we still must try to spell out the specific issues in this case. That is why, to answer this question, we must be precise about what we mean by the term *priesthood* as applied to Christ (the High Priest) and to all Christians (the royal priesthood), and what the term means when it refers to one of the tasks of the Christian ministry. Note that I said just *one* of the tasks, because this is something we will have to ascertain: one of the reasons—not the only one, and perhaps not even the main one—why the title of *hiereus* is not assigned to ministers in the New Testament is that it does not suffice to express the totality of their role. But I will return to that.

OUR PLAN AND OUR METHOD

From the first results gathered thus far and from the questions they raise, we evidently have to try to specify what is included in the two expressions just mentioned: *royal priesthood* and *priestly ministry*. However, neither of these two realities comes first, nor do they provide their own self-justification; thus, we return to their common source. This is why we will begin by speaking of the priesthood of Christ (chapter 1). Here, as elsewhere, we must return to Christ if we want to become aware of each and every aspect of our Christian life. Only then will we look at our first term, the *royal priesthood* of all Christ's faithful (chapter 2). This royal or baptismal priesthood is a reality of the order of grace, and, therefore, it prevails over the ministerial priesthood, which exists to serve grace, as its name indicates, coming from the Latin *minister*, which means "servant." (We will see later that Vatican II has also retained this order of exposition in its Constitution on the Church, *Lumen Gentium*.) Next we will explore the term *priestly ministry* (chapter 3). I will explain why it is preferable to speak of priestly ministry rather than of ministerial priesthood; however, to delineate this priestly quality of Christian ministry carefully, we must undertake a much longer, more delicate, and broader investigation. That is why this chapter has the most detailed title: "The Ministers of the New Covenant and Their Different Functions: From the New Testament to the Beginning of the Third Century." There will be various subsections in this chapter, but I will introduce their headings in due time. Finally, we will look at the teachings of Vatican II to enable us to synthesize what we have learned (chapter 4).

As for the method I intend to follow, it would have been theoretically possible to take as my point of departure the liturgical ceremony for the ordination of bishops and priests. But there is a fundamental reason for not doing it this way. Predictably, the ordination ceremony refers to little else but ministers, and so it would have been difficult to derive much information from it about the royal priesthood; by the same token, the theological approach would have been skewed. Thus, it seemed more judicious to engage in a more historical—or genetic, if you will—investigation. So I will follow more closely the data from the New Testament and the first Christian writings. Nevertheless, references to liturgical documents will not be dropped altogether, and I will return to them on occasion; but by remaining in the perspective already sketched out in this introduction, my method will let us see more clearly at what point the Catholic theology of the priesthood of the faithful and of the ministers is solidly based on the oldest Tradition.

I

CHRIST, SOURCE OF ALL PRIESTHOOD

"Christ is the source of all priesthood." This expression, which comes from Thomas Aquinas (*Summa Theologica* III q. 22, a. 4), ably sums up both the certitude of our faith and the theological principle that must shed light on our investigation. If the whole Church is a priestly body, it is obvious that its most noble part, the Head, is itself not only the recipient of this priestly quality, but, in addition, the cause of that quality. The Church only exists thanks to the grace that God communicates to us through and in Christ, and nothing of what constitutes the Church is untouched by this mediation and recapitulation in Jesus Christ. Wherever our roving investigation may take us and whatever nuances may have to be changed in our oversimplified conception of priesthood, we must never forget, at the risk of losing sight of what is essential, that the priesthood in its double form can never be explained apart from this orientation to Christ. When it is a question of baptismal priesthood, this goes without saying: Grace is found in us with the same qualities that it already has in Christ (at our own level, of course). When it is a question of the priestly ministry, things are no less simple, and one can just say that it includes in its own unique way a double reference to Christ: first, to Christ as Head; then to Christ in his ecclesial Body. As each of the two aspects is always accompanied by the other, we will be spared the danger of underplaying either one to the benefit of the other.

Since we are dealing with Christ in his quality as Head, "from whom the whole body, joined and knit together by every ligament with which it is equipped, as each part is working properly, promotes the body's growth in building itself up in love" (Eph 4:16), we must first recall what theologians mean by speaking of "capital" grace. It is not an expression borrowed directly from Scripture, but there is nothing mysterious about it, since "capital" comes from the Latin *caput* ("head") and has the advantage of conveniently summing up a number of things that will be useful for us to know as we continue our exposition. We can then get into a more tangible sense of capital grace by surveying Holy Scripture more broadly. Finally, even while following Scripture, we will be able to discover the main characteristics of Christ's priesthood. These things are easy to understand, but it is important to have a clear view of how they are interconnected.

PRINCIPLE AND CAUSE OF ETERNAL SALVATION FOR ALL THOSE WHO OBEY HIM

The title of this section, which comes from a verse of the Letter to the Hebrews (5:9), sums up exactly what Christ is for the faithful; at the same time, it expresses precisely what theology means by the phrase *capital grace*. Theologians have been led to speak of capital grace because in reality, when it comes to Christ, they have formed the habit of distinguishing (comfortably, but not quite exactly) a triple grace.

1. *The first is what is called the grace of union.* This means that God's entering into union with humanity in Christ (the hypostatic union) was the first grace that the humanity of Christ received, and that this gift was the effect of God's gratuitous love. In that sense, it definitely was a grace, and even an infinite grace, since it was the gift that God made of himself, in the person of the Word, to a creature. But it is readily apparent that this is not the usual sense in which we speak of grace; it is something absolutely different.

2. *The second is Christ's habitual grace,* his personal grace— and this time it is in the same sense as when we speak of being in a state of grace. But one cannot help asking: Why did Jesus need this new grace in addition to the grace of union? Well, because even in its state of

hypostatic union with the Word, Christ's human nature remained strictly human. Since the Council of Chalcedon in 451, we know that this union took place "without confusion of natures"—in other words, Jesus did not lose his human nature, which was transformed to the point of becoming divine. If that had happened, Jesus would not have been truly human, and we could not confess in the Creed that he was true God and true man. Without becoming a divine nature, Christ's human nature still needed to be divinized in itself. That took place by the gift of sanctifying grace (also called habitual grace because we possess it in a stable manner), which is a participation in the divine nature. Put another way, it was a matter of harmonizing his psychology and his ontology. This was absolutely necessary because, without grace, Christ's humanity would not even have known that it was the humanity of a divine person.

3. *The third is then what is called capital grace.* But it is not above and beyond personal grace. It is not a new grace to be added on to the earlier kind, but the same personal grace considered under a different aspect: no longer insofar as it is given to Christ as a private person (the way it is given to each one of us), but rather insofar as it is given to him as Head of the Church. We are given grace as a treasure, not to keep jealously for ourselves alone, but to share as much as possible. This applies to Christ in an eminent and even unique fashion. As the "mediator between God and humankind" (1 Tim 2:5), Christ had to possess grace in such a way that it would pour out over all those of whom he is the Head. He is "full of grace and truth....From his fullness we have all received" (John 1:14, 16).

One can readily understand why this distinction is essential, and hence theologians have taken the greatest pains to elaborate on it. Thomas Aquinas, for example, explains that grace was given to Christ "as to a universal principle in this kind—the category—of all those who have grace" (*Summa Theologica* IIIa q. 63, a. 3). The word *principle* must not be understood here in the sense of a life maxim, but as an equivalent of *source* and *cause* (which is exactly the sense as in the Letter to the Hebrews 5:9, the verse that we took for the heading of this section). One can also translate it as a universal principle that governs all categories of those who have grace. This is essential for everything that remains to be said. Grace has been granted to Christ as to a universal principle of justification for all of human nature. It is from him that grace flows, as water pours from its source; and it is he who causes it and freely disseminates it.

We must insist on using this notion of principle (source, cause), because it has the advantage of stressing the active role of Jesus' humanity in the production of grace. This humanity is not just a channel through which grace coming from the Trinity simply passes, but rather is an instrumental cause that brings its own contribution. One can altogether truthfully compare the role of Christ in the "production" of grace to that of God himself in the production of being: "Christ is in some manner the *principium* of all grace according to his humanity, in the way that God is the *principium* of all being" (Thomas Aquinas, *On Truth* q. 29, a. 5).

This way of underlining the role of Christ's humanity has more than just a theoretical interest. It gives rise to two points that are particularly germane to our topic. On the one hand, we can get a better grasp of the "Christic" and Christian character of grace; it is not only about participating in the divine nature abstractly (see 2 Pet 1:4: "participants of the divine nature"), but also in the divine nature as has been concretely lived by Christ—that is, our Christian grace, which has specific modalities that we shall soon encounter again. On the other hand, we do full justice to the value of Christ's humanity and we give full substance to his role as Head.

This manner of underlining the role of Christ as Head plays out in two main realms. The first is that of grace's *internal* inflow, of which I have already spoken, and on which there is no need to insist. But it still has to be stressed that this role is absolutely reserved to Christ; this internal inflow of grace is the very source to which we must link the *basileion hierateuma* mentioned in the

First Letter of Peter: the body participates in the qualities of the Head and notably in its priestly quality. The second main realm where Christ as Head plays out is that of the *external* government of his ecclesial body. In this second domain, Christ alone is, strictly speaking, the Head; but he has made humans participate in this function, and they will in their turn be placed at the head of this body. One could even say that they are its "heads," although in a derivative and secondary way, and entirely by reference to the Head from which they have their authority, as well as for the good of the body whose servants they are. They do not have the capacity to give grace by internal inflow as Christ does; but they can prepare people for it and guide them to it as ministers of Christ, whose word and sacraments they dispense.

It is to this specific point that we must anchor the next stage of our investigation of how the ministry is linked to Christ. I have mentioned St. Thomas, but this is not a type of a priori argument. His doctrine is really nothing more than a slightly more technical elaboration of a distinction that we find back in the Letter to the Ephesians (4:7–16). That whole passage should be read in its entirety, but for anyone who does not remember it, let me recall the two aspects that are of particular interest to us. The author (if it is not St. Paul, it is one of his immediate disciples) recalls the gifts that Christ has given to his ecclesial body, and he divides them into two categories (v 7): "Each of us was given grace [*charis*] according to the measure of Christ's gift." The issue here is the grace properly so-called that is given to us, one and all. But a little further on (vv 11–12), he adds another category of gifts: "The gifts he gave were that some would be apostles, some prophets, some evangelists, some pastors and teachers, to equip the saints [that is, the faithful] for the work of ministry [*ergon diakonias*], for building up the body of Christ."

We note here some of the categories mentioned earlier, but there is no need to linger over this. It is more interesting to know that this division of the gifts of Christ into two categories corresponds to the two meanings of the word *head* (*kephale*) in St. Paul: the sense of a vital principle that he inherited from the Greek world and that of authority, tied in with the idea of head-leader that he got from his Jewish roots. This distinction is altogether central, and it is no surprise that it has come down through the centuries all the way to us. It gives us the best understanding of the Church's structure, and so Vatican II predictably addressed this theme in *Lumen Gentium* 10: "The common priesthood of the faithful and the ministerial or hierarchical priesthood are nonetheless interrelated: each of them in its own special way is a participation in the one priesthood of Christ." This text is not, to be sure, an infallible definition, but the use of this theory at least indicates that the Council recognized a certain validity to it. It is in this same sense that Saint Thomas long ago wrote the phrase used for the title of this chapter, one that he repeats under a slightly different form: "The whole ritual of the Christian religion derives from the priesthood of Christ" (*Summa Theologica* IIIa q. 63, a. 3).

To return to capital grace, we can say this: In the strict sense, Christ's capital grace is his personal grace considered under its aspect as sanctifying grace, which is given to him not just for himself, but for the members of his ecclesial body. But in the broad sense, his capital grace also includes all the gifts and charisms, all the privileges granted to Christ to fulfill his mission as Head. It is this totality of various gifts and charisms in which Christ makes his ecclesial body participate, although in a differentiated manner. According to the felicitous expression of Pius XII in his fine encyclical *Mystici Corporis*: "All the gifts, powers, and extraordinary graces found superabundantly in the Head as in their source flow into all the members of the Church, and are perfected daily in them according to the place they hold in the Mystical Body of Jesus Christ" (77).

Among these gifts given by Christ to his Church, some have been the object of particular attention by Tradition, because they were already stressed in the Bible; and these are the ones that must be examined now.

THE MESSIANIC CHARACTER OF CHRIST'S CAPITAL GRACE

What I am about to say in this new section is at once well known and ignored: well known in the sense that these are things

22

Q: What does Christ's Messiaship mean for the Differentiated Communion of the Church?

that all Christians are thought to be familiar with ever since they studied their Catechism; ignored in the sense that it is seldom applied systematically to Christ and to Christians. I am talking about a doctrine that we hold from Christian antiquity, one that Augustine and many others taught to the faithful in their preaching, and that St. Thomas himself considered self-evident: "With other men, one is a lawgiver, another a priest, another a king. With Christ, however, all these prerogatives are united as in the source of all graces" (*Summa Theologica* IIIa q. 22, a. 1, sol. 3). But here once again, long before the theologians, it is the Bible that gives us this teaching.

It is sufficient to open the New Testament to note how Jesus, the emissary of his Father, receives in a privileged fashion the title of Christ, that is, the Messiah, the Anointed One. This is already true before his resurrection: "You are the Messiah," says Peter in his confession of faith at Caesarea Philippi in Matthew 16:16. But it is only Christ's resurrection that consecrates the title: "God has made him both Lord and Messiah, this Jesus whom you crucified" (Acts 2:36). It is not just Peter who speaks this way; it is also Paul. When Paul begins to preach, it is to proclaim that Jesus is the Christ (Acts 9:22). The announcement is made to the Jews, but also to the pagans; to the centurion Cornelius, Peter sums up the Gospel message by saying that Jesus received the messianic anointment: "God anointed Jesus of Nazareth with the Holy Spirit and with power" (Acts 10:38). The notes supplied by both the Jerusalem Bible and the Ecumenical Translation provide enlightening information on these passages.

If Jesus receives the title of Messiah so emphatically, we can assume a priori that he also possesses all the powers that go with it and that he exercises the ministries bound up with anointing in the Old Testament. But we are not simply forced to deduce this. The texts allow us to have complete certainty here; they attribute to Jesus the three functions conferred by anointing:

1. *The king is by excellence "the Lord's anointed"* (2 Sam 19:21; see 1 Sam 10:1–10). Starting with David, each king descended from him becomes Messiah in turn; thus Jesus is acclaimed by the crowds as the "Son of

→ A: Christ is the union from which diversity of vocations + flows is oriented.

David," which means that he is recognized as Messiah (Matt 9:27).

2. *The priest also receives anointing.* We will see in particular the anointing of Aaron and his sons for the priesthood in Exodus 29:4–9. Scripture scholars explain here that, although initially reserved for the king, anointing was later conferred on the high priest, beginning in the Persian era (538–332 BCE), then progressively extended to the other priests. For the application of the priestly title to Jesus, one needs to consult the Letter to the Hebrews (see especially 3:1 and 5:1).

3. *Finally, the prophet too is thought of as having been anointed.* In 1 Kings 19:16, Elijah receives the order to anoint Elisha to replace him as prophet, but for a prophet it is more often a question of anointing in the figurative sense. The coming of the Spirit who takes hold of him with the aim of entrusting him with a mission is compared to an anointing that confers the prophetic investiture: "The Spirit of the Lord God is upon me, / because the Lord has anointed me [some Bibles translate this as "he has made a Messiah of me"], / ...to bring good news to the oppressed" (Isa 61:1–2). This text has to be carefully noted, because Jesus picks it up in his reading at the synagogue in Nazareth, where afterward he applies it to himself, saying: "Today this scripture has been fulfilled in your hearing" (Luke 4:16–22, at v 21). The crowds likewise do not hesitate to proclaim that Jesus is a prophet (Matt 16:14; 21:11).

We can distinguish the three titles of king, priest, and prophet as we have just done for the sake of clarity. In reality, things were not always so clearly defined, and a certain reciprocal overlapping of these titles was present. Hence, if the anointing began to be given to the high priests after the exile, that was because at the time there was no more king, and the task of being head of the people was passed on to the high priest. Thus, messianism, which was originally royal, also became priestly. This is why the prophetic texts closely associate priesthood and royalty for the eschatological times (Jer 33:14–18; Ezek 45:1–8; Zech 4:1–14; 6:13). Also, when the Letter to the Hebrews repeatedly gives Jesus the title of *archiereus*, this is a way of saying that he gathers together in his person the titles of priest and king. In fact, the word expresses at once authority (*archē*) and priesthood (*hiereus*), but with the stress on priesthood. For the author of Hebrews, it is clear that *archiereus* is truly the name of Christ. One can note, however, that the distinction between the two functions must have been rather strongly felt or regretted because the community of Qumran awaited two messiahs: the Messiah-priest who would be preeminent, and the Messiah-king who would rule over temporal affairs.

As for the connection between the word and priesthood, it is equally manifest. Aaron, the head of the priestly line, is Moses' spokesman (Exod 4:14–16); the Book of Ecclesiasticus (or Sirach) does not fail to stress this in its praise of Aaron (Sir 45:17). The same thing happens for Levi and his sons: "They teach Jacob your ordinances, and Israel your law" (Deut 33:10). One of the frequently voiced reproaches by the prophets against the priests is precisely that they are not dispensing the word as they are bound to do: "My people are destroyed for lack of knowledge; because you [O priest!] have rejected knowledge [that is, the Torah, which the priest had to teach to the people], I reject you from being a priest to me" (Hos 4:6). The point is underlined by another interesting text: "For the lips of a priest should guard knowledge, and people should seek instruction from his mouth, for he is the messenger [*angelos*] of the Lord of hosts" (Mal 2:7).

Here once more, to speak of the way that Christ the High Priest has retained and fulfilled the link between priesthood and the word, we cite the Letter to the Hebrews. It does not give Christ the title of prophet (as other New Testament writings do), but it calls him "the apostle and high priest of our confession [= profession of faith]" (Heb 3:1). Scholars have shown in a convincing fashion that in this context *apostolos* stands for *angelos*: both words mean "emissary" or "messenger"; and we find the same term in the Greek text of Malachi 2:7. Hence, this verse from Hebrews has to be translated as "spokesman and high priest of our profession of faith." The sense of the passage thus becomes quite clear: It presents Jesus as the one whose word we must listen to. That is important, because this connection with the word forbids us to define Christ's priesthood and that of Christians solely in terms of sacrifice.

The point is often made as evidence based on the history of religions that the priest was defined as the man of sacrifice, understood in the mostly strictly cultic sense (sacrifice of the victim on the altar); but that does not do justice to the complexity of what the Bible reveals to us. Christ is incontestably presented to us at once as high priest, that is, as priest and king, but also as prophet and teacher. We must keep all that in mind when we speak of Christ's sacrifice; and, as we shall see, the notion of the spiritual sacrifice that we will soon focus on explodes these overly narrow categories wherever it meets them.

The distinction between prophet and teacher just mentioned aims to do justice to the distinction between the "official" or "ministerial" teaching of the priest as we have recalled it, and the "charismatic" teaching of the prophet who comes to supplement the former, or perhaps even contradict it, when it does not conform to the Torah—but this distinction must not be pushed too far. As I see it, the word *prophetic* includes, generally speaking, this double aspect: hence, there is no reason to oppose the world of the prophet to that of the priest. As we have just seen, the prophet does not speak against the Law; he reproaches the priest for not teaching the Law. The word of both of them comes from the same God and aims at the same goal: to keep the people faithful to the Word of God. In the New Testament, the apostles, who are the teachers sent by Christ, are also called prophets. When the Letter to the Ephesians uses the phrase "the apostles and prophets" (2:20; 3:5), that must be understood as the apostles who are also prophets. This is equally true for Christ, who is simultaneously the prophet and teacher par excellence.

Novelty of
Christ's Priesthood

THE PRINCIPAL CHARACTERISTICS OF
CHRIST'S PRIESTHOOD

As always, or at least often enough, when dealing with the transition from the Old to the New Testament, the hard part is not to show the continuity—that is evident—but rather to see where the novelty is. To be brief, here too I will continue to rely on the Letter to the Hebrews and stress three points: the reference to Melchizedek, the reference to the relationship to Moses, and the thoroughly unexpected fulfillment of the priesthood in Jesus.

The author of the Letter to the Hebrews loves to develop the idea that Melchizedek represents the very figure, the type, of Jesus' royal priesthood: Melchizedek, "priest of the Most High God" is also the king of "Salem" (recall Gen 14:8–20); but Hebrews also underlines the thoroughly exceptional fact that Melchizedek is "without father, without mother, without genealogy, having neither beginning of days nor end of life" (Heb 7:3), which allows the author to see in him the prefiguration of Christ's eternal priesthood (7:17, 21–25). One also recalls Psalm 110:4: "You are a priest forever according to the order of Melchizedek." So the point is a familiar one, and yet we do not always see enough emphasis laid on the fact that Melchizedek is a stranger to the chosen people. This detail is crucial because it signifies that God's action can extend beyond the framework of the Covenant in the strict sense. The same can be said about Job and Noah; the Covenant with Noah after the flood takes the form of the rainbow to show that it extends to all the earth (Gen 9:12–16). And so, asserting that Christ is a priest according to the order of Melchizedek does not mean simply that we are dealing with something different from the Levitical priesthood, but that his action is not limited to those who explicitly invoke him.

The second principal reference from the Letter to the Hebrews naturally directs us to the figure of Moses (3:1–5): the prophet without peer (Deut 18:15; 34:10); the priest who sacrifices (Exod 24) and intercedes for his people (Exod 32:31–32); and also, if not the king in title, then at least the guide and liberator of his people. Moses is the only one, along with Jesus, who is given the title of Mediator (Gal 3:19–20); in turn, scholars have

27

noticed that a number of passages from the New Testament allow us to speak of Jesus as a new Moses (one can see a body of such references and allusions in the *Doubleday Bible Dictionary*). This means that Jesus, who is the Mediator of the New and definitive Covenant, gathers these functions together in his person and brings them to a perfection never reached before and never to be reached again: "For there is one God; there is also one mediator between God and humankind, Christ Jesus, himself human" (1 Tim 2:5). In the eyes of St. Thomas, this definition of the Mediator is, of course, a prerogative absolutely reserved to Christ; but Thomas does not shrink from conceding to others a certain role as subordinate mediators. In the economy of salvation as he understood it, as well as in the organization of the purely natural world, God chose to have need of secondary causes. This is a masterpiece of the Thomistic theology of providence, as well as of his theology of the Church.

If mediation is the most specific feature of priesthood, we can readily understand why the Letter to the Hebrews did not attribute to Christians the title of priest. We have to recall that unique quality of the Mediator of the New Covenant before defining, as people used to like to do, the priestly function of the Christian minister solely by mediation. The one and only priest in the full sense of the term is Christ. Such is the supremely novel thing about Christianity. I have mentioned this before, and I will return to it later. The First Letter of Peter and the Book of Revelation do not hesitate to give Christians the title of priest, but one fact does not weaken the other, nor does it allow us to contradict the way in which Hebrews affirms so forcefully the unique priesthood of the Christian faith.

The altogether unheard-of form taken by the fulfillment of the priesthood in Jesus is already evident from what I have said. But the point asserts itself if we consider the particular character of the sacrifice offered (Heb 9:14): "Christ, who through the eternal Spirit offered himself without blemish to God." This simple phrase expresses the most specific feature of Christ's offering. He offered not only "prayers and supplications" (Heb 5:7), but also himself.

Three further aspects must be pointed out to assess better what is truly new in Christ's sacrifice:

1. The author of Hebrews is synthesizing here two elements of Christian catechesis that are already found
in earlier New Testament writings. First, there is the
presentation of Christ as a sacrificial victim: "Our
paschal lamb, Christ, has been sacrificed" (1 Cor
5:7); "[We were ransomed] with the precious blood
of Christ, like that of a lamb without defect or blemish" (1 Pet 1:19). Second, there is the aspect of vol-
untary self-giving, of freely chosen personal action
that characterizes the passion of Jesus. We see this at
the moment at which he institutes the Eucharist
(Matt 26:26–29), as well as in Gethsemane (Matt
26:39). The Letter to the Hebrews groups these two
aspects together, but in doing so, it emphasizes the
ritual aspect of the offering by using the verbs *ana-
pherein* and *prospherein,* which come from the liturgical vocabulary, meaning to "offer a sacrifice" (see
Heb 7:27; 9:14, 25). This aspect is further underlined by use of the expression "unblemished victim"
(*amomos*). We find in the passage from Hebrews 9:14
the same expression as in 1 Peter 1:10, which itself
borrows verses from the Pentateuch concerning the
qualities of the victim to be immolated (see Exod
29:1; Lev 1:3, 10): for animals, no physical flaw; for
Christ, no moral fault, no sin (see Heb 4:15; 7:26).

2. The passage from Hebrews 9:14 expresses yet
another feature of the extraordinary novelty of
Christ's sacrifice, in that he is both active and passive:
he is not only the priest who offers, he is also the victim offered. This oneness of priest and victim was
absolutely unthinkable in a Jewish setting, where it
would be reminiscent of a ritual suicide. Readers of
the Letter to the Hebrews know that Jesus did not kill
himself; but it is here that the idea of sacrifice completely changes and takes on a new meaning: It is the
offering of self by Jesus himself, and not his being put
to death by the executioners, that is the sacrifice
properly speaking. We move from the ritual sacrifice

of the Old Testament, which was no more than a symbolic, powerless prefiguring, to the only really efficacious sacrifice: the one that made humanity agreeable to God by transforming us internally. As some writers have aptly put it, one can say that this is an existential and not just a ritual sacrifice.

3. This idea of an existential sacrifice is the third novel aspect of Christ's sacrifice. It essentially consists in transforming existence itself by bringing divine charity into play. Christ has done this perfectly in a double fashion by his total obedience to the will of the Father (Heb 5:8; 10:7–10), and by the total gift of himself to his brothers and sisters (Heb 2:14–18; 4:15). And this is precisely what Christians, thanks to Christ's mediation, are invited to do in their turn. It is quite remarkable that the same expression that first defines the sacrifice of Christ—"to do God's will" (Heb 10:7, 9)—is later used to define the Christian vocation (Heb 10:36; 13:21). In the same way, the attitude of dedication to one's brothers and sisters is itself characterized as a "sacrifice" (*thusia*) (Heb 13:10). Thus, by imitating the attitude of Christ, Christians will be in their turn priests and victims of the spiritual sacrifice that they are invited to offer.

THE IMPORTANCE OF TERMS

There is no need to summarize everything just described; it is clear enough. But it may be useful to emphasize a few matters that should not be lost sight of in what follows.

The uniqueness of the title mediator has to make us careful not to use it lightly for anyone besides Christ. While Thomas Aquinas is not himself absolutely opposed to a certain extension of this term, he still stresses that we cannot talk about priests as mediators except to the extent that they are ministers, servants of the true mediator, in their sacramental function. The uniqueness of the priest and the victim in the cult of the New Covenant is likewise a point that has to be taken very seriously. If Christian ministers are never called priests (*hiereis*) in the New Testament, that is partly lest we be tempted to liken them to the Jewish or pagan priests, but also to safeguard the uniqueness of Christ's priestly role. But if, on the other hand, the faithful are called *hiereis* or *hierateuma,* that is by virtue of the fact that they belong to the ecclesial Body of Christ. Their being members of that Body, through the grace received from their Head, confers on them a mystical identity with Jesus the *archiereus.*

The unity amid the distinction of the three messianic privileges equally draws our attention to the necessity of not separating them: the grace of Christ is priestly, royal, and prophetic in its source, and it remains that way when communicated to others. Similarly, the authority of Christ over his body is simultaneously priestly, royal, and prophetic; and this triple aspect recurs in his ministers. When we call his ministers "priests" out of old habit, without paying much attention to it, we are actually using the poetic figure of speech called *synecdoche,* which consists in taking a part for the whole (for example, "all hands on deck" to mean "everyone on deck"). The priestly function is meant to designate all three functions, but it threatens to eclipse the other two. So, it is better to use the term *minister* or *servant* (*diakonoi*), which is very well attested, or yet another current term to unify this complex whole.

One such term is *poimen,* pastor. We have already encountered it; but two things remain to be said about it. First, like *hiereus,* this title is applied to Christ with a superlative: Christ is the *poimen megas,* the "great shepherd [pastor] of the sheep" (Heb 13:20), and even the *archipoimen* (like *archiereus*), the "chief shepherd" (1 Pet 5:4). This manner of speaking links up with other similar names, such as *archegos* ("leader," "prince," "pioneer"), which occurs several times in different forms: *archegos tes soterias,* "the pioneer of salvation" (Heb 2:10); *tes pisteos archegon,* "the pioneer of faith" (Heb 12:2); "the Author of life" (Acts 3:15); "Leader and Savior" (Acts 5:31). So we can consider this title of *poimen* as equivalent to *archiereus,* and as summing up in a single word the whole of Christ's titles. Similarly, the term *poimen* is also applied to the apostles, along with the function of *poimanein* (feeding the flock). It is likewise a word that Tradition has been pleased to keep, to characterize the role of minister. This begins with *The Shepherd of Hermas* and the Letters of Ignatius of Antioch, both from second-century authors, and it continues without interruption all the way to the Second Vatican Council. We cannot ignore it.

II

A ROYAL PRIESTHOOD
TO OFFER SPIRITUAL
SACRIFICES

This chapter aims to probe more deeply into the meaning of the reality that Holy Scripture calls *basileion hierateuma*, which exclusively shares with Jesus the adjective *priestly*. We must examine this first if we want to understand what priesthood represents in Christianity. We are dealing with an original reality, and we cannot impose on it any a priori definition; revelation alone can teach us about its nature. Clearly, this is going to have consequences for the way we conceive and speak about the priestly role of ministers; but, far from compromising it, this should rather contribute to giving it a more solid foundation. Our effort is going to play out in accordance with these approaches. First, we will engage in greater detail with the *basileion hierateuma*, which we mentioned in the first pages of this book. Then we will examine the notion of the spiritual sacrifices that are constantly associated with it, so as to finish describing, if not defining, priesthood by the function that it carries out. Finally, we will gather some witnesses from the ecclesial Tradition on the royal priesthood, as well as on the spiritual sacrifices. Far from being a recent approach, which might give rise to suspicions of a dubious modernist element, this way of seeing things is, on the contrary, at the heart of our faith and is deeply rooted in Christian antiquity.

A ROYAL AND PROPHETIC PRIESTHOOD

As I have already said, the expression *basileion hierateuma* refers to an organism, a community, a priestly body. The accent here is on the collective character of the priesthood. But if we stay with that, we have not said all we need to say, and three further complementary points have to be detailed: (1) the relationships between the persons who make up that community with its shared priestly quality; (2) the royal character of that priesthood, which is perhaps not addressed often enough; and (3) its *function*, often summed up in the word *prophetic*, which consists in proclaiming God's great deeds. All three will be now examined.

A Shared Priestly Quality

The first item to discuss involves clarifying the status of the persons in the priestly community. In drawing on the collective sense of the term *hierateuma*, it is sometimes said that since the word evokes the function of the entire Church, it does not speak to the particular office of each Christian. That is partly true, but putting it this way can lead to error if it suggests that individuals do not personally participate in the priestly and royal dignity of the People of God. That would be a contradiction; the members of a wholly priestly community are themselves priests. According to the Letter to the Hebrews, "we have become partners of (*metochoi*) Christ" (3:14). What we can and must say is that we are not really priests except to the degree that we are members of this community, that is, to the degree that we participate in what makes us priestly in this particular scheme. To confirm this reading, we have the parallel passages of Revelation 1:5 and 5:10, which also depend on Exodus 19:6, but we have kept the concrete Hebrew sense of the word *priests* (*hiereis*) instead of the Greek collective noun (*hierateuma*): "He has made us a kingdom of priests" (or rather a "kingship of priests").

We may recall from comments by Scripture scholars that these verses do not attribute to all Christians the *ministerial function* of priest or the *public office* of priest. A closer look reveals that these authors are aiming to dispel the classic Lutheran reading—

which some Catholics have also had a tendency to adopt—that attributes to each of the faithful the rights and functions that are de facto those of the ministers. In the same sense, certain authors claim that spiritual sacrifices are not cultic acts. Everything depends on how one defines *cult* (or *worship*).

If one takes the word *cult* to mean the public celebration of external acts by specially appointed official ministers, it is evident that this is not what these passages chiefly have in mind. But this definition is just too narrow; the use of the word *cult* poses a problem analogous to that of the word *priest*. We were accustomed to certain definitions that were not quite those of the New Testament, which is why the exegetes warn us. But one must not be misled by other overly absolute formulas. Hence, I maintain that this collective priesthood of the whole Church is also possessed by each member, not in the form of a function or an office, but of a dignity, an honor (a *timē*, as 1 Pet 2:7 says). This dignity is the one we received at baptism that makes a Christian a member of a body that is priestly in its entirety and that is consequently bound to act by virtue of this dignity—that is, in a priestly manner—in a sense that remains to be defined. One can embrace the opinion of a reputable exegete (C. Spicq), who says that the use of the term *spiritual* "should suffice to eliminate all disputes about the existence or exclusion of a hierarchical and sacramental priesthood that is envisaged neither by Peter nor by the Letter to the Hebrews: the worship is spiritual, in a spiritual society, where spiritual sacrifices are necessarily offered by a spiritual priesthood."

The Royal Character of This Priesthood

One has to agree with the same exegete when he asserts that modern commentators are guilty of ignoring the royal quality of this priesthood, and when he stresses that this quality is nevertheless anchored in the Jewish faith. "All Israelites are the sons of kings," said Rabbi Simeon (*Mishnah, Shabbat* 14, 4). "They are true kings and true priests," says another text, and still other documents apply to the chosen people as a whole what Deuteronomy 17:17–20 prescribed for the king alone.

So when 1 Peter picks up on this royal quality and applies it to Christians, it is only expressing a familiar notion. This is proved by the parallel passages already cited from Revelation 1:5 and 5:10, to which can be added Revelation 20:6, which is situated in the already-realized eschatology of the world to come: "They will be priests of God and of Christ, and they will reign with him a thousand years." These passages can be tied in with Luke 22:29–30: "And I confer on you, just as my Father has conferred on me, a kingdom, so that you may eat and drink at my table in my kingdom, and you will sit on thrones judging the twelve tribes of Israel." This allusion to the messianic banquet suggests that the incorporation into the royalty of Christ takes place thanks to participation in the Eucharist (see also Rom 5:17); the gift received from Christ will come to fulfillment through the kingdom of life in his company. These are only a few texts among others that add a little detail to the royal nature of that priesthood. Without dwelling on this point at length, two things must be mentioned here: first, the element of novelty in relation to the way in which Jewish tradition could understand this royalty; second, its field of operations.

The novelty in relation to Jewish tradition is that this royalty is obtained from the imitation of Christ in his trials. Thus, the author of Revelation presents himself to the Christians of Asia as "[sharing] with you in Jesus the tribulation and the kingdom and the patient endurance," and a little further on he says that "the crown of life" is won by faithfulness till death (Rev 1:9; 2:10 [RSV]). This context is exactly the same as that of 1 Peter, which alerts us to the fact that this title has nothing triumphalist about it. Furthermore, Christ is himself charged with forewarning about this temptation: "My kingdom is not of this world" (John 18:36 [RSV]). The apostles have left no illusions on this point: "It is through many tribulations that we must enter the kingdom of God" (Acts 14:22 [RSV]). So, if it is true that our royal quality implies participation in the lordship of God and Christ, it is obtained by the victory over oneself and one's passions. To avoid misunderstandings, we must not forget that our king wears a crown of thorns.

The field of operations for this royalty is, in the first instance, that of victory over the evil in ourselves and in the world; this dimension has always been perceived in Christian tradition. In the relatively recent past, it has also been connected to the passage from Genesis that describes humanity, made in God's image, receiving from him the command to dominate and subdue the earth itself (Gen 1:26, 28). As the Book of Wisdom makes explicit: "By your wisdom [you] have formed humankind / to have dominion over the creatures you have made, / and rule the world in holiness and righteousness" (Wis 9:2–3). It is a participation in the lordship of God and Christ, and this theme has been happily worked out by Vatican II (see, in particular, *Lumen Gentium* 36 and *Gaudium et Spes* 33–39). But here as well it is only too clear that people can misuse this dignity, and that Christians must act so as to prevent the devastation caused by greed and excess, which never stop disturbing the divine plan for the world.

I will not emphasize this any further because it is not our main subject, but it was important to underline this link between priesthood and royalty: this is what serves as the theological foundation for the Christian mission in the world. The intrinsic connection between Christians and the secular world, of which they are all components by the very fact of being human, is taken up and transformed by reason of their Christian existence; and the same is true for the following theme.

Priestly, Royal, and *Prophetic*

Unlike *priesthood* and *royalty*, the word *prophecy* itself is not found in the text of 1 Peter 2:4–10. But it is the term that spontaneously comes to mind when one has to delineate the function received by the newly baptized person: "You may proclaim the mighty acts of him who called you out of darkness into his marvelous light" (v 9). This obviously supposes that prophecy cannot be reduced to simply predicting the future, a reduction that would be absolutely unbiblical. Two words at least need to be underlined in this verse: first, *exangello*, which means "announce," "proclaim," "make public." This is the only time the word is used in the New Testament, but it is frequently used in the Psalms, where it is synonymous with "magnify" (for example, Ps 79:13). This implies that the proclamation of this message takes place amid exultation, and that it is one of the tasks incumbent on this chosen people: "the people whom I formed for myself so that they might declare my praise" (Isa 43:21). The second word to be noted is *aretas*, translated here as "mighty acts." The liturgy of the royal sacrifice is to sing the *aretai*; literally, the "divine virtues." The term is known in secular language, where *aretai* are feats or acts of valor, but are also the intervention by the gods in favor of human beings and the means used in that intervention. In the Bible, *aretai* are works that can only come from God: not just miracles, but his acts of mercy in favor of the elect.

This verse thus allows us to catch a glimpse of the fact that, in addition to those spiritual sacrifices, and even within those spiritual sacrifices, the royal priesthood has for its mission to declare the wonders of God. The exercise of this prophetic grace by the faithful is manifested above all by the witness of their holy lives. It does not need to take shape in extraordinary acts, but it is true that Tradition has viewed martyrdom as the supreme witness, the extreme form of confessing the faith. So the prophetic function is not limited to a simple discourse; it leads to the imitation of the prophets and of Jesus himself, who sealed their witness with their blood. Here we are quite close to a passage to which we will return, but that I need to point out now to call the reader's attention to its connection with our verse. This is Romans 15:16, where Paul presents himself as "a minister [*leitourgon*, 'officiant'] of Christ Jesus to the Gentiles in the priestly service [*hierogounta*; literally, 'accomplishing a cultic function'] of the gospel of God, so that the offering [*prosphora*; here, again, a liturgical term] of the Gentiles may be acceptable, sanctified by the Holy Spirit."

The vocabulary is undoubtedly sacrificial and cultic (see Rom 1:9), but experts hesitate to say that it is specifically priestly. To my mind, that is being too scrupulous, but I will return to the question. All we need recall about this verse in our context now is that the triple function of this royal and prophetic priesthood does not come down to a purely ritual cult—in the sense that the Levitical cult, so often attacked by the prophets, sometimes could.

If we now try to synthesize the results of our first approach, we can hold onto three main points:

1. In keeping with our initial texts, we have concluded that in the first instance it is the community that is priestly, and that the persons who comprise it are priests only by participation. But they *are* priestly, and we have the counterproof of this with the texts from the Book of Revelation. The only thing remaining—it was obvious, but it still had to be done—was to underline the fact that this community is what it is only because it is the Body of Christ himself, who in his quality of Supreme Pastor reunites the triple priestly, royal, and prophetic features.

2. We will no longer have to return, except incidentally, to this royal and prophetic quality of the *hierateuma,* the holy priestly community of Christians; but it is very important never to lose sight of the way these three qualifications go together. It is their participation in the unique grace of Christ—itself priestly, royal, and prophetic—that makes his disciples priests, kings, and prophets.

3. The link bonding priesthood to royalty and prophecy reminds us not to define it solely by its relation to sacrifice. The *hiereus* in the line of Christ (*hiereus* and not yet *presbuteros*, but that, too, will hold good for him) is not the man of the sacred realm or of cultic doings in the manner of Jewish or pagan *hiereis*; the notion of worship can and must be expanded considerably. That is precisely what we will do with the notion of spiritual sacrifices.

TO OFFER SPIRITUAL SACRIFICES

The passage from which we started out and to which we must continuously return (1 Pet 2:4–10) explains to the newly baptized that they have become a holy priesthood "to offer spiritual sacrifices acceptable to God through Jesus Christ." The phrase *spiritual sacrifices* is the translation for the Greek *pneumatikas thusias*. We recognize "spirit" (*pneuma*) in the first word; as for the second, *thusias*, it can be translated either as "sacrifice" or "victim." The passage from one to the other is self-evident: The victim is the object of the sacrifice, and a sacrifice presupposes a victim. In this passage, Peter does not explain what he means by spiritual sacrifices. So we must refer to other passages of the New Testament or to parallel texts of Jewish literature, as we did for the idea of priesthood, to get a clearer view of what the expression implies. We will follow up on this consideration by asking whether the notion of *spiritual* sacrifice excludes or, on the contrary, allows one to include, the idea of *ritual* sacrifice. In other words, is there a ritual sacrifice that can also be a spiritual sacrifice in the sense that I am about to define?

The territory covered by the expression *spiritual sacrifice* is really quite vast, and in the New Testament we find various uses of *thusia* that shed a special light on the passage from 1 Peter. The first is found in Romans 12:1–2: "I appeal to you therefore, brothers and sisters, by the mercies of God, to present your bodies [literally, 'to offer your persons'] as a living sacrifice, holy and acceptable to God [*thusian zosan haghian*], which is your spiritual [*logiken*] worship." The word *spiritual* here is not an equivalent translation of the Greek, but *logikon* is used in Peter to render "the *pure* milk of the Word" (1 Pet 2:2); so we remain in the same context. "Do not be conformed to this world," St. Paul continues [see 1 Peter 1:14: "Do not be conformed to the passions of your former ignorance…"], "but be transformed by the renewing of your minds, so that you may discern what is the will of God—what is good and acceptable and perfect." It is clear to Paul that the sacrifice that must be offered to God is one of a holy life, completely conformed to his will and acceptable him, an essential quality for the sacrifice to be welcome.

Thanks to a second passage in the Letter to the Hebrews, we can further expand and spell out the notion of sacrifice: "Through him [Jesus], then, let us continually offer a sacrifice of praise [*thusian aineseos*] to God, that is, the fruit of lips that confess his name. Do not neglect to do good and to share what you have, for such sacrifices [*thusiai*] are pleasing to God" (Heb 13:15–16). This verse is remarkable in more than one way: it contains at least two quotations from the Old Testament, along with an equally important reminiscence and suggestion. The first quotation, "sacrifice of praise [or thanksgiving]," comes from Psalm 50, where it is found twice (vv 14, 23). The second, "the fruit of lips," comes from the prophet Hosea (14:2), where it is specifically contrasted with the idea of a purely external sacrifice: "Instead of bulls we will dedicate to you our lips"; the same contrast, by the way, is found in Psalm 50. As for the reminiscence, it is the passage from Matthew 9:13, where Jesus sums up the teaching of the prophets: "I desire mercy, not sacrifice" (see also Mark 12:23 and Hos 6:6.) Once again, in this passage from Hebrews, we must note an interesting suggestion that gives a glimpse of a new dimension: The word translated here as "share what you have" is in fact *koinonia* (literally, "communion"). The Jerusalem Bible translates it as "sharing your resources." According to this verse, the category of spiritual sacrifices extends not only to prayer, but also to alms and community sharing, and it fits into the lineage of the great prophetic tradition, taken up and accomplished by Christ himself. Alms are mentioned again in a third text, in which St. Paul thanks the Philippians for their gifts, which he calls "a fragrant offering, a sacrifice acceptable and pleasing to God" (Phil 4:18). Different translations of the Bible rightly stress here that, on the subject of these fraternal gifts, Paul is going back to the cultic language of the Old Testament as spiritualized by the New.

A fourth Pauline text takes us very close to Romans 12:1: the offering of a person to God by him- or herself: "...Even if I am being poured out as a libation over the sacrifice and the offering of your faith, I am glad and rejoice with all of you" (Phil 2:17). In the Greek text we find here *thusia* for "libation," but also "the sacrificial offering [*leitourgia*] of your faith"; and both of these terms come from the cultic vocabulary. The "liturgy" of the Philippians' faith (that is, either the faith itself, with all its effects, or Paul's life as consecrated to their service, or both) is therefore considered a sacrifice, to which is added the offering of blood that Paul is preparing to pour out for them (see 2 Tim 4:6: "I am already being poured out as a libation"). So once again we have a spiritualization of a cultic vocabulary, and we can conclude from this that in proclaiming the Gospel, St. Paul is accomplishing one of the cultic acts in spirit, which is that of the New Covenant. It is, by the way, Paul himself who speaks of "worship in the Spirit of God" (Phil 3:3). We can see with increasing clarity how artificial it is to oppose spiritual and ritual sacrifice; the faith with which the sacrifice is offered allows us, in fact, easily to reconcile them (Heb 11:4): "By faith Abel offered to God a more acceptable sacrifice [*pleiona thusian*] than Cain's." What Abel offered was effectively a ritual sacrifice, but the internal disposition of the one making the offering made him acceptable to God, while his brother lacked that disposition.

A final text enables us to find the model proposed to Christians for acting in a fashion acceptable to God: "...Live in love, as Christ loved us and gave himself up for us, a fragrant offering and sacrifice [*prosphoran kai thusian*, "offering and victim"] to God" (Eph 5:2). This text is replete with reminiscences and parallels, and readers can find them in the footnotes and margins of their Bibles. We will look at the two most obvious passages. First: "the Son of God, who loved me and gave himself for me" (Gal 2:20), which emphasizes that love is the source of that sacrificial offering by Christ. Second: "We have been sanctified through the offering of the body of Jesus Christ once for all" (Heb 10:10); here *body* is the translation of *soma*, as in Romans 12:1— not the body as distinct from the soul, but the whole man, the person acting by his or her body.

We would not have said everything about the text from Ephesians if we did not underline the fact that it invites us at the same time to imitate Christ and God: "Therefore be imitators of God, as beloved children, and live in love, as Christ loved us and gave himself up for us, a fragrant offering and sacrifice to God" (Eph 5:2). It is striking to note that in this way we are led to the privileged text of 1 Peter, and that it too is framed by two references to Christ that undoubtedly situate us in the same context of his sacrifice and his imitation. The redemptive sacrifice of Christ is clearly mentioned: "You were ransomed...with the precious blood of Christ, like that of a lamb without blemish or spot" (1 Pet 1:18–19). The word *thusia* is not there, but the idea unquestionably is; and with a great deal of coherence Peter moves on to the "spiritual sacrifices" that Christians must offer in their turn, that will also be "acceptable to God through Jesus Christ," because the spiritual sacrifice is accepted by God to the extent that it receives its value and welcome character from the sacrifice of Christ. As for the second reference, it can be found a few verses further on in 2:21–24, where Peter proposes the imitation of Christ's sacrifice: "For to this [suffering patiently] you have been called, because Christ also suffered for you, leaving you an example, so that you should follow in his steps....He himself bore our sins in his body on the cross, so that, free from sins, we might live for righteousness; by his wounds you have been healed." The text concludes (v 25) by recalling the two titles of Christ whose pertinence one can appreciate in this context: "For you were going astray like sheep, but now you have returned to the shepherd and guardian of your souls [*poimen kai episkopos*]."[1]

There is no need to belabor the specific contribution of these two last texts; it is plain that the spiritual sacrifice of the Christian is situated in relation to the sacrifice of Christ. So we can sum up the results of this section in the following fashion:

1. The notion of spiritual sacrifice (with or without the adjective) has a considerable range: it covers not just alms, sharing, prayer, faith, and other virtues that could be listed, but also the very person of the disciple who is throughout all his or her life the object itself of that sacrifice.

2. At the heart of the spiritual sacrifice, therefore, lies the offering of oneself to God. That offering of self has been eminently realized by Christ: "Sacrifices and offerings you have not desired, but a body you have prepared for me [*soma*, as in Rom 12:1 and Heb 10:10]....Then I said, 'See, God, I have come to do your will, O God" (Heb 10:5–7).

3. It is thus by Christ's example, with Christ and through Christ, that Christians offer themselves in their turn to God in a sacrifice in which they are at once priests and victims. Later I will indicate in more

43

detail how we can explain that; but it is already clear now that it is by the imitation of Christ that this sacrifice acquires its value—that is, essentially by his obedience to the will of the Father and by the love that prompted him to give his life that way. This is indeed the existential sacrifice I spoke of.

But there remains a final question to consider so as to finish, at least in a provisory fashion, the description of spiritual sacrifices. Does 1 Peter include the Eucharist in those *pneumatikai thusiai*, or must it be excluded? Scripture scholars are at least as divided on this point as they are about the *basileion hierateuma*. As far as I can judge, it seems that those opposed to the idea of including the Eucharist in the group of spiritual sacrifices share an a priori notion that makes them claim that the spiritualization of sacrifices, as I have thus far defined it, necessarily excludes any idea of external cult. Now if we read closely all the texts just cited, we can see at once that this is a mistake: One can very well maintain the spirituality of those sacrifices without rejecting the possibility that the inner feelings they imply can express themselves externally, that what is at stake here are all the acts just mentioned, up to and including the offering up of one's own person, all that indissolubly connects the corporal and the spiritual.

One need not be a great philosopher to understand that what we have here is an anthropological necessity. Body and soul, humans can never give shape to an inner feeling without translating it into outer acts at the risk of remaining with an "imagined" religion. The Letter of James says this with a certain brusqueness: "Show me your faith apart from your works, and I by my works will show you my faith" (2:18). The First Letter of John says more or less the same thing: "...Those who do not love a brother or sister whom they have seen, cannot love God whom they have not seen" (4:20). That is why I follow without hesitation the great majority of Scripture scholars who think that the Eucharist is an integral part of those *pneumatikai thusiai*.

Two major reasons can be put forward to justify this position:

1. The first comes from a proper notion of external sacrifice (ritual). When the prophets and Christ after them rose up against the sacrifices to which they preferred mercy, what they were really targeting was sacrifice taken in an overly material sense, a soulless act, an external rite without interior worship. One could quote many texts, but it is enough to mention the ending of the *Miserere* (Ps 51:18–19): The contrite heart suffices if the ritual sacrifice is impossible when the Temple is destroyed. Without that broken spirit, the ritual sacrifice is nothing, but the psalm does not exclude it for all that. In the New Testament, the rejection of the old ritual cult in the Letter to the Hebrews is not the same as the rejection of the new sacramental cult, and Christ shows this in an eminent fashion. He offers a sacrifice as real and external as possible, because he gives his own life, but his obedience, penetrated by love, makes that action a fully spiritual sacrifice. The cultic, ritual sacrifice, understood and performed as it should be, thus includes the spiritual sacrifice.

2. The second reason that the Eucharist is an integral part of the *pneumatikai thusiai* derives from the total context of 1 Peter. It is generally agreed that this letter is based on a baptismal liturgy; scholars have even managed to distinguish in it four different baptismal hymns. The part that concerns us is likely to have reworked, even literally quoted, a homily once addressed to the neophytes (the "newborn infants" of 2:2). In any case, the catechetical elements in it are many. Thus, it is perfectly possible that this initiation ceremony included the Eucharist. Apart from the already-cited allusions to the ransom achieved by Christ on the cross, one could also mention the verse in 1 Peter 2:3, "You have *tasted* that the Lord is good."

It is true that there is no formal mention of the Eucharist, but neither is it excluded. On the contrary, given the context, we can assume that if the individuals baptized are priests and victims of the sacrifice that they offer, this sacrifice is only made possible by the unique sacrifice of Christ. So we must refuse the fallacious dichotomy of spiritual interpretation vs. eucharistic interpretation. Peter's text implies the union of both aspects. Undoubtedly, the real sacrifices are the existential acts, which consist in the transformation of the life of the baptized person by the action of the Holy Spirit in union with the sacrifice of Christ. The Eucharist could not be absent because it is the condition of their possibility. The inspiration that animates Christians in their existential sacrifices has its origin in the sacrifice of Christ, made present in the Eucharist; and their culmination in God is only possible through the mediation—itself made present in the Eucharist—of Christ's sacrifice.

SPIRITUAL PRIESTHOOD IN
THE ECCLESIAL TRADITION

To illustrate what I have just said, I would now like to introduce some texts borrowed from the Fathers of the Church and from the great theologians of the past, who constantly put these truths to work in their preaching and teaching. A paradoxical fact has to be noted here: While this teaching about the royal and prophetic priesthood of the faithful practically disappeared from catechesis from the Reformation up until Vatican II, it had been, on the contrary, widely honored during the first Christian centuries, which were faithful on that score to the teaching of Holy Scripture just recalled. Jesuit Paul Dabin devoted himself to the worthy task of gathering these texts from over the course of twenty centuries.[2] His survey begins with Pope Clement of Rome (AD 95–98), that is, practically in the apostolic era, with St. Ignatius of Antioch (martyred ca. 107–10) and St. Justin Martyr (d. ca. 165), and it continues until the present time, with the inclusion of St. Augustine and St. Thomas in particular. It is worth the trouble of reading a few of these witnesses here, but they are no more than a few samples chosen from among the most significant, most ancient, and most explicit texts.

"Not Every Priest Is a Saint, But Every Saint Is a Priest"

Clement of Rome and Ignatius of Antioch simply pick up the affirmation from 1 Peter 2:5–9. But St. Justin, to whom we owe such a wealth of details about the liturgical life at Rome in the middle of the second century, is already more explicit:

> We are the true high priestly race [*archieratikon genos*] of God, as even God Himself bears witness, saying that in every place among the Gentiles sacrifices are presented to Him well pleasing and pure. Now God receives sacrifices from no one, except through His priests. Accordingly, God, anticipating all the sacrifices which we offer through this name, and which Jesus the Christ enjoined us to offer, that is, in the Eucharist of the bread and the cup, and which are presented by Christians in all places throughout the world, bears witness that they are well pleasing to Him. (*Dial.* cxvi–cxvii)

This text lends itself to three comments: (1) "We" evidently refers to those who believe "like a single man" through Christ. What follows is explained by this unity in Christ. (2) The link between sacrifice and priesthood is also extremely clear: "God never accepts sacrifices except through his priests." (3) These sacrifices offered in every place have no value except in the Eucharist of bread and wine. The point presupposed in 1 Peter is clearly developed here.

St. Irenaeus of Lyon (martyred ca. 202–3) is very positive and unambiguous. In relation to the episode of the apostles' rubbing the ears of wheat on the Sabbath and the explanation that Christ gives, Irenaeus invokes the example of David and his men eating the "show bread" reserved to the priests (see 1 Sam 21:3–6 and Luke 6:3–4): "Every just king has the rank of a priest." That is to justify David's attitude, but he continues: "All the disciples of the Lord were priests too, those who had as their heritage here below neither fields nor houses, but who continuously attended to the service of the altar and God" (*Haer.* 4.8.3). It is interesting to note that the Latin translation slightly strained the original text: It invoked the quotation "Every just king has the rank of a priest," but actually omitted it. So one might discuss whether Irenaeus allows this generalization; in any event we find it quite often later on, independent of him. St. Ambrose (339–97), for example, writes: "All the children of the Church are priests. We receive in fact the anointing for a holy priesthood, offering ourselves to God as spiritual victims" (*On Luke* 5.33). We recognize the quotation from 1 Peter, which need not be emphasized; but it is more important to comment that the gift of the holy priesthood is a consequence of the baptismal anointing.

We find a similar formula in St. John Chrysostom, a contemporary of St. Ambrose (347–407), who unhesitatingly puts it in the mouth of St. Paul: "[The Apostle] declares that *everyone is a priest* by the mortification of his flesh and by his way of life." This statement is found in his commentary on Paul's Epistle to Romans (see Homily 20.2 on Romans 12:1). Chrysostom is also credited with a celebrated formula that has come down to us in a Latin translation: "Not every priest is a saint, but every saint is a priest" ("Non omnis sacerdos sanctus, sed omnis sanctus sacerdos"). Actually, it is from a disciple of Chrysostom, but basically that does not change anything, because this expression ably sums up the common opinion (*Unfinished Commentary on Matthew*, Homily 43). The formula is celebrated because of St. Thomas's mention of it, but while he approved its truth, he also explained how it had to be understood lest it be misinterpreted.

It is not necessary just now to enumerate additional authors or to quote still more texts. The most authorized and recent version of that traditional doctrine has been made by Vatican II in its Constitution on the Church (*Lumen Gentium*); see text 6 in the Appendix for a relevant selection. The conciliar text is naturally more nuanced and presents the royal priesthood as closely connected to the priestly ministry—something I will do as well—but it is, after all, the same doctrine.

The Anointing of Kings, Priests, and Prophets

So far we have read texts that could be called "priestly." There are many others that broaden the perspective and recall a doctrine that by now is quite familiar to us. Here we will leave aside the lesser-known authors (who have nonetheless left us some very beautiful texts, such as that by the Bishop Fastidius—or possibly by Pelagius—(text 1 in the Appendix), to turn our attention to two of the best-known authors in our Latin tradition.

First is Augustine, whose *Expositions on the Psalms* have spiritually nourished generations of believers through the centuries and continue to be reissued:

> At that time [of David], the anointing was reserved for the king and the priest....[In] these two persons was prefigured one to come who should be both King and Priest, the one Christ holding both offices, and called the Christ by reason of his Anointing. Not only has our Head, however, been anointed, but we ourselves also who are His Body. Now He is King because He rules and leads us, Priest because he makes intercession for us....
>
> Like a spotless lamb, He redeemed us by the shedding of His blood, incorporating us with Himself, making us His members, that with Him we may make one and the same Christ. That is why all Christians share in the anointing which formerly under the Old Testament was the exclusive prerogative of two men. From this it is evident that we are Christ's Body, because we all share in the anointing and in him we are all both Christ's and Christ, since in a certain way the whole Christ consists in both Head and Body.[3]

Augustine's reasoning presupposes that his listeners are familiar with the etymology of the word *Christ* as well as of the word *Messiah*, both of which mean "anointed," that is, one who has received anointing. The only difference between them is that *Christ* comes from the Greek and *Messiah* from the Aramaic. As for the chrism or oil used for the anointing that Christians have received, it is evidently an allusion to the rite of holy chrism administered at baptism even today with these words: "He [God the Father] now anoints you with the chrism of salvation. As Christ was anointed Priest, Prophet, and King, so may you live always as a member of his body, sharing everlasting life." When one knows the theological and traditional background of such a rich formula, one has to regret that celebrants so often perform it without the least commentary, which could be used to underline its implications.

After St. Augustine, it will be common to connect the priestly, royal, and prophetic nature of the faithful to the baptismal anointing. Thomas Aquinas offers a fine example of this, because he too had much to say about this doctrine. We can take a single text here, one particularly rich in biblical allusions that best teases out the dogmatic implications of anointing. In his commentary on Hebrews 1:9 ("God, your God, has anointed you"), Thomas first recalls the practice of anointing in the Old Testament and the way this applies to Christ, who is likewise a king (according to Isa 32:1 and 33:22), a priest (Ps 110:4), and a prophet too (Deut 18:15). That is why it was fitting for Christ to be anointed with the oil of sanctification and joy, because from him come the sacraments, which are means of grace (according to the Vulgate text of Isa 22:24). Then Thomas continues:

> This anointing also befits Christians, for they are kings and priests: "You are a chosen race, a royal priesthood" (1 Pet 2:9); "You have made us a kingdom and priests for our God" (Rev 5:10). Furthermore, they have the Holy Spirit, Who is the spirit of prophecy: "I will pour out my spirit upon all flesh; and your sons and your daughters shall prophesy" (Joel 2:28 or 3:1). Therefore, all are anointed with an invisible anointing: "Now he that has confirmed us with you in Christ and that has anointed us is God: who has also sealed us and given the pledge of the Spirit in our hearts" (2 Cor 1:21); "But you have the unction from the Holy One and know all things" (1 John 2:20). But what comparison is there between the anointed Christ and anointed Christians? This comparison, namely, that He has it principally and first, but we and others have it from Him: "Like the precious ointment on the head that ran down upon the beard, the beard of Aaron" (Ps 132:2). And, therefore, he says,

before thy comrades: "Of his fullness we have all received" (John 1:16). Hence, others are called holy, but He is the Holy of holies; for He is the root of all holiness. But he says, with the oil of gladness, because spiritual gladness proceeds from that anointing: "The kingdom of God is not meat and drink, but justice and peace and joy in the Holy Spirit" (Rom 14:17); "The fruit of the Spirit is charity, joy, peace" (Gal 5:22).[4]

I wanted to cite that text at some length because it is typical of the way St. Thomas comments on Holy Scripture. This passage is no less theological than many others in the *Summa*, but the texts of Scripture that the reader makes out only faintly in the *Summa* appear in a bright light here. If the results we achieve strike some readers as surprising, they will know that our findings have a solid foundation.

We can readily see in this commentary the key elements that I took as the point of departure in our investigation: Christ, the source of all priesthood and the universal principle in the order of all those who have grace, is also the one who first and foremost possesses the anointing, as the source and cause of all holiness. The persistent presence of the Holy Spirit is no less meaningful, because through it Christ continues to act in our heart. Thomas does not hesitate to say, "The anointing is the Holy Spirit." Notice a detail that is not sufficiently stressed: The presence of the Spirit is synonymous not only with charity and peace, but also with spiritual joy. That too teaches us to read Thomas carefully; he rarely neglects to talk about the spiritual resonances of his teaching.

In Thomas, as in Augustine and so many others before and after him, this doctrine flows from baptism. The Christian is king, priest, and prophet, like Christ, because he or she has received the anointing as Christ did. The formula attributed to St. Cyprian is thus completely accurate: "The Christian is another Christ" ("Christianus alter Christus"). Thomas is no less explicit than Augustine on this point: "Just as the Church is anointed, the faithful too are anointed with a spiritual anointing so as to be made holy. Without this, they would not even be Christians, because *Christ* means 'anointed.' And this anointing is the grace of the Holy Spirit" (*Exposition on the Apostles Creed*, a. 9).

So there is a direct line between this doctrine and the sacrament of baptism. If time permitted, we might have continued our study of Tradition by investigating the liturgical texts, which would yield an abundant harvest. In particular, one could point to the Mass of Consecration of the Holy Chrism, on Holy Thursday, where our triad occurs more than once. The blessing of the oil for the sick on the same day also mentions the martyrs, along with the priests, kings, and prophets. In fact, Scripture bears frequent witness that the prophetic witness goes all the way to the supreme witness of martyrdom.

Sacrifice in *The City of God*

Like the royal and prophetic priesthood, the theme of spiritual sacrifices was also too prominent in Scripture to be ignored by the Fathers and theologians. The one who spoke most eloquently about this—at least in the West—is St. Augustine. Any Christian desiring a theological formation ought to read the selection from Augustine's *City of God* cited in text 2 in the Appendix. Here is a summary of the basic points of his meditation:

Augustine's intention begins to take shape in a preparatory chapter (10.5–6), in which he recalls that the sacrifices of the Old Testament "signified the things which we do for the purpose of drawing near to God and inducing our neighbor to do the same"—and concludes that "[a] sacrifice, therefore, is the visible sacrament or sacred sign of an invisible sacrifice." What, then, is this invisible sacrifice? To answer with the words of Scripture that we have already encountered, it is the "contrite heart" (Ps 51). In fact, the Lord demands that people "do justice,…love kindness, and…walk humbly with your God" (Mic 6:6–8). So when the prophet says, "I desire steadfast love and not sacrifice" (Hos 6:6), he means that "mercy is the true sacrifice." Augustine derives that first definition from the Old Testament. He does not conclude from it that external sacrifices were useless, but that they were signs of another reality and existed on a double level: signs of the interior sacrifice that is always necessary, because it is the soul of all external sacrifice; also, signs of the New Law, the sacrifice of the cross that is always effective and fertile in the sacrament of the Eucharist.

Augustine then comes to his own personal vision of sacrifice: "Thus a true sacrifice is every work which is done that we may be united with God in holy fellowship, and which has a reference to that supreme good and end in which alone we can be truly blessed" (10. 6). The definition is extremely broad, as are the examples given to support it: "True sacrifices are works of mercy to ourselves or to others done with reference to God." One cannot help noticing that St. Augustine calls a sacrifice exactly what St. Paul does in Romans 12:1, that is, offering oneself as "a living sacrifice, holy and acceptable to God, which is your spiritual worship." Augustine's idea of sacrifice thus takes us back to what I earlier called the "existential sacrifice." Every act of charity that expresses our obedience to the double commandment of love is a sacrifice, and through that charity is realized the union, the communion, with God that is the very purpose of worship. This text may be read in its entirety later on: there really is a beautiful continuity between Paul and Augustine.

Yet, there is something new in Augustine. Or rather, he sums up and specifies things that are more implicit and diffuse in Paul: It is not just the persons who are the object or material of this sacrifice, but the whole Church:

> It follows that the whole redeemed City, that is to say, the congregation or communion of the saints [Augustine says *societas*, but this is plainly a translation of the Greek word *koinônia*], is offered to God as our sacrifice through the great High Priest, who offered himself to God in his passion for us, that we might be members of this glorious Head, according to the form of a servant. For it was this form he offered, in this he was offered; because it is according to it he is Mediator, in this he is our Priest, in this the Sacrifice. (*City of God* 10.6)

This text is not only beautiful—a simple taste of Augustine's lyricism, one might be tempted to say—it actually lays down the absolute condition that prevents us from distorting the notion of spiritual sacrifice.

In bygone days this doctrine was misused to the point of a mean-spirited caricature; for example, little children were taught to make "little sacrifices" that could be jotted down in a little notebook. This individualistic, bookkeeping attitude has nothing to do with the profound Christian reality about which we are speaking. Augustine recalls that only insertion into the ecclesial Body of Christ constitutes the concrete environment for exercising the commandment of love. The sacrifice of mutual charity and the reciprocal service in mercy are possible only to the extent that we are a single Body in Christ.

At this point in our reflections, it is evident that the spiritual sacrifice finds its fulfillment in the eucharistic offering. What one could no more than glimpse in 1 Peter has been perfectly perceived and expressed by Augustine, which is why he ends that chapter by recalling the liturgical sacrifice, the place where Christians celebrate their spiritual sacrifice:

> This is the sacrifice of Christians: we, being many, are one body in Christ. And this is the sacrifice of Christ, which the Church continually celebrates in the sacrament of the altar, known to the faithful, in which she teaches that she herself is offered in the offering she makes to God. (10.6)

THE REALITY OF THE SPIRITUAL PRIESTHOOD

Until Vatican II, many preconciliar theologians had difficulty in situating precisely, and even simply naming, the reality we have just dealt with, as expressed by the greatest minds of our Latin tradition. This reality had so completely disappeared from the theological horizon since the Reformation (and, in part, as a result of it) that the term *priesthood*, being exclusively reserved to ordained priests, seemed impossible to apply to the faithful who had not received the sacrament of holy orders. One had to be familiar with the discomfort felt by certain members of the clergy when the postconciliar, new-sounding vocabulary appeared, to measure the astonishment and disarray it sometimes caused. We are still not at the end of this process, and many questions are still being asked. The most important of these questions undoubtedly concerns the relation of the royal priesthood to what is generally called the ministerial priesthood (which I prefer to call the priestly ministry). But it would be better to wait and have a leisurely discussion of that ministerial priesthood before addressing the relation between the two. Similarly, at that point we can ask ourselves from a closer vantage point about the best terms to designate each of them. For now, by way of a provisional conclusion, I would like to dissipate a misunderstanding that weighs down the use of these words.

A Metaphorical Priesthood?

It has sometimes been said that *sacrifice* and *priesthood*, in the context in which we have just applied them, are only usable in a metaphorical sense; therefore, one has to resist the temptation to substitute "that kind" of priesthood for the only real priesthood, which would be ministerial priesthood. After all the texts that we have just read, it is easy to understand that this manner of speaking is inaccurate. I emphasize just two points:

1. Hinting that spiritual priesthood or sacrifices are not real opens the way for "real" to become to be synonymous with "material" or "exterior." The only "real" things in this view would be what is visible and palpable. This cheapens the life of the spirit itself in its broadest sense; spiritually speaking, it means denying any reality to religious feelings in general and to mystical phenomena in particular, which so many saints have told us about, since by definition spirituality is all about acts that come from the soul and escape direct observation.

2. More seriously, speaking of a metaphorical priesthood or sacrifice suggests that the first term of comparison (theologians would call this the "first

analogue") according to which priesthood is judged would be the ministerial priesthood. Now this is an unquestionable error: The royal priesthood *is* called that in connection with a first priesthood; *but* that first kind is the priesthood of Christ. It is from him that the royal priesthood derives its reality and its name. This is equally true for the ministerial priesthood, something we must not lose sight of. But in that case we are dealing with another type of participation in the first kind, and it is a mistake to believe that this second participation is superior to the first. The opposite is true: The priestly ministry is meant to serve the reality of grace that the royal priesthood expresses by spiritual sacrifice.

A "Real" Priesthood?

To solve the preceding difficulty—only an apparent problem, but a persistent one—we must return to the priesthood of Christ. For us Christians, there is no a priori definition of sacrifice that would apply equally to Jewish priests, pagan priests, and Christian priests. It seems that it was actually to prevent such confusion that the first Christian writings avoided using the word *priest* to designate Christian ministers. Thus, the only definition of priesthood that is normative for us is the one we can gather from the writings of the New Testament and, more precisely, from those that speak of Christ's priesthood and of royal priesthood. There is no room for doubt here: Even if such an extended sense of priesthood and sacrifice seems disconcerting, it is, to be sure, spiritual; it is also thoroughly real. Such consistency in using the cultic vocabulary, as well as in reserving the word *hiereus* for the officiant of that interior worship, forbids us to consider it metaphorical. Again: it is plainly spiritual, but it is also altogether real. One could even maintain non-paradoxically that *this* priesthood and *this* sacrifice are the only "real" ones, that is, the ones fully entitled to derive from the order of reality (*res* in Latin, whence our word *real*), but from the reality that is ultimately at stake here—in other words, from grace, from the divine life. We recall how Augustine puts it in *The City of God*: "The visible sacrifice is the *sacramentum*...of the invisible sacrifice"; and a little further on: "That which in common speech is called sacrifice is only the symbol of the true sacrifice" (10.5). St. Thomas picks up precisely this passage and concludes, as Augustine does, "Everything that is offered to God with a view toward bringing the spirit of man to God can be called a sacrifice" (*Summa Theologica* IIIa q. 22, a. 2). Even in the treatise on religion, where Thomas seeks to define sacrifice in its external reality, he never abandons that Augustinian heritage; rather, one would say that he "fiercely strives to keep it" (*ST* IIa IIae q. 85, a. 3, sol. 1–2).

Nor does St. Thomas hesitate either to use the title *sacerdos* ("priest") for the ordinary faithful. With specific reference to the famous phrase of Pseudo-Chrysostom that "every saint is a priest," he explains: "Every good man or woman is called a priest, because in a mystical fashion he or she offers to God a mystical sacrifice, that is to say, himself or herself, I as a living victim to God, in keeping with Romans 12:1" (*Sentences* IV d. 13, q. 1, a 1, sol. 1, ad 1). Nevertheless, he makes distinctions that are imperative, as I myself will do when the time comes. Still, with reference to the same authority of Pseudo-Chrysostom, he further explains in another place:

> The just *layperson* [note that the perspective here is intra-ecclesial, he no longer speaks of "everyone" (*omnis homo*); yet neither does he repudiate that first statement] is united to Christ in a spiritual bond by faith and charity, not by sacramental power. And this is why the layperson possesses a spiritual priesthood that permits him or her to offer spiritual sacrifices like those spoken of in Psalm 51:19 ("The sacrifice acceptable to God is a broken spirit") and in Romans 12:1 ("Present your bodies as a living sacrifice"). And again that is what 1 Peter 2:5 talks about: "a holy priesthood to offer spiritual sacrifices." (*ST* IIIa q. 82, a. 1, sol. 2)

St. Thomas himself came to grips with this difficulty, which is why he proposes another distinction to account better for that same text of Pseudo-Chrysostom:

> Chrysostom uses the term "priest" according to the *interpretation* of the name, that is, according as "priest" means one who gives sacred things. In this sense, *all just persons* have the reality of the priesthood in that they give their holy merits to others to help them. We, however, speak in accordance with the [current] *meaning* of the name. In fact, this name of "priest" has been reserved to those who give sacred things in the dispensation of the sacraments." (*Sentences* IV d. 24, q. 1, a. 3, sol. 3, ad 1)

There is no better way to point out that the ecclesiastical usage of the term *priest*, which Thomas alludes to here as the "current meaning of the name," has limited its first sense. But he nonetheless recognizes it as still valid, in keeping with Chrysostom.[5]

The Some-All Relationship

We still have two points to emphasize as we conclude the chapter. They are raised by the last texts of St. Thomas that we have just read, but they also apply to the entire foregoing argument. First, there are indeed two meanings of the word *priest*, or *priesthood*, in Christianity. The fact that, despite several periods of neglect, the Church of Christ has always retained these two different meanings simultaneously makes it clear that Christians saw no contradiction between them. Thus, one cannot invoke the new emphasis on the royal priesthood to deny the value of the ministerial priesthood. Second, one has to distinguish between these two priestly titles or else risk being bogged down in harmful ambiguities. All are priests, but some are priests of a different sort.

This becomes clearer if we recall an episode from the Old Testament that is both curious and enlightening. In it we see two ringleaders, Dathan and Abiram, rise up at the head of 250 men to protest against what they see as an abuse of power by Moses and Aaron. "You have gone too far! All the congregation are holy, every one of them, and the LORD is among them. So why then do you exalt yourselves above the assembly of the Lord?" (Num 16:3). Yet God pronounces in favor of Aaron and his sons, whom he has chosen and consecrated for the priestly anointing; and the rebels are cast down still alive into Sheol for having dared to "seek [the functions of] the priesthood" (Num 16:10). Much later, the Letter to the Hebrews draws this lesson from the episode: "One does not presume to take this honor, but takes it only when called by God, just as Aaron was" (5:4).

The story certainly voices a real political difficulty on which we need not dwell; but it also recalls a fact that the Church Fathers would not forget: in this wholly priestly people, certain individuals exercised the priesthood as an official function. Even if the nature of the priesthood changes in the New Covenant, we must acknowledge the existence of an analogous relationship between the priestly body of each of its members and of the ministers chosen from among them, who take on a priestly function among others. It is these ministries that I will now address.

III

THE MINISTERS OF THE NEW COVENANT AND THEIR DIFFERENT FUNCTIONS

From the New Testament to the Beginning of the Third Century

The purpose of this chapter is to identify the role played by the ministers in an ecclesial body that is wholly priestly. This new investigation is directly related to the two major facts brought out in the Introduction during the attempt to find the right language for our subject: first, the diversity of offices or functions—or, at the very least, the multiplicity of names—attributed to the Christian ministers of the New Testament; second, the absence of a priestly vocabulary in the context of those ministerial functions.

This second discovery directly asks whether and how the ministers can be called priests. That is the principal question I want to answer in this chapter, since the primary object of the book concerns the priesthood in all its fullness, among the ministers and among the faithful. We will return to this later and begin by examining the questions raised by the ministry in general as it appears in the texts of the apostolic era and immediately afterward. Two main questions then emerge: (1) Did these various ministries really originate in the apostolic era? (2) How did the transition occur from that abundance of ministries with different names to the strict three-part classification with which we are familiar today: bishops, priests, and deacons? In keeping with the approach followed in this book, I am going to look for the answer in sources that are already well known, but in which a more attentive rereading will allow us to discover less-familiar features. First, however, I will make some preliminary clarifications.

PRELIMINARY REMARKS

These observations might have been proposed at the very beginning of the book, but they are more directly applicable to what follows. They come from noticeably different spheres, but they share an important, if not decisive, influence on our investigation.

Method

I do not intend to go into detail on everything that can possibly be said about the ministries in the New Testament. There are some very fine works on this subject, and I can only refer readers to them. Despite appearances, my aim is not exegetical, but theological. I do *not* want to do a narrowly philological reading of these texts as if they were our only resource. We cannot forget that these texts are merely the fragmentary and discontinuous echo of a life in the Church, which they describe at times in some detail but about which they do not tell us everything. To understand them, they must be positioned against a complex background that involves at least three main elements.

The first is the life of the primitive Christian community that has had to learn to carry on after the departure of its Lord (whom, it seems, Christians expected to return very quickly). It therefore has to take measures to get organized in response to its growing mass and diversity. The first and most evident example of this is found in the Acts of the Apostles 6:1–6 in the election of seven men to fulfill two specific objectives: first, to free the Twelve from the material problems posed by the distribution of aid to an indigent community that was becoming larger and larger, so that they themselves could remain completely available for the proclamation of the Word; second, to solve the "political" problem caused by friction between the Hellenist and the Jewish faithful.

We learn here in credible detail that the need to set up functions of government and assistance was very quickly felt by the apostles. In fact, we see them "laying hands" on persons chosen by the assembly of the faithful and delegating to them some of their own functions. This is not a simple episode of secondary importance; we will find many analogous cases in which the need generates the function. This elementary state of affairs that becomes necessary for all groups of any significance is also found in the community of the primitive Church.

So the life of the early Church constitutes part of the background against which we reposition what the texts say because that life shows us their meaning. It is this vital tissue, enduring through the new generations of Christ's faithful, that will allow us at times also to conjecture about what the texts do *not* always say, but whose existence we can readily suspect. To be sure, one must not abuse this sort of conjecture, but the procedure can be legitimate and at times I will have recourse to it.

The second element in our investigation of this background is that this first community is itself related to a larger environment, that of contemporary Judaism. This is self-evident, but there are ways of referring to just the letter of the New Testament that might make us forget it. Like Jesus himself, the first disciples were Jews—in religion and in culture. They were slow, sometimes very slow, in coming to grasp their specific Christian identity. For example, the first Christians and St. Paul himself continued to frequent the Temple and practice Jewish customs until the decade of the 50s; the Letter to the Hebrews was plainly written to fortify old Jewish priests' nostalgia for the Temple cult. Now, what is true for such persons is also true for the community, and the institutions that the early Church established closely resemble other Jewish institutions that we know. We will see this once we discuss the apostles, who correspond to an otherwise familiar Jewish institution, the *schelihim*. The same goes for the elders, who are the Christian continuation of the council of the elders that presided over every Jewish community. This continuity with institutions already existing in the Hebrew environment allows us to refer to them so as to understand better the mode of governance of the growing Christian community. Thus we can sometimes make up for the silence of our texts by appealing, for example, to the texts from Qumran. We will not conclude from them that there is no difference—far from it! But, in certain cases, this can shed decisive light on the issues.

The third element of the background that we must keep in mind is the historical community that existed between the time of Jesus and the Twelve and the time of the various ministers that we will encounter again in the postapostolic era. Just as the primitive community did not live within a closed milieu, isolated from the world around it, so the years when the New Testament was edited cannot be understood as marking off a closed period unconnected to those that preceded and followed it. True, the books of the New Testament have a unique authority for us, but it is quite clear that they are incomprehensible without the Old Testament, to which the protagonists of the New constantly refer (beginning with Jesus and Paul). In the same fashion, the last books of the New Testament had not yet even been written when the "new" Christian books of the Apostolic Fathers began making their appearance. This is the case, for example, with the *Didache* (written between AD 50 and 70, according to some scholars, or, in any case, before the end of the first century), and of *First Clement*, written by Clement of Rome (pope 95–98). Historically speaking, these "new" writings can claim at least some of the authority enjoyed by the canonical texts, and can be used to confirm what the most critical exegetes observe in the New Testament. Thus, for example, it is obvious that in the thought of St. Luke, as seen in Acts, the new ministers have the precise goal of assuring the continuity from one stage to another of the history he recounts.

This continuity even allows us to discover the problem to which it is responding: the assurance of the succession of the apostles. So it is not surprising that the ministers appear at a relatively late epoch, or at least that they are better documented then. It is the disappearance of the apostles and of their first delegates that leads (and has already led) those men to look for successors—successors who will themselves stand before the community and in its midst to vow fidelity to the Gospel message. It is no accident that we encounter the finest expression of this concern in the Second Letter to Timothy (written around the year 80, but possibly sooner, if one takes the Pastoral Letters to be authentically Pauline, as used to be the case): "What you have heard from me through many witnesses entrust to faithful people who will be able to teach others as well" (2 Tim 2:2).

The importance of this verse comes from the fact that it clearly announces three links in a succession of ministers: Paul (or one of his immediate disciples), Timothy, and the "faithful people." But even this chain does not close upon itself: it can and must be lengthened out in both directions. St. Paul himself solemnly looks to the past on two occasions: "I received from the Lord what I also handed on to you" (1 Cor 11:23, on the celebration of the Eucharist); and, "I handed on to you as of first importance what I in turn had received: that Christ died for our sins in accordance with the scriptures" (1 Cor 15:3, for the first catechesis on the resurrection). Paul also looks to the future, not just the "faithful people" in 2 Timothy 2:2, but their very clear assignment to instruct others and to confide the same teaching mission to those whom they will have taught.

For the theology of what will later become the apostolic succession, this verse from 2 Timothy is of capital importance. If we now broaden the perspective and say not just "teach," but "do" (which is the context of the verse that recalls Christ's commandment: "Do this in remembrance of me" [1 Cor 11:24–25]), we have the exact framework that we need for our investigation, and that will let us deal suitably with our problem. This framework is that of Tradition in action, such as the Second Vatican Council defines it:

> Now what was handed on by the Apostles includes everything which contributes toward the holiness of life and [an] increase in faith of the peoples of God; and so the Church, in her teaching, life and worship, perpetuates and hands on to all generations all that she herself is, all that she believes. (*Dei Verbum* 8)

No doubt we now understand better why these first remarks have been placed under the heading of "method." Their purpose can be summed up in this way: If one isolates the various pieces of evidence that we are going to gather from this movement of lived transmission, which is at once doctrinal and "real" (by "deeds"—notably baptism and the Eucharist—the "reality" of salvation is transmitted), these pieces of evidence are often just discontinuous fragments with significance in themselves, and yet whose range one will always be afraid of overestimating. However, by contrast, if these indications are placed back in their relation to the whole that supports them, they assume their full importance and appear for what they are: testimonies to the life of the newborn Church. We wish there were more of them, of course, but they are already precious.

The Date of the Letters of Ignatius of Antioch

Bishop of the most prestigious Church after the one in Jerusalem, Ignatius was, according to the early fourth-century historian Eusebius of Caesarea, second successor to St. Peter as the head of that community, where Christ's faithful first received the name of "Christians." Ignatius was arrested during the reign of the emperor Trajan (AD 98–117), along with other Christians, and transported to Rome to be thrown to the beasts in the Coliseum. His journey to execution was marked by a series of seven letters addressed to the Churches through whose territory he passed. These letters not only express the moving spirituality of martyrdom that animated him; they are also very precise testimonials about the life of the Church at that time and, in particular, about its internal organization and the various ministries operating there. The date of his martyrdom, generally given as around 107 to 110, makes this collection of letters a major witness to the beginning of the second century. It is also exceptionally clear about the existence of a three-step Church hierarchy, exactly like the one we know today (bishops, priests, deacons); and, likewise, very clear about the connection of these ministers with the Eucharist.

The clarity and power of this testimonial in favor of the single episcopacy makes it a bothersome witness for all the non-Catholic historians who challenge the legitimacy of the Church's hierarchical structure. Thus, for about two hundred years, these letters have been subjected to discussions and critiques; the result has been a veritable dance of varying hypotheses that successively contradict one another. Take, for example, the two most recent ones, put forth more or less simultaneously in 1979. Their authors have in common the notion that there was a forger—living some fifty years after the real Ignatius—who either manipulated the authentic letters or fabricated the entire lot. The second of these authors, who is the more radical, thinks that the first man's thesis will not stand up under examination. The critical recensions that I have read do not shy away from pointing up the disagreements between the two authors; indeed, they stress the excessive part played by gratuitous reconstruction in each of the theories. These theories are, in fact, more ingenious than convincing, and one of the authors has, furthermore, retracted part of his case.

When we think about the different ministries that appear in the New Testament texts, witnesses as old and as clear as the letters of Ignatius in favor of a single bishop in each local Church really have something amazing about them, as we can see. However, even if one had to concede that the disputants were right about the date of the letters (which still remains to be proven, despite the recent attempts just mentioned), their contents cannot be disqualified, for all that. Even if the texts as they have come down to us are placed in 165 and not 110, they remain unimpeachable witnesses to what the Church's organization in Asia was at that date.

But this remains nothing more than a hypothesis, and it ought not make us forget that these letters were attested to very early on, and that those who introduced them raised no doubts as to the identity of their author. To cite only three witnesses to these letters: The oldest and most important, the first to talk about them, is St. Irenaeus of Lyon (shortly after 180). He does not name Ignatius and simply calls the author "one of ours," but he quotes literally, without any possible misunderstanding, a passage from Ignatius's letter *To the Romans* in his own work *Against Heresies* (5.28.4). The second witness is Origen of Alexandria (around AD 240), who quotes Ignatius by name on two occasions and anonymously on a third, in three different works (*Commentary on the Canticle*, Prologue 2.36; *Homilies on St. Luke* 6.4; *On Prayer*

20). The third witness is, once more, the celebrated historian Eusebius of Caesarea, to whom we owe so much information about the first three centuries of Christianity and, in particular, many titles and long quotations from works that have by now disappeared (*Ecclesiastical History* 3.36; before AD 303). Taken together, these letters of Ignatius are a document that is incontestably from the second century. Even if we admit that we must resign ourselves to using them with a certain amount of incertitude, that does not make any fundamental difference. This would simply mean pushing forward by some years the period of definitive dating for the institutions of the Church that we are now about to discuss.

THE MINISTRIES IN THE SUCCESSION OF THE APOSTLES

The Twelve

We can use as our point of departure verse 8 from Psalm 109 quoted by Peter at the moment when a successor has to be nominated to replace Judas, who had betrayed Jesus: "Let another take his position of overseer" (Acts 1:20). The word that has been translated here as *overseer* is *episkopē*. As we know from other sources, *episkopē* means an office of supervision, of inspection, a duty that has attached to it the right to make visits, with the right, as needed, to reprimand. This quite general meaning will become more specific in the course of our investigation, but this verse shows us at the outset that the group of the Twelve, which had to be made complete, exercised an *episkopē*. To become part of this group, certain conditions had to be met, which Peter specifically lists: "So one of the men who have accompanied us during all the time that the Lord Jesus went in and out among us, beginning from the baptism of John until the day when he was taken up from us—one of these must become a witness with us to his resurrection" (Acts 1:21–22). This was written by St. Luke around the year 80 (the probable date for the final editing of Acts); but all four of the evangelists tell us about this group of the

Twelve, chosen by Jesus. We see that it still existed as such at the time of the appearances of the Risen One (see 1 Cor 15:5, where Paul picks up an ancient tradition concerning the appearances; Paul's letter itself dates from AD 56/57, but the account of the apparitions that he adopts probably goes back before the year 40).

To describe briefly the concrete content of the work of *episkopē* exercised by the Twelve, we can take the final scene from the Gospel of Matthew (28:16–20), which places in the mouth of the risen Christ the order calling for a universal mission addressed to the remaining eleven apostles; this mission consists in making disciples of all nations by announcing the Word to them and baptizing them. We find the equivalent of this sending forth at the end of Mark and Luke. But Luke twice adds a significant note: "You are *witnesses* of these things" (Luke 24:48; Acts 1:8). The word is important because it emphasizes not only an idea held dear by Luke, who carefully sought out documentation from eyewitnesses to write his Gospel (see Luke 1:1–4), but also the fact that this is a prerogative of the apostles that absolutely cannot be transmitted: no one after them will ever be able to be a witness in that manner.

In fact, we later find express references to the activity of certain individuals from that group, restored to twelve members by the addition of Matthias, who himself had been an eyewitness. In reality, we see only the first four, the two pairs of brothers: Peter and Andrew, James and John. Thus, Peter and John are specially involved in the oldest preaching (Acts 3:1; 4:13; 8:14). They reappear in the year 49 in a position of authority with James: they are the "pillars" of Jerusalem to whom Paul will report about his mission (Gal 2:9). This James is the "brother of the Lord," not of John, who died a martyr a little earlier in that same decade (see Acts 12:2). Of these Twelve, only Peter engages in any activity outside Palestine. We find him in Antioch (Gal 2:11) and perhaps in Corinth (1 Cor 1:12), where we hear about those who appeal to Paul and those who appeal to Cephas. In 1 Corinthians 9:5, we read of Cephas, who is accompanied by a sister. We do not know anything about the *individual* preaching of other members of the group—even if the first Christian traditions attributed to them, early on and with some probability, apostolates in various countries of what we now call the Middle East and even farther afield.

Still, in the absence of individual activity, we often see the Twelve exercising a *collective* role, as in the moment when they lay their hands on the seven men chosen to attend to the needs of the poor in the first community (Acts 6:2), or at the Council of Jerusalem in AD 50, when differences had to be settled between Paul and Barnabas, on the one hand, and the Jewish faithful on the other, concerning the admission of the first pagans (Acts 15:6). It is likewise as a body that the Twelve received the power to bind and to loose, whether to admit people into the community or to lay down obligations (Matt 18:18). The same is true when they receive from Jesus, after his resurrection, the power to remit sins (John 20:21–23). The acknowledged preeminence of the group of Twelve recurs in the heavenly Jerusalem where they reappear as the twelve foundations of the City (Rev 21:14).

Within this body, Peter has a place apart: he is the only one of the Twelve whom one sees acting outside of Jerusalem. He is also the only one who has had the office of binding and loosing, which has been entrusted to the Twelve in common, communicated to him in a personal fashion by Jesus (Matt 16:19). On the days after Jesus' resurrection, Peter is seen as the natural spokesman, not only of the Twelve, but of the assembly of the faithful. He is the one who takes the initiative for the selection of Matthias (Acts 1:15–22), who addresses the crowd on the morning of Pentecost (Acts 2:14–36), and who, with John, represents the community before the authorities (Acts 4:1–22). Again, he is the one who announces the punishment of Ananias and Sapphira, who have been found guilty of trying to deceive the others about the price of the field they had sold (Acts 5:1–6). Among many other texts in which we see him thrust forward in this way, we still recall the passages that show Peter receiving from the Lord the mission to strengthen his brothers (Luke 22:32) and the assignment to *feed* (*poimainein,* "guard," "nurture," "guide") the flock of Christ (John 21:15–17).

This is all surely familiar since the texts recur regularly in our liturgical celebrations (especially during Eastertide). But this cumulative reference here allows us to grasp better the strong preeminence and authority attached to the group of the Twelve and, among them, the special role that falls to Peter. I will not return to that last subject because it does not fit in with the purpose of this book. But it is highly interesting to follow as closely as possible the principal stages of the transmission of their authority to the ministers who, under different titles, will succeed the Twelve.

The Seven

The first example of the transmission by the Twelve of some of their prerogatives is the one reported by the Acts of the Apostles (6:1–6). According to the specialists who have sought to discover the sources to which Luke had recourse in composing Acts, this passage is all the more interesting in that it reproduces a very old document. The growing numbers of the Jerusalem community and its diversity are what led to the institution of the Seven. In the very beginning, Luke seems to be speaking about a rather banal dispute between Hebrews and Hellenists over a simple question of obtaining help for poor widows. In reality, according to a number of experts, the persecution to which the Hellenists would soon be subject suggests that a much more serious conflict was involved.

In any event, we see the apostles refusing to abandon "the service [*diakonia*] of the word" (6:2 and 4, which adds "prayer") to devote themselves to the cares of the local Church of Jerusalem. And that is why, with a view to continuing to take care of their own specific task, they ask the assembly to choose seven men to whom they can entrust the supervision of the Hellenist group. The author does not use the term *diakonos* with respect to the Seven, but he repeats the term *diakonein*, and it is possible that he sees in them the "deacons" who are also mentioned elsewhere (Phil 1:1, and various other places). Nevertheless, these men are not deacons in the precise sense that the word will assume later, because we see them preaching and teaching (as Stephen and Philip do in Acts 7 and 8), which is definitely a participation in the "service of the Word," the *diakonia tou logou*, which is the apostles' primary function.

The most interesting thing about this passage, however, might be found in what it does not say clearly. In all probability, we are witnessing here the actual founding by the apostles of two parallel hierarchies, in that the Seven are all Greeks (as we see from their names), and they are proposed for the group of Hellenists. The text does not tell us whether the Hebrews also got a similar group to take care of them, but everything suggests that they did. Later in the Book of Acts (11:3), we are told about a group of *presbuteroi* in charge of the Church of Jerusalem—that same Church from whom the Hellenists had been driven out by the persecution—and on several occasions these *presbuteroi* are mentioned at the same time as the "apostles" (that is, in Luke's language, the Twelve). Thus, we see side by side "the apostles and the elders [*presbuteroi*]" (Acts 15:2, 4, 6, 22–23; 16:4).

This apostles-elders (*presbuteroi*) combination reminds us of another coupling often found in Luke when he speaks of the Jewish authorities: "the rulers of the people and the elders" (Acts 4:5, 8); "the chief priests and the elders" (Acts 23:14; 25:25). The text of Acts does not say—nor does any other text, by the way— but it is highly possible that the growing Church provided itself with an organization parallel to the one functioning in the Jewish communities of its day. The highest authority, that of the apostles, was passed along in the local communities by a lower-level authority, that of the elders. The parallel does not stop there. In the group of the apostles, Peter plays the part of spokesman (at the very least); in the group of Jerusalem elders, it is James who takes on that role. He, in fact, is the one who, surrounded by the elders, receives Paul when he comes on pilgrimage (Acts 21:18). It is James again who plays a leading role in the Council of Jerusalem in 49/50 (Acts 15:13–21, 23–29). And in his Letter to the Galatians (2:9), Paul even mentions James before Peter and John, who, after all, were two of the Twelve. (On this James, see also Gal 1:19; 2:12.)

One might think for a moment that James had succeeded Peter as the head of the Church of Jerusalem, but this apparently is not correct, and scholars recall that the passage about the appointing of the Seven emphasizes the refusal by the apostles to take over the leadership of a local Church. Besides, the simultaneous presence of Peter and James on several occasions cancels out the hypothesis of succession. That simultaneous presence is explained much better if the positions they hold are different. The presence of James and the elders among the Hebrews thus corresponds to the same type of necessity that led to the institution of the Seven among the Hellenists: the need to have an authority at the head of the local Church. By that very fact, the apostles could continue devoting themselves to what they considered their own role, and thus they were probably also set free to pursue an itinerant ministry. As for the Twelve, while only Peter appears explicitly in this case, there is nothing to indicate that the others did not do the same. In any event, it is the image that Tradition has kept of them; one can see in this sense what Clement of Rome says about it in his letter to the Corinthians (*1 Clement* 42; text 3 in the Appendix). The *Didache* also speaks of traveling apostles in 11:3–6, but that is not about the Twelve. Some critics like to stress that, except for Peter, we have no historical proof that any of the Twelve ever left Jerusalem. That is true, but the opposite has been said as well.

The story of the founding of the Seven allows us to see how, very soon after the departure of the Lord (that is, around 35 to 40), there was a concrete transition from the authority of the apostles to that of those in charge of the local Church. This took place in two ways: by the group of elders with James at their head and by the group of the Seven. Did this latter group have a president? Was it Stephen? We cannot answer these questions because Stephen died too soon for us to be able to follow his path, as we can with James. The two groups are clearly going to evolve differently with respect to their attachment to Judaism, and it is ultimately the group of Hellenists that will insure the expansion of Christianity. If it is likely that their challenge of Jewish customs was the cause of the persecution that drove them from Jerusalem, it is absolutely certain that this expulsion lies at the providential origin of the beginning of the worldwide mission. It is also clear that this episode of Acts is the only passage in the New Testament in which we see the Twelve intervening so intimately in the nomination of heads of a local Church. Thus, we can understand much better the importance of this text, because with it we go back to the witnesses of the historical Jesus. With it we have access to the first link of the Tradition spoken of in 2 Timothy and 1 Corinthians. Similarly, the evolution that follows and that I will soon discuss is solidly rooted in its historical legitimacy.

The First Ministers Appointed by St. Paul

If we now choose another example of succession and transfer of authority, it cannot be on the part of the Twelve but of St. Paul, whose rank as an apostle does not have to be demonstrated: He took charge of it himself. For him, the vision of the risen Christ substitutes for what life with Jesus was for the Twelve (who were also, of course, witnesses to the risen Christ). But it must be noted that, in spite of his polemical claims, Paul then receives the message from the already-existing Church. He is sent to Damascus to learn from Ananias what he has to do (Acts 9:6, and parallel passages). He has to be baptized (Acts 9:18). He is extraordinarily concerned with obtaining the agreement of the Twelve and of Jerusalem (Gal 2:1–10). Even if relations between him and Peter were sometimes stormy, there is no doubt about the continuity between Paul and the Twelve. And he himself says that he then handed on what he received (1 Cor 11:23; 15:3).

In the same way, there is a similarity between the *episkopē* of the Twelve and the one exercised by Paul: He teaches, he exhorts, he reprimands, he judges the bad members of the community. It is pointless to enumerate the references; his letters are full of these examples. He undoubtedly considers himself the first person responsible for the communities that he founded, and he promises that when he visits them, he will act, if necessary, "unsparingly" (2 Cor 13:2). He even expels from the community those who refuse to obey his letter (2 Thess 3:14). So he behaves with the full authority of a ruler, and yet we do not see him bound up with Corinth or Ephesus, despite his long stays in both places as the local person in charge.

On the contrary, from the very beginning of his mission we see that he names people to be responsible for the communities he has founded. The first dated mention is found in the First Letter to the Thessalonians (5:12), around AD 50, several months after Paul had passed through: "Respect those who labor among you, and have charge of you in the Lord and admonish you." These persons in charge of the community are the *proïstamenoi*, whom we will meet again later. The second passage occurs in Philippians 1:1, which is addressed to the community as well as to its *episkopoi* and its *diakonoi*. This passage is of interest to us for specific reasons. It proves that the title of overseer was already in use at that period, so close to the origins (around 56 to 57); it also introduces the pairing *overseers-deacons* that we will meet again in other ancient writings: the *Didache* (15:1) and Clement of Rome's letter to the Corinthians (*1 Clement* 42:4–5; see text 3 in the Appendix). As for the third citation, it too is very old; it is found in 1 Corinthians 12:28 in the listing of charisms at work in Corinth, where Paul speaks of the gift of *kybernesis* (meaning "guidance," "leadership," "governance," or "administration"— depending on the translation). At this point we are in the spring of the year 57. To these various passages from his letters, we can add Paul's exhortation at Miletus to the *presbuteroi* of the Church of Ephesus who have been appointed as "*episkopoi* to care for [*poimainen*] the church of God which he obtained with the blood of his own Son" (Acts 20:17, 28), which attests to the existence of these ministers at Ephesus when Paul passed through en route to Jerusalem in 58.

Thus we have four convergent indications between 50 and 60 that clearly point to the fact that Paul's practice corresponds to what he says in 1 Thessalonians 5:12: He puts persons in charge before leaving the newly founded community to itself. We have, incidentally, a confirmation of this practice in Acts 14:23, where Luke, speaking of Paul and Barnabas's traveling evangelization, declares: "They had appointed elders for them in each church." Even if the title of elder is slightly anachronistic at this period, the very action of appointing people in charge corresponds to reality. That is why, incidentally, we cannot accept the oft-repeated but unverified claim first made by nineteenth-century, liberal Protestant scholars that there were no persons in charge in the Pauline communities, only charismatics. Just because such ministers are not explicitly named at Corinth does not permit us to conclude that they did not exist. Some even propose to identify them with Stephanas, Fortunatus, and Achaicus, who are the very same ones who brought to Paul the news of the disturbances against which he reacted. It is with good reason that he recommends, "Give recognition to such persons" (1 Cor 16:15–18).

Nevertheless, we must not overestimate what we know about such ministers. We still do not know what their exact role was in that ancient period and how their function as overseers fit in with the other charisms Paul speaks of (1 Cor. 12). We will learn more from the slightly later epoch of the Pastoral Letters.

The *Presbyters-Overseers* in the Pastoral Letters

Without lingering on it, we cannot completely ignore a preliminary question: What is the date of the Pastoral Letters, that is, Titus, and 1 and 2 Timothy? There used to be many good authors who argued for their Pauline authenticity and so placed them around the year 65. But these authors were already in the minority, and most exegetes today consider them deuteropauline (that is, not written by Paul himself, but by his disciples), and instead date them from the 80s. For our purposes, this issue of dating has only a relative importance. The essential thing is that the Pastoral Letters already reflect a postapostolic situation, which clearly shows how preoccupied that epoch was with assuring the continuation of the Church and providing for its organization after the loss of the apostles. In fact, Peter, Paul, and James all die in the middle of the 60s, and it is perfectly understandable that the problem should have become more acute at that moment. It is quite as understandable that people would have sought to ensure fidelity to the apostolic work and to attribute to the authority of the apostles the measures that were taken at the time. However, whether it is Paul himself who speaks or someone who speaks in his name, the author is always inspired to tell us what the community did and, with the assistance of the Holy Spirit, to respond to the Lord's commandment to proclaim the Gospel until the end of time.

With the Pastoral Letters, then, we become acquainted with a changed situation, and this is manifest even in the appearance of a new category of ministers. Until now, we have seen the

Twelve or Paul himself directly naming the persons in charge in the local Church. In the Pastoral Letters, we see the emergence of the apostles in the broad sense, the second-generation apostles. We are already aware of them because the account of the apparitions of the risen Christ, after mentioning the Twelve, alludes to a larger group: "then to all the apostles" (1 Cor 15:7; see also Acts 14:4). In a more specific fashion, we meet the apostolic delegates Titus and Timothy. Sylvanus is also probably one of them (see 2 Cor 1:19), as is Barnabas. The first two, however, are the best known because of the letters addressed to them. We will be content here to note the information they give us.

The clearest teaching of these letters in relation to our topic is that the apostolic delegates are to do the same thing that the Twelve and Paul did, namely, install people to manage the local Church: "I left you behind in Crete for this reason, so that you should put in order what remained to be done, and should appoint elders in every town, as I directed you" (Titus 1:5). Two noteworthy items stand out in this verse: First, beyond Titus and through his intermediary, the recommendation is addressed to all the Churches, because it is a well-known fact that Paul's letters were passed on from community to community (see Col 4:16). We already encountered an analogous situation in 2 Timothy 2:2: "And what you have heard from me…entrust to faithful people who will be able to teach others as well," and so on. Second, we also see from this verse that the appointing of ministers is to be done by Titus himself, whereas in the account from Acts, the Seven had been chosen by the people before the apostles laid hands on them. It is probably in this same sense that "Paul" recommends to his disciple not to be hasty in the laying on of hands with a ministry in mind (1 Tim 5:22). So Titus and Timothy are to do what Paul himself did, and to facilitate this appointing of competent persons, the author lists the conditions they must fulfill (see Titus 1:6–11; 1 Tim 3:2–7; 2 Tim 2:24–26). Similar rules are also given for the deacons (1 Tim 3:8–13).

We will return to the qualities expected from the ministers (for example, eloquence), but two things can be remarked upon immediately. First, there is a certain interchangeability of the terms *elder* and *overseer*. The same phrase can begin with *elder* and continue with *overseer* (for example, Titus 1:5, 7). The same thing happens in Acts 20:17, 28. Similarly, the elders in 1 Peter 5:2–3 must tend the flock of Christ like true overseers (*episkopountes,* that is, exercising *episkopē*). We cannot take these overseers to be exactly what today's bishops are, but we can see in the elders a participation in the office of overseer. Second, among the rules governing the choice of these elders-overseers there are, to be sure, moral qualifications, but there are already rules that one could call "canonical": Overseers must not have been married more than once; they must have believing children (a manifest sign of a second generation); they must not be recent converts; and so forth. Recommendations of this sort are so many indicators of an organization that has reached a certain degree of complexity.

The Letter of Clement to the Corinthians

The well-known document *First Clement* represents the subsequent stage of the process that I am trying to reconstruct. Writers constantly refer to it because it occupies an intermediate position between the New Testament and the later period, and it lets us understand better what becomes of the Church's organization at the end of the first century. Let us briefly recall the context: The Corinthians, turbulent as ever, feel authorized to dismiss their ministers. Invoking the authority of the Church of Rome, Clement undertakes to show them the seriousness of this act. Passages 42 and 44 should be read in their totality (text 3 in the Appendix), because it will be necessary to return to them often. Generations of scholars have scrutinized them from all angles.[1] I will limit myself here to what interests us:

1. Clement too does not make any distinction between *elders* and *overseers.* When he explains to the Corinthians that it would be unjust to reject their ministers of *episkopē*, he is talking about the elders. So he is perfectly in keeping with Acts 20:17, 28 and with 1 Timothy 3:2 and 5:17.
2. Clement has a very clear awareness that these ministers have been appointed by the apostles, and he

unhesitatingly applies to them the notion of the *schali-ach* discussed earlier in the book. In his own words: "Christ comes from God, the apostles come from Christ." Armed with the Holy Spirit, the apostles set out to announce the good news: "And thus preaching through countries and cities they appointed the first-fruits of their labors to be overseers and deacons of those who should afterwards believe" (*1 Clement* 42:2, 4). It is striking to see that the word *firstfruits* had already been used by Paul to designate the first con-verts of a region to whom the new believers had to submit (Rom 16:5; 1 Cor 16:15–16).

3. The letter does not simply recall the fact of the apos-tolic succession; it creates the theory of it and asserts that the apostles promulgated a rule on the issue—that after the death of those first ministers, other tested men would succeed them in their office. The grave fault of the Corinthians comes from their hav-ing broken this apostolic rule (*1 Clement* 44: 2).

4. There is no exaggerating the importance of this text, dated 95–98. It speaks in an "archaic" manner (as indicated by the interchangeability of the terms *over-seers* and *elders*), but one can also stress its proximity to the sources (the theme of its concluding portion is the same as St. John's). At the same time, Clement presents a carefully reflected position, since he is the first to declare the principle of apostolic succession. This is much more important than the name *ministers* itself or the relative vagueness of their functions. These last elements arise out of growing precision in the organization of the community, which can be more or less advanced, depending on the case. On the other hand, it is crucial to hear Clement express his deep conviction that, through these ministers, who succeed the apostles, one goes back to Christ who sent them, and to God himself who sent Christ: "Whoever welcomes you welcomes me, and whoever welcomes me welcomes the one who sent me" (Matt

10:40). As we know, the Gospels offer many other parallels to this verse.

5. One last detail ought to be emphasized in these texts: the role played by the community. The ministers in fact were *established* by the apostles (or by their first successors) *with the approval of the whole Church* (*1 Clement* 44:3). This is not quite the Pauline manner of direct appointment by the apostolic delegate, but something resembling more what we have seen in Jerusalem in the choosing of the Seven by the Church, then the laying on of hands by the apostles. There is a pattern here that was long followed in the West. Theoretically nothing would prevent us from putting it into practice again now, but one must not be deceived by the democratic appearance of the process. The choice by the community is just preliminary—important, to be sure—but in reality and in the final analysis, the "enabling" of the minister comes from the laying on of hands.

How Did They Arrive at the Sole Overseer of Ignatius of Antioch?

Clement's letter does not suggest that the Church of Rome was already familiar with the confirmation as president of a sole overseer in the college of elders. Still, at the same period or perhaps a little earlier, we find evidence for a sole overseer in Asia Minor. In fact, the Book of Revelation—which scholars attribute to the end of Domitian's reign (91–96) as a probable date, although certain parts could go back to the year 70—begins with a series of seven letters to the Churches of Asia (see Rev 1–3). We learn there notably that each of the Churches is presided over by an angel, generally identified as the spiritual head of the community. It is not immaterial that the phenomenon occurred in Asia Minor, because the Church of Jerusalem may have exported its model of government, according to which James would appear as the exemplary type of sole overseer surrounded by the elders.

Even without putting too much weight on this hypothesis or

on the text from Revelation, which remains hard to interpret and only expresses a possibility, we find the proof of this sole overseer shortly after Clement (ten or fifteen years later, around 101 to 110) in the letters of St. Ignatius of Antioch. He is, in effect, the first explicit witness to the existence of a three-step hierarchy like the one we are familiar with today: the bishop surrounded by his diocesan priests and the deacons. It would take too long to quote the texts, because they are numerous, but I have reproduced at the back of the book a summary made by an expert in this topic (text 4 in the Appendix, titled "Ignatius of Antioch: The Bishop and the Presbyterium"). My intention is to try to answer the question that never fails to arise in the reader's mind: How did the transition take place from the multiplicity of the elders-overseers attested to in Scripture, as well as in Clement, to the single overseer whose authority is exercised in a very strong fashion on the presbyterium subordinate to him?

The explanation that seems to be most generally accepted today was formulated fifty years ago, with the help of solid documentation, by Fr. Pierre Benoit of the École Biblique in Jerusalem (I have borrowed from him the string of quotations in the paragraph below).[2] In a more rapidly sketched-out form, this position has been notably adopted by the well-known American Scripture scholar Raymond Brown, except that Brown stresses the influence of Qumran in the appearance of the overseer, whereas Benoit did not want to exaggerate it, but nonetheless found place for it in his view.

Recall, to begin with, the meaning of each term: "The *presbuteros* is an elder, a notable, a dignitary, acting through the collective channel of the Council of which he is a member." This is a direct legacy from the synagogue, where each community was ruled by a group of elders, of *zekenim* (the Hebrew term for *presbuteroi*) who handled together the community's affairs. From the outset (both in the Jewish and the Hellenistic setting), the nature of the presbyterium was collegial, and it would remain so. As for the overseer, he was a "functionary, an employee, assigned to some specific job in administration, most often an office of inspection or management." In the Greek of the Septuagint, *episkopos* is used as the translation for words derived from the

Hebraic root *pqd* and is always applied to a "personage assigned to precise tasks in the administration of the community. The same is true in the Greek world." The closest Hebrew equivalent to *episkopos* is *paqid*, which designates a "person charged with surveillance or administration." It was just like that at Qumran, where the *paqid* was "the elder *put in charge* of the Community Council." In the transition from the *presbuteros* to the *episkopos*, therefore, one was moving from the deliberative to the executive. The two titles, however, were not incompatible. It was quite possible and even normal to choose among the members of the council someone who would be charged with a specific task; in this case the *presbuteros* does not stop being a *presbuteros*, but he also becomes an *episkopos*. The two titles are and remain different; but the same man carried out two different offices, somewhat as in the American system, the vice president becomes on occasion a voting member of the Senate. Father Benoit stresses, however, that he has never found a non-Christian text that puts the two terms side by side like this. Thus, the theory is plausible, but it is good to know that it was developed to try to make sense of a specifically Christian fact.

In their Christian use, the term *elder* definitely seems to go back further, while *overseer* does not appear until later. That is easily understood. In the beginning, everything is still undivided; but as the community grows, its tasks have to be given to specialists. Thus, the *episkopos* or *episkopoi* appear as the executive organ of the council of elders. In this sense we have an interesting indication in 1 Timothy 5:17: "Let the elders who rule well be considered worthy of double honor, especially those who labor in preaching and teaching." So there are different categories: elders who preach and others who do not; elders who rule and others who do not. The elders who rule and who preach are the ones who will become overseers. Benoit proposes to identify them with "those who are over you" (*proïstamenous*) from 1 Thessalonians 5:12 and with the "leaders" or *higoumenes* in Hebrews 13:7, 17, 24.

The Qumran texts allow us to add an extra degree of probability to this hypothesis. There we meet a person called the *meqabber*, whose functions, at once economic, judicial, and spiritual, rather resemble those of the future Christian bishop. The very name, which means "inspector," is close to the title of over-seer. A number of scholars have welcomed the idea of a possible importing of this function by the entrance of Essene converts into the Christian community; such persons might have brought with them some of their customs. There is a striking example of this in a writing from the early third century, the *Didascalia Apostolorum.* The document has come down to us in different versions, the most interesting of which is the *Syriac Didascalia*, which describes the Christian overseer with the features of the *meqabber* and cites Bible passages that are also found in the Qumran texts.[3] Now there is only one *meqabber* in each community, just as there will be only one bishop, Ignatius of Antioch. If we note, by the way, that the *Didascalia* is an Antiochian text, and that Antioch is where the monarchical bishop appears for the first time, then there is nothing unlikely about this line of descent. We cannot dwell much longer on this subject, but it has to be acknowledged that this explanation, by its historical origin, does not lack coherence. We have here a convincing verification, I think, of the possibility, raised in the introduction to this chapter, of appealing to non-Christian sources to supply what the rarity of Christian references could not.

OBSERVATIONS ON THE FIRST EIGHTY YEARS

This first stage of our investigation concludes, then, at the beginning of the second century, that is, eighty to eighty-five years after the death of the Lord, and fifty to sixty years after the deaths of, if not all the Twelve, then at least Peter and Paul. It has allowed us to make a few observations of the highest importance that can be summarized as follows:

There is, to begin with, the massive, irrefutable fact that there were ministers from the earliest time, that is, in the six or seven years following the death of Christ. Jesus was crucified on April 7 in the year 30, and the election of the Seven in Jerusalem took place before the martyrdom of Stephen and the conversion of Paul, which have been dated to 36 or 37. This fact is not negated by what follows; on the contrary, it takes on a growing importance to the point where it becomes an institution in the Pastoral Letters. It is, at least, what we can determine from reading the texts that have come down to us; however, nothing prevents this institutional arrangement from having occurred sooner than its appearance in the texts. It is a well-known historical constant that writings come after the facts. People only write about things that exist already; this occurs most often when there is some difficulty or when it is a matter of codifying a practice that has already been developing for a certain amount of time. In all probability, therefore, the situations described in the Pastoral Letters had taken shape before they were written down.

Apart from the mere fact that there were various ministers, we have also observed the presence of a way of thinking that understands these ministries within a process of succession. This is plain from the Acts of the Apostles onward and, even more so, in the Pastoral Letters and in *1 Clement*. It would be premature to see already present in these writings a theory of apostolic succession in the strong sense that this expression will later acquire, but we can certainly note in them the *fact* of ministers succeeding the apostles. This emerges as far back as Clement on the level of a thoughtful awareness, but the first lists of bishops will follow very rapidly, appearing with Hegesippus, who draws up the first list of the bishops of Rome around 150, then in 180 with Irenaeus, who specifically creates the theory of apostolic succession to argue against the heretics in favor of the Church of Rome's superiority "by reason of its more excellent origin," that is, with Peter and Paul (see Irenaeus, *Against Heresies* 3.3.2, but at greater length in 3.3–4).

Thanks to this continuity between the ministers and the apostles, we can definitively go back all the way to Christ himself, who sent out the apostles. We have seen that action in the case of the Jerusalem Seven; but Clement will be the first one to formulate clearly the notion: "Christ, therefore, was sent forth by God, and the apostles by Christ. Both these appointments, then, were made in an orderly way, according to the will of God" (*1 Clement* 42). This was not a novelty without roots, because the theme of sending forth is very much present in St. John as it is in the Synoptics; the final scene in Matthew 28:18–29 also expresses the same conviction. We likewise recall the Jewish institution of the *schaliach* and its translation into Greek as *apostolos,* whose meaning I have empha-sized above. Hence, we can and must speak, not only of an *apostolic origin of "the" ministers,* but equally of a *christological origin of "the" ministry.* So, if it is clear that Christ did not found the episcopacy and the presbyterate as we know them today, it was nevertheless his will that lay at the root of the sending of the apostles and of the measures taken by them with the authority with which he entrusted them so that their mission could be pursued in the Holy Spirit, who also gave them authority.

It is nonetheless worth noting that the accomplishment of Christ's will was realized in the most human, historical way possi-ble. So historians are right to stress the wholly natural character of the measures taken to make the community last. The assign-ment of ministers responded to a very concrete need: the growth of the community, its geographical dispersion, the diversity of the tasks to be done, the disappearance of the first generation, and so forth. As Christians, we surely believe that the Holy Spirit watched over this process; but nothing prevents us from acknowl-edging the reality and importance of the human factor. God acts in the life of the Church in a manner analogous to the way he acts in the life of each believer: by various events and encounters, which only reveal their divine potential over time.

This last statement allows us to fully value community. I said earlier that the continuity of ministers permits us to trace the path back to Christ as the source of the ministry. This is the chris-tological reference, more precisely the reference to Christ the Head, that was announced at the very beginning of this book as one of the two essential aspects to be considered in our investi-gation. Now we add the relation to the community, that is, the ref-erence to Christ in his ecclesial body, as the second aspect.

We have found that the community "intervenes" in the choice of ministers. This is not always said clearly, but, given the "democratic" structure of the council of elders, one can assume that this happened elsewhere as well. Above all (this is not said either, but it is obvious), the community "finalizes" the ministers. It is in order for its service of the Word to be correctly assured that it takes pains to look to continuity and the conditions of its legitimacy. It is striking to observe that the same word *diakonia* is used for the service of the Word and that of the community. These two aspects have to be kept in mind simultaneously, which the texts invite us to do. The community chooses, but the apostles consecrate. We have gotten out of this habit, but the scheme will last a long time in history. The best-known cases in the West are those of St. Ambrose of Milan and St. Augustine of Hippo; that is how our double reference to Christ will be articulated.

This relation to the community, to its rootedness in a place, a milieu, and its concrete needs, allows us once again to understand how the transition occurred from an initial plurality of ministers to an increasing concentration in the person of the bishop. It is permissible to draw an approximate parallel here to today's situation. In a parish where the priest cannot handle everything, we see the faithful taking on a growing number of services. Some do the readings, others distribute the Eucharist, others visit the sick and bring them communion. They are perhaps temporary ministers, but are we sure that all the ministries mentioned in the New Testament had the permanent character that we are tempted to give them? The elders-overseers ended up becoming established because they already had a certain preeminence, itself inherited from the Church's original Jewish milieu. If the path went from the council of elders to the single bishop, that was no doubt under the influence of other Jewish customs; but it is equally a law of the group that it needs to identify itself with a head. Only in our case the Head is Jesus Christ; thus, the sociological need also corresponds to a mystical necessity. Ignatius of Antioch has given it an incomparable formulation: to submit to the bishop is to submit to the Father of Jesus Christ, who is the bishop of all (*Magnesians* 2.1–2). And also: "The bishop holds the place of God, the elders hold the place of the senate of the apostles" (*Magnesians* 6.1).

We need to be aware that the process just described allows us access to a certain vision of the birth of the Church. There has long been a "fundamentalist" way of speaking about Christ establishing the Church by searching in this or that Gospel statement of his for the "charter" founding, as had been done for each of the sacraments. In the name of history, scholars have challenged and still challenge this inaccurate view; and on their own scientific level they are right. That is why, before proposing a response here, it is more judicious to ask first what we should include under the name *Church*. If we are thinking of the community of grace and life with Christ, which realizes among human beings who believe in him the anticipated coming of the kingdom, then it is quite certain that Christ founded it. It has existed since the very first disciples followed him on the roads of Palestine. That is true, at least if one is not thinking of the Church under the rule of the New (and definitive) Covenant. But if one thinks of the Church Universal of salvation history of which Vatican II speaks, then it has to be said that it began with Abel the just (and even with the repentant Adam and Eve) and will end with the last person chosen. On the other hand, if we consider the Church in its aspect as an institution of salvation, then the situation has to be looked at differently. Its core is certainly found in the group of the Twelve and the disciples. In that sense it does goes back to Jesus, and we must stick with this. But that was no more than the seed of what was called upon to deploy itself progressively in the structured manner just sketched out. To present things in this way certainly does not contradict what we believe. Vatican II has undoubtedly authorized us to do so (see *Lumen Gentium* 18–20), but Pius XII was already addressing the three stages in the foundation of the Church in *Mystici Corporis* 26:

1. Christ began to build it by his preaching.
2. He continued to build it when he died on the cross, as the water and blood flowed from his pierced side, symbols of baptism and the Eucharist, source of all the sacraments that the Church is made of.
3. The coming of the Holy Spirit upon the apostles gathered at Pentecost constitutes, so to speak, the public and finished proclamation of the Church.

It is enough to develop what is implied in that third stage to arrive at the process that I have just described.

THE SACERDOTALIZATION OF THE CHRISTIAN MINISTRY

We already know that the ministers of the New Testament are never given the title of priests and that the direct priestly vocabulary is never used when speaking of them. Even in Ignatius, who still strongly insists on the link between the overseers and elders to the Eucharist, the word *hiereis* is only used once for the priests of the Old Covenant, to whom the unique *archiereus* of the New Covenant must of course be preferred (*Philadelphians* 9.1). Yet, very early in the history of the Church, this situation would change, and that vocabulary would unhesitatingly be used for those same ministers. Thus, we must first investigate the first evidence of this "sacerdotalization" of the ministry. I will return later to statements in the New Testament to try to verify if it is possible to justify that evolution. Actually, even if we cannot prove this priestly quality of the ministry with enough certitude by means of New Testament exegesis, the existence of the priestly ministry remains a fact for us, and we have to establish its legitimacy to understand its meaning. At the very least, it would be difficult for a Catholic theologian to think that the Church was mistaken on that point for twenty centuries. So, we must question the texts, but meanwhile remember how we have already found out that the texts do not tell us everything. This will be a fresh occasion to put into action the methodical principles presented at the beginning of this chapter.

Tertullian

The oldest explicit evidence for the use of the priestly vocabulary apropos of Christian ministers occurs in Tertullian (end of the second century/beginning of the third). It must be said specifically that this is the first-known and first-certain instance of that vocabulary, for he makes such abundant use of it that we have every reason to think that the reality of the matter is for Tertullian a *fait accompli*, and that he is using the language current in his day and in his African Church. Here are some texts among others:

On the power to perform baptism, he says:

The highest priest [*summus sacerdos*; as we know, *sacerdos* is the Latin translation of the Greek *hiereus*], who is the overseer [if he is there], has of course the right to confer it; then the presbyters and the deacons, not, however without the overseer's authority, out of respect for the church: when this respect is maintained, peace is secure. But besides, even laymen have the right to baptize. (*Treatise on Baptism* 17)

Tertullian could not be clearer on the different degrees of the ministry and on the distinction between clergy and laity. This is the only passage in which he uses the expression *summus sacerdos*, which is why some scholars propose to translate "if he is there" (*si qui est)* in a different manner, as "if one can call him this," but that does not change anything for us.

Elsewhere, he blames the heretics, whose

ordinations are carelessly administered, capricious, changeable. And so it comes to pass that today one man is their overseer, tomorrow another; today he is a deacon who tomorrow is a reader; today he is a presbyter who tomorrow is a layman. For even on laymen they impose the functions of priesthood [*sacerdotalia munera*]. (*Of the Prescription of the Heretics* 41.6–8)

In this text the word *ordination* already has the technical sense that it will keep to our day, when we speak of ordination to the priesthood. Here we once more discover the three degrees we have already met in Ignatius; and it is clear that the phrase *functions of priesthood* refers to them.

There are many other passages in which Tertullian uses priestly language, but in a different context. He uses it on the subject of Christ, the *sacerdos Patris* ("the priest of God the Father" in *Against Marcion* 4.9.9; *On Monogamy* 7.8; and *Exhortation to Chastity* 20.10). This allows him to stress the universal role of Christ in the liturgy. He also uses it apropos of pagan priests, but that does not concern us. More curiously, this language is used with regard to laypeople themselves, but in two different senses. We know that around AD 207 Tertullian went over to Montanism, which he had once fought so vigorously; hence, his texts have been classed as coming before or after this. In his orthodox period, he backs the common doctrine of the priesthood of the faithful: "We are the true adorers and the true priests [*veri sacerdotes*]" (*On Prayer* 27, 28). In his Montanist period, Tertullian grants all the faithful the power to exercise the "priestly functions [*munera sacerdotalia*]," which he had denied them when he was still a Catholic (*Exhortation to Chastity* 7.3–4). In fact, however, these texts are difficult to interpret, and scholars disagree about how to understand them. But we do not have to take a position on this point. All we need to know is that the priestly vocabulary was already in use at that time, and we have another example of this in a Church Father immediately after Tertullian.

Hippolytus of Rome

As readers may know, Hippolytus of Rome is the only antipope venerated as a saint, because he died a martyr around 235 after being reconciled with his adversary. Among his other writings, he has left us a precious little book titled *The Apostolic Tradition*, generally dated around 215, which transmits very specific information about the Roman liturgy of that epoch. (Even though the book was written in Greek, it has only come down to us in Latin and several other Eastern languages.) Our present-day second Eucharistic Prayer is found here practically complete. We also find the prayer for the consecration of a bishop:

> Grant, Father, who knows the heart, to your servant whom you chose for the episcopate, that he will feed your holy flock [*episcopatum; pascere gregem*; one recalls 1 Pet 5:2: *poimainein*], that he will wear your holy priesthood without reproach, serving night and day, incessantly making your face favorable, and offering the gifts of your holy church; in the spirit of high priesthood [*spiritu primatus sacerdotii*] having the power to forgive sins according to your command [John 20:23];

to assign lots [offices] according to your command; to loose any bond according to the authority which you gave to the apostles. (3.4–5)

Anyone who has ever attended the consecration of a bishop will be at least slightly familiar with this text; apart from a few details, it is exactly the same as the one found today in the Roman Pontifical. When the liturgy is said to be an organ of Tradition, this is no empty phrase.

One specific item to note in the text above: The Eucharist is first mentioned as "offering the gifts," and the first act of a new bishop, as Hippolytus describes in the next paragraph, is precisely to celebrate the Eucharist with "the whole council of the elders" (4.2). This, then, is at the same period as Tertullian, and we find here a fully cultic and priestly vocabulary. Hippolytus also reports the prayers for the ordination of elders and of deacons, but they cannot be quoted here in full. One should observe, however, that the title *sacerdos* is reserved to the bishop, and that the other ministers are called *presbyteri* or *diaconi*. But whereas the elders participate in the priesthood of the bishop, that is not the case with the deacons, who are ordained only for the service of the bishop (8.1–5).

A hundred years after Ignatius of Antioch, therefore, we meet with texts in Rome that are exactly like his. Even if the language has evolved, since it has now become explicitly sacerdotal, the continuity is perfect. This is all the more notable because fifty years earlier (before 165), Justin, likewise writing in Greek, describes the Eucharist quite exactly, but without using the words *episkopos* or *diakonos*.

Cyprian of Carthage

The extension of the word *sacerdos* to the elders will be a settled affair for St. Cyprian (died 258, less than fifty years after Tertullian and Hippolytus). In one of his letters, he says that "the elders are joined with the bishop in the honor of the sacrifice [*cum episcopo presbyteri sacerdotali honore coniuncti*]" (*Letters* 61.3.1). Elsewhere, in a context dealing with both bishops and presbyters, he asserts:"The *sacerdotes* and the ministers of the altars must be pure and without blemish" (*Letters* 72.2.2). There may be another application of *sacerdotes* to *presbyteri* in *The Unity of the Church* (n. 17), in which Cyprian distinguishes between the *episcopi* and the *Dei sacerdotes*. Apart from that, we find in his writings many uses of *sacerdos* in connection with the bishop. For example:

> For if Jesus Christ, our Lord and our God, is himself the chief priest of God, the Father, and has first offered himself a sacrifice to the Father, and has commanded this to be done in commemoration of Himself, certainly that priest truly discharges the office of Christ, who imitates that which Christ did and he then offers a true and full sacrifice in the Church to God the Father, when he proceeds to offer it according to what he sees Christ Himself to have offered. (*Letters* 63.14.4)

In another letter (69.8.3), Cyprian speaks once again about the bishops as *sacerdotes Dei* to encourage obedience toward them, contrary to what had happened with Dathan and Abiram, who refused to obey Moses and Aaron.

Origen

In the East, the priestly vocabulary appeared at about the same time that it did in the West, since toward the end of the second century, Bishop Polycrates of Ephesus called St. John a *hiereus* (as witnessed by Eusebius in *Church History* 5.24.3). But it is above all Origen, the exact contemporary of Cyprian (himself a martyr, dying in 254), who is our best source. In this homily on Joshua, Origen does not hesitate to compare the eucharistic liturgy to the liturgy of the Temple:

> When, indeed you see nations enter into the faith, churches raised up, altars sprinkled not with the flowing blood of beasts, but consecrated with "the precious blood of Christ"; when you see priests and Levites [*sacerdotes et levitas*—we do not have the Greek original] ministering not "the blood of bulls and goats," but the Word of God through the grace of the Holy Spirit, then

say that Jesus received and retained the leadership after Moses.[4]

In this same collection of homilies on Joshua, Origen advises the faithful not to hide anything about their way of life "especially from the priests and ministers" (*maxime sacerdotibus et ministris*, Homily 7.6). There is another very clear passage where Origen connects the pair clergy-laypeople in the Church of his day with the dyad of Israelite-clergy in the Old Testament. To consecrate themselves entirely to their ministry, the *sacerdotes et levitai* must be able to count on the help of the *laici*. These words are repeated several times in Homily 17.3; the same distinction and the same vocabulary, but in Greek, are found in the *Commentary on St. John* 1.9–11). One can equally look at the *Homilies on Numbers* (2.1), where Origen forcefully chides the bishops and deacons who fail in their duties of "the priestly and Levitical order." These texts, incidentally, raise the issue of what Origen thought about the ministry, since he seems to say that "[o]nly the true saints are capable both of carrying out the churchly functions, as well as of validly receiving the episcopacy or the priesthood."[5]

Whatever may be the case with that last item, we can conclude from our brief investigation that, beginning in the early third century (and perhaps even in the late second century), specifically priestly language was used with evident ease by Christian authors in the East as well as in the West, and, what is more, by the liturgy for the consecration of a bishop in Hippolytus. Even if we admit that the liturgy did not yet have the fixed form that we are familiar with today, we have at least an indication that this vocabulary was recognized as appropriate to the way things were actually done. From that epoch onward, it is true, and even before then (as we will see with Clement of Rome), the comparison with the Levites and priests of the Old Testament was heavy with an ambiguous development. But we can say that this mode of expression was definitively adopted.

The question that arises now is how the Church arrived at this point. It is not easy to offer a certain answer because, despite their importance, the elements that I have just cited are not enough to advance any decisive explanation of how this manner of speaking evolved. Nevertheless, we can hazard a hypothesis about how things progressed by exploring the texts one more time in accordance with these different, but ultimately convergent, lines. These three paths are those of the three great messianic functions; there is nothing surprising about that, since the mission of the apostles and that of the ministers whom they appointed continue the very same mission of Christ as prophet, priest, and king. One might have thought a priori that the use of the priestly vocabulary would have appeared exclusively in the context of the sacraments. In fact, it was not at all like that, and the two other functions, "word and government," show that they too were subject to sacerdotalization, which thus spread gradually until it became the name of the ministry itself.

THE SERVICE OF THE WORD AND ITS CULTIC DIMENSION

Here we will consider two main points. I will first recall the primacy of proclaiming the Gospel in the ministerial functions by summing up the principal themes of the New Testament. I will then examine an expression of St. Paul that Vatican II has taken up on its own account in *Presbyterorum Ordinis*, the Decree on the Ministry and Life of Presbyters (not the "Life of *Priests*," as it is usually translated).

The *diakonia tou logou* (Acts 6:4)

To be faithful to the texts, one must assign first place to the proclamation of the Good News. Jesus' first public act was in fact "proclaiming the good news of God" (Mark 1:14). A little further on (Mark 1:38), Jesus himself explains: "Let us go on to the neighboring towns, so that I may proclaim the message there also; for that is what I came out to do" ("came out," not from Capernaum, as is sometimes said in a flatly reductive fashion, but "from the bosom of the Father"). And the last word the risen Jesus will say to his disciples picks up the same terms: "Go into all the world and preach the Gospel to the whole creation" (Mark 16:15).

This priority of the Word is perceived by the apostles to have such power that they refuse to abandon the "service of the Word" (*diakonia tou logou*) to busy themselves with the administration of the Jerusalem community (Acts 6:1–6). Paul will use even stronger language: "Christ did not send me to baptize but to proclaim the gospel" (1 Cor 1:17). In a clear sign of the importance of the Word, the various lists of charisms always give first place to those of teaching in its various forms (prophecy, instruction, exhortation: see 1 Cor 12:8; Rom 12:6–8; 1 Pet 4:11; Heb 13:7). This stands out in sharp relief in the Pastoral Letters, where the function of the elders-overseers takes on an intense doctrinal coloration (1 Tim 3:2; 4:6, 13; 5:17; 2 Tim 2:2; Titus 1:9; 2:15). But it is also the case in the Acts of the Apostles, which devotes the same attention to this aspect of the post of elders-overseers.

To better grasp this primacy of the prophetic mission, we have to recall that this Word of the Gospel is the very Word of God, which continues the *dabar* of the Old Testament with its creative and life-giving power. Incarnated in Jesus, it remains present and active through the Spirit in the apostolic message (1 Thess 1:5). It has the power, the *dynamis*, to raise the building, that is, the Church (Acts 20:32). To proclaim the Gospel is to give birth to the faithful in Christ Jesus (1 Cor 4:15). James says the same thing: "He gave us birth by the word of truth" (Jas 1:18; and in the same sense, 1 Pet 1:23). To transmit and receive the Word is to transmit and receive the life that comes from God. Proclaiming the Gospel is thus something altogether different from giving a simple talk, and Paul himself compares this proclaiming to celebrating the liturgy.

The Sacred Service of the Gospel

In Romans 15:16, St. Paul uses an expression that has given some trouble to his translators. Recall, first, this verse as a whole. Paul assures his addressees that if he is writing them with a certain boldness, it is "because of the grace given me by God to be a *minister* of Jesus Christ to the Gentiles in the *priestly service* of the gospel of God, so that the offering of the Gentiles may be acceptable, sanctified by the Holy Spirit." This verse has been and still is today translated rather differently, depending upon the time period and the different translators. All Bibles feel the need to make their translation more explicit with a footnote spelling out the literal meaning of the terms. There are, in fact, two words here that come from the cultic vocabulary: the first is *leitourgos*, which the Jerusalem Bible and the Ecumenical Translation render as *minister* (in the sense of "officiant"), whereas other translations have kept it as *servant*. The second word is *hierourgounta*, the present participle of *hierourgein*, whose root is *hiereus* or "priest," with which we are well familiar. The Jerusalem Bible proposes *minister* for this as well, but adds in a footnote, "Literally; 'in accomplishing a cultic function.'" The Ecumenical Translation of the Bible adds language from the previous verse (Rom 15:15) and comes up with "consecrated to the ministry." C. Wiéner, the author of the most precise study on the subject,[6] offers a more complete formulation: "presenting as a sacrifice the proclamation of the Gospel of God." Meanwhile A. Vanhoye proposes: "accomplishing a sacred work." As one might guess, it is the second word, above all, that causes problems.

Until very recently, this verse has been understood as expressing a priestly activity. Thus, in its first edition (1956), the Jerusalem Bible unhesitatingly translated: "I was given grace to be a minister [Fr. *officiant*, priest] of the Gospel of God, so that the Gentiles might become an acceptable offering, sanctified by the Holy Spirit." At the same time, another author (A.-M. Denis), in a very careful study, explained the reasons for this translation as follows: "St. Paul says that he is vested like the priests of the Old Covenant with a service that is a stable function with regard to the Gentiles. He clarifies his thought: 'Which I do by accomplishing the sacred act of the Gospel of God.'"

Contrary to what one might be tempted to think, that was not a Catholic position in the denominational sense of the term. Wiéner quotes John Calvin, who commented on this passage:

> [Paul] then makes himself the *priest* or the sacrificer
> who offers in sacrifice the people he has won for God,

> and in that way serves the sacred mysteries of the Gospel. And hence here is the *priesthood* or making holy of a Christian pastor, to sacrifice (in a manner of speaking) men to God in subjecting and reducing them to the obedience of the Gospel.[7]

For this author, who has reviewed in his erudite note all the accessible uses of the two terms, there is no doubt about *leitourgos*. In itself the word is not specifically priestly or even specifically "liturgical" in the sense that we understand now (because it can also serve for a purely civil celebration). But, linked to the second word, as it is in this verse, it does mean a cultic service. Nor is there any doubt about the word *hierourgein*. It means "offer sacrifices" in the broadest sense "without specifying whether the author of the action is the priest or the believer who turns to him."

This brief review of discussions among exegetes was perhaps a little difficult, but it has at least the advantage of imposing a certain prudence on us and warning us against putting too much weight on this text. For as long as critics were not alerted to the New Testament's reserve concerning the priestly vocabulary, they used the word *priest* without a problem. Now nobody dares to. Vatican II itself was equally cautious. It takes up this verse of Paul and gives it an important role, as we shall see, since it extends it to the ministers of today, but it says simply *sacro Evangelii munere fungentes* ("carrying out the sacred service of the Gospel," Decree on the Ministry and Life of Presbyters 2, which avoids the word *sacerdotes* and speaks of *presbyteri*).

It is easy to understand the prudence of these scholars and, in their wake, the Council. Still, it remains possible to ask whether the reading of the two terms in the complete context of this verse and of Pauline thought does not allow us to be more affirmative. According to one renowned exegete (A. Vanhoye), we have to pay attention to the end of the verse, on which most critics do not linger. The usual translation accords the Gentiles (pagans) a passive role, "so that the offering of the Gentiles may be acceptable." In reality, in the context of Pauline thought, this role is active, because the Gentiles provide the victim of the sacrifice, and Paul considers himself the officiant of this cult, not one believer among others. The means by which he has sanctified this victim is the fire of the Holy Spirit through the proclaiming of the Gospel. But we see that he has shied away from using the word *hiereus* so as not to suggest that his ministry was like that of the Jewish priests. The difference between this new sacrifice and the old ritual sacrifices is enormous. So is the difference between this conception of the priest and the old one. Without using the word *hiereus*, Paul nonetheless prepares to offer this interpretation of the priesthood.

Leaning on this interpretation, we can invoke a verse from Philippians that we have already met: the blood of Paul poured out as a libation "over the sacrifice and the offering of your [the Philippians'] faith" (2:17). Still more explicitly in the sense of our verse, from the beginning of the Letter to the Romans (1:9), Paul declares: "God, whom I serve with my spirit by announcing the gospel of his Son, is my witness" (1:9); our Bibles are particularly abundant in notes on these words. Once again this is not explicitly priestly language, but we are close enough to it. We can make yet another curious connection, which ultimately might be the most suggestive of all:

> Do you not know that those who are employed in the temple service [here it is not *hierourgein*, but *hiera ergazomai*] get their food from the temple, and those who serve at the altar share in what is sacrificed on the altar? In the same way, the Lord commanded that those who proclaim the gospel should get their living by the gospel. (1 Cor 9:13–14)

In the same sense, we also have to remember that at the moment of sending out his disciples to preach the Word, Jesus tells them: "Laborers deserve their food" (Matt 10:10). It was in fact the custom of the teaching rabbis to live on the gifts of their disciples. The same was true for the priests: according to Deuteronomy 18:1–2, the priests have no patrimony because they live on the gifts offered to the Lord. True, this is just a comparison, but it is an eloquent one. Paul likens his work of evangelization to work for which he deserves payment, just like the task of a priest officiating at the altar.

The least one can say is that these texts shed a precious light on our initial verse and seem to merit consideration. I do not think I am forcing their sense by arguing that we have here one of the ways by which the sacerdotalization of the Christian ministry has traveled in its prophetic mode. As has been well said:

> The Word of God is not spread about in the way that ordinary human discourse is. Like a seed, it brings life, pardon, and justice. Gospel, faith, and baptism are indissolubly bound together. To eat and drink at the table of the Lord means "proclaiming" his death until he returns. And the ministry of pardon and reconciliation, according to Paul, is that of the Gospel (2 Cor 5:18–21). Because we have forgotten the effectiveness of the Word of God, we have opposed to it the Word of the sacraments; whereas it is in them that the Word works. Hence, the ability to celebrate the sacraments seems implied in the ability to communicate the Word. Philip evangelizes and baptizes. The prophets and teachers of Antioch celebrate worship and lay on their hands. In the assembly the prophets pray and give thanks.[8]

This synthetic judgment happily sums up the unity in the distinction of the various offices that we have found in previous stages of our investigation. It is important not to forget this in the following ones, at the risk of slipping into false problems.

THE SERVICE OF THE SACRAMENTS AND ESPECIALLY OF THE EUCHARIST

We have now arrived at the trouble spot of our operation. Clearly it is in the relation of the ministers to the Eucharist that their priestly character will best affirm itself. There is no shortage of Scripture scholars who claim that the texts do not say anything about this bond between ministers and the Eucharist. In my opinion they are wrong, but we still have to examine their arguments and at least show the plausibility of that bond. The task is a delicate one, because it is constantly up against a double danger: The first is maximalism, which consists in making the texts say more than they actually do, to the point of introducing a further set of problems in the explanation one gives of them. The second is the peril of minimalism, which systematically aims at the lowest level, to the point of refusing a priestly interpretation even of texts that incontestably lend themselves to it. True, talking about worship does not automatically mean talking about priests; however, we must not fall into a "positivistic" conception of history that pays attention only to what the texts say explicitly. This all-too-reductive perspective leads us to an idea of history as conceived around the beginning of the twentieth century that has long since been abandoned because it blocks all forward movement. If it will not limit itself to laying texts end to end or to merely counting up the witnesses from the past, and if it wants to make that past ever so slightly intelligible, history cannot do without rationally justified reconstructions, including, at times, even hypotheses.

An example may help here. On the question of the breaking of the bread, which is generally taken to mean the Eucharist, we have two very clear cases in the Acts of the Apostles (2:42 and 20:7). In the first, the apostles are mentioned; in the second, it is Paul. We read these texts spontaneously thinking that those persons are presiding over the celebration and that their role is reserved to them by virtue of the authority with which they have been vested. Many exegetes read it that way; however, there are some who argue that the texts do not say it expressly, and that claiming that they do goes beyond the facts. I am not the only one to think otherwise, and I argue that it does not do justice to the texts when you refuse to see in them what they imply. In the first case, it is the apostles who are presiding over the assembly; in the second case, it is Paul.

Thus, we have to try to use the narrow space that lies between these two extremes and try to say which route appears the most plausible. The enterprise is difficult, but the material collected is defensible. We could pursue the evidence along three different lines, the first two of which are already found in the Gospel. That would be the Eucharist, on the one hand, and, on the other, the ministry of forgiveness entrusted to the apostles. The third, that of the laying on of hands to ordain new ministers, appears in the Acts of the Apostles and other New Testament writings. I have spoken enough about this last not to need to return to it. So I shall just say a few words on the ministry of forgiveness and then I will stay with the Eucharist. That will allow us to center our research better and treat the issue at greater depth.

The Institution of a Ministry of Forgiveness by the Pre-Easter Jesus

The clearest expression of a priestly activity entrusted to the apostles is found in the Gospel itself and in the mouth of Jesus. Authors who have dealt with problems in the founding of the Church and in what relates to its ministry in the words and actions of the historical Jesus have made some interesting discoveries. It seems, in fact, that we can distinguish two periods in Christ's public life: the first, where Christ seems to have envisaged the coming of the kingdom as a proximate event; the second, where he has understood that a long future is yet to be expected and he prepares his disciples for this lasting mission. This second period opens with Peter's confession: "You are the Christ" (Mark 8:29). This is still the pre-Easter Jesus, but in the second phase of his existence. Things are less clear than will be in the declarations of the post-Easter Jesus, where the disciples may have projected more of their own practice onto the text; but it is enough to provide a solid "basis" in Christ's earthly life for these later developments.

On the existence of a ministry of forgiveness, we have two very clear facts, one from before Jesus' resurrection, the other afterward. The first is the celebrated saying of Jesus to Peter: "Whatever you bind on earth will be bound in heaven, and whatever you loose on earth will be loosed in heaven" (Matt 16:19). This same promise, made here to Peter as head of the Twelve, is picked up again two chapters later, addressed this time not to Peter alone, but to all the disciples accompanying him, that is, the Twelve whose leader he is: "Truly I tell you, whatever you bind on earth will be bound in heaven, and whatever you loose on earth will be loosed in heaven" (Matt 18:18). This is not just a doublet; it is a matter of extending the area covered by the first verse. According to some scholars, in all likelihood the editor of Matthew placed the second verse in his compilation shortly after the year 44, that is, after the persecution of Agrippa, which cost the life of James and probably that of his brother John as well. Peter himself must have fled Jerusalem at that time, no doubt for good. Deprived of its leaders, the community would then have given itself a collegial government (we have already seen it at work), and the second verse reflects that extension, benefiting the heads of that "college" or council, with privileges that an older tradition attributed to Peter and the Twelve. Rudolf Bultmann insisted that Jesus' saying to Peter was not an authentic word of Jesus. But if this verse is dated before 44, as Bultmann himself dated it, there is no denying that it brings us very close to Christ, and there is no valid reason not to credit it to him.

This is our first evidence of a ministry of forgiveness, entrusted by Jesus during his pre-Easter life to the apostles, who are the first ministers of the Church whom we see in action. The second is the appearance of the risen Christ at the end of John's Gospel, who says: "Receive the Holy Spirit. If you forgive the sins of any, they are forgiven them; if you retain the sins of any, they are retained" (20:12–23). The text no doubt reflects the conviction of the post-Easter community as to the origin of this ministry, which was already being exercised in the Church at the time when the Gospel of John was edited. It is a distinct witness of the Church's faith from that epoch and of its continuity with what the pre-Easter Jesus said and did. That is more than enough for us.

The Institution of the Eucharist by the Pre-Easter Jesus

The second expression of a priestly activity entrusted to the apostles—and again, one where our consideration must travel cautiously between minimalism and maximalism—is the command that the pre-Easter Jesus gives to the Twelve: "Do this in memory of me." There is no need to linger here on the meaning of *memory*, which is not just the pious repetition of one of Christ's past acts, but rather is its saving reactualization for today (as the ancient Hebrews commemorated the events of the Exodus: "It is today that God leads us out of Egypt").

It will be useful to recall that we have four different accounts of the Last Supper: that of 1 Corinthians (11:23–25) and the three reports of the Synoptic Gospels (Matt 26:20–25; Mark 13:22–25; Luke 22:21–23). These four versions break down into two slightly different groups: Paul and Luke on one side, Matthew and Mark on the other. We can pass over the details of the scholarly analyses that lead experts to reconstruct the archaic account that the two versions are based on. For our purposes, we need to keep just the following points in mind:

1. The command to repeat what Christ did during the farewell meal (a command that is repeated twice, after the breaking of the bread and after the blessing of the cup), that is, to repeat what can be called the symbolic, sacramental, and anticipatory celebration of his own death, is a supreme religious celebration that consists in mentioning the body given and the blood poured out to seal the New Covenant. That Christ should have envisaged his apostles being able to renew that celebration of the Last Supper after his death, not as a simple repetition but as the reactualizing memorial of the grace obtained by that death, in the way the Hebrews celebrated Passover—there is nothing improbable about that in the context of a Paschal meal.

2. We must emphasize that this command is addressed to the Twelve, not as simple members of the kingdom, but as future leaders of the Church. So we must not see here the simple fact of eating and drinking that would concern ordinary communicants, but rather the fact of celebrating the meal or festival of Passover, that is, of celebrating an entire rite of which the eating and drinking are the central

elements, but not the only ones. At this moment Jesus thus sees the Twelve as future presiders over the table and at the same time he suggests their functions of authority within the Church.

We do not have any words of the post-Easter Jesus to confirm this last interpretation by a later intermediary marker; but scholars note two interesting details in the accounts of the multiplication of the loaves. First, the story of the miracle is modeled on that of the Eucharist (especially in Matt 14:21, but also in Mark 6:41): Jesus lifts his eyes to heaven, pronounces the blessing, breaks the bread, and gives it to his disciples. Second, it is the disciples who distributed to the crowds the miraculously multiplied bread, and, according to many exegetes, the apostolic Church undoubtedly saw in this a symbol of the hierarchical, mediating role of her ministers in the eucharistic celebration. "Hierarchical" is perhaps excessive for this moment, given the meaning that this word subsequently took on; but "mediating" is surely welcome. According to an author who has long studied this question (J. M. R. Tillard), what is certain in any case is

> the accuracy of the traditional opinion that linked the appearance of the "priesthood" to the Last Supper. If what I am saying is true, it is within the experience of the Eucharist that we see the appearance not of the ministry certainly, but of its "priestly" quality.

The Eucharist in the First Christian Communities

What texts allow us to assert that the celebration of the Eucharist is reserved to the ministers of the Church, whether to the apostles or to their successors? In that absolute form ("reserved"), the question has only one answer: No text says this expressly. Since we are already familiar with the discretion of the New Testament, we have to phrase the question in a different way, so it is better to ask: Is it possible to see a connection between ministry and celebration of the Eucharist? We can then answer: Yes, there are at least three texts that permit us to see this.

The first is Acts 2:42, which describes the first believers as "devoted...to the apostles' teaching and fellowship, to the break-ing of bread and the prayers." The breaking of bread is generally identified with the Eucharist; and the spontaneous tenor of the text shows us that the apostles are the celebrants; but I will come back to that reading.

The second text also occurs in Acts (20:7–12). Paul is at Troas: "On the first day of the week [Sunday, the day of the res-urrection], when we met to break bread...." We recall what fol-lows: Paul preaches for so long that a young man, seated on a windowsill, falls asleep and tumbles down into the street to his death. Paul interrupts his talk and restores Eutychus to life. "Then, Paul went upstairs, and after he had broken bread and eaten..." (v 11 [RSV]). The critics who refuse to see Paul as pre-siding over the Eucharist in this passage stress that, in order to be sure of his role as liturgical leader, we must be able to read in the text that he "broke bread *and distributed it.*" Otherwise, one would instead have to understand that all the assistants imitated Paul, broke the bread, and ate it. These writers say that the attention of Luke, the narrator of this episode, is focused on Paul's preaching, not on his liturgical function. We can grant this last point without being obliged to accept the first one. If we recall the solemnity with which Paul passes down the account of the institution of the Last Supper (1 Cor 11:23ff.) and the way in which he clings to his prerogatives, it is difficult to explain why he would not have presided over the meal, since he already had the leading role in the assembly. We can see at work here the sort of positivist read-ing that I spoke of a while ago, which ultimately condemns itself to seeing no more than an incomplete truth.

The final text we can cite comes from Hebrews 13:7–17. The first and last verses explicitly mention the "leaders" who are at the head of the community, the *higoumenes* who proclaim the Word of God, and who must be imitated and obeyed because "they are keeping watch over your souls and will give an account." The lan-guage is very strong, and fairly describes what will later be called the "care of souls." These two verses frame a description of Christian worship under its spiritual aspect ("a sacrifice of praise to God, that is, the fruit of lips that confess his name. Do not neglect to do good and to share what you have"; vv 15–16).

Eucharistic worship forms part of this, since the letter also mentions "an altar from which those who officiate in the tent [the old worship] have no right to eat," whereas Christians have access to the blessings won by the sacrifice of Christ (vv 10–12). A number of scholars have been struck that the reference to these leaders is so close to the allusion to the Eucharist, and conclude from this that their task must have extended to celebrating it (there is another reference to the Eucharist in Heb 10:19–25).

So there we have the three main passages that most closely link the ministers to the Eucharist. It has to be admitted that these texts are hardly explicit. Then what authorizes us to read them as if the apostles or the men they have appointed must necessarily be presiding over the eucharistic meal? The strongest reason one can cite is that there were no Jewish religious meals without a president and even without a priest. As for the first passage mentioned above (Acts 2:42), the Jerusalem Bible judiciously remarks: "Taken by itself, the expression [breaking of the bread] evokes a Jewish meal where the individual presiding pronounces a blessing before sharing the bread." This is precisely what Christ did, as we have just recalled, and that is what he bade the apostles do in memory of him.

The Contribution of the Qumran Texts

We find many examples of these Jewish meals with a obligatory president in the literature of Qumran. In the *Rule of the Community*, the following is prescribed:

> Wherever there are ten men of the Council of the Community there shall not lack a priest [*kohen*, no doubt] among them and they shall all sit before him according to their rank and shall be asked their counsel in all things in that order. And when the table has been prepared for eating, and the new wine for drinking, the Priest shall be the first to stretch out his hand to bless the first fruits of the bread and new wine.

Another text, this from *The Messianic Rule*:

And [when] they shall gather for the common table, to eat and [to drink] new wine, when the common table shall be set for eating and the new wine [poured] for drinking, let no man extend his hand over the first fruits of bread and wine before the Priest; for [it is he] who shall bless the first fruits of bread and wine, and shall be the first to extend his hand over the bread. Thereafter, the Messiah of Israel shall extend his hand over the bread [the context explains this specific touch: the Priest is the Messiah of Aaron, who takes precedence over the King, the Messiah of Israel] [and] the congregation of the community [shall utter a] blessing, [each man in the order] of his dignity. It is according to this statute that they shall proceed at every me[al at which] at least ten men are gathered together.[9]

It would be easy to quote other texts, but it is not necessary. Those above do not say that Christianity borrowed from Qumran; however, they certainly do show that Qumran and primitive Christianity are component parts of the same Jewish milieu. The meal of the Christians is not the same as that of the Essenes, and its content is quite different, but in all probability the external form is, if not the same, at least very close, one to the other.

One might ask why the texts of Qumran are so specific when the Christian texts hardly ever are. There are likely two explanations for this: First, the people at Qumran had no reason for avoiding the word *priest*, while the Christians had many. As I already said, it is a question of the uniqueness of Christ's priesthood; Christians also had to avoid confusion with the Jewish and pagan priests. Second, the texts of Qumran are community rules, which list and foresee all details quite minutely. The Christian writings, by contrast, were written for various occasions (letters, sermons, or testimonies), and they do not say everything. Far from it! I shall have to repeat that more than once. We have to remember, for example, that we have no evidence of the celebration of the Eucharist before the year 56 (the date of Paul's First Letter to the Corinthians). If there had not been troubles in Corinth over this matter, we probably would have had to wait even longer to know. We can imagine the reaction of critics if we had nothing before the 80s. In the name of the positivistic history mentioned before, critics might have concluded that the Eucharist had never been celebrated before, and so it was a pure creation of the community. Arguments drawn from the silence of the texts are hard to manage one way or another, but the Christian texts are not all silent.

The Witness of the *Didache*

We have to leave behind the canonical writings to find indications as clear as those from the Qumran texts; but we are not, for all that, leaving behind the epoch of the New Testament. In fact, the *Didache*, a short writing composed of several, originally independent pieces, dates entirely from the first century, and many authors propose a range of AD 50 to 70 for some of its parts. This means that it is, on the whole, contemporary with the date of the editing of the oldest Letters of Paul (1–2 Thess, 1–2 Cor, and Rom). Now it happens that the *Didache* gives a good deal of information about baptism, the Eucharist, and the ministers who serve in the Church (see chapters 7 to 10 for liturgical questions, and chapters 11 to 15 for disciplinary matters.) We can leave aside the parts concerning baptism, as well as the details about the Eucharist. By contrast, what relates to the ministers and their function is of direct interest.

The *Didache* is familiar with two kinds of ministers: the traveling ministers and the resident ones. Among the first, it mentions the apostles (who must not be confused with the Twelve: The apostles are rather their coworkers in the first generation), the prophets, and the teachers; and the text mostly talks about the prophets. Now this naming system for ministers corresponds to the one that was in use in Antioch around the 50s (see Acts 13); and we see in this fact evidence pointing to a Syrian origin of the *Didache*. So what we get here is a glimpse into the oldest form of the ministries. The text gives various indications as to the manner of distinguishing between true and false prophets. But the most important thing is to notice the bond established between the prophet and the eucharistic liturgy (10:7; 11:7), as well as the order to honor the prophets and give them the firstfruits, "because they are your chief priests" (13:4: *archiereis*; unless I am mistaken, this is the earliest use of priestly language for ministers by a Christian text). It is interesting to note that a later document, the *Apostolic Constitutions* (around 350), which includes the *Didache* in its collection, felt obliged to substitute the word *priests* for the word *prophet*, in order to harmonize this teaching with the changed situation, and thereby to erase the apparent anomaly (*Apostolic Constitutions* 7.29, and *Didache* 13:3).

Prophets and teachers thus carry out liturgical functions, but what happens when the traveling ministers leave the community? The *Didache*'s answer is very clear: "Appoint, therefore, for yourselves, bishops and deacons worthy of the Lord, men meek, and not lovers of money, and truthful and proved; for they also render to you the service of prophets and teachers. Therefore, do not despise them, for they are your honored ones, together with prophets and teachers" (*Didache* 15:1–4). These few lines are rich in information:

1. The situation they describe is obviously later than the preceding one: There is a new generation of ministers, indigenous and stable, which succeeds to that of foreign, itinerant ministers.

2. "Overseers and deacons" is a consecrated expression that we have already met both in Philippians 1:1 and in *1 Clement* 42.4–5. It does not mean that the bishops follow the prophets and the deacons follow the teachers. Rather, it is a global expression used to designate the community's ministers as a whole. Why are they not called "presbyters," as in Clement's letter? The majority of scholars think that there was no difference in the role played within the community, but that the expression "overseers and deacons" was used for the ministers of new communities emerging from paganism, while the word *presbyters* referred to the ministers of the Judeo-Christian communities.

3. As to the functions of these ministers, they are easily discerned from the context. It is immediately after

the description of the arrangements for Sunday (14:1–3) that we find overseers and deacons mentioned, whence the *therefore* in the phrase "*therefore*, do not despise them." Furthermore, their office is presented as a liturgy (*Didache* 15:1), which, by the way, is not just Sunday worship, but also includes catechetical teaching (chapters 1–6), the administration of baptism (7), and presiding over the eucharistic meals (9–10). As for the diaconate (the "service," 15:1), it is a way to recall that they must be disinterested.

4. On the subject of the eucharistic meals, the formula runs: "But every Lord's Day gather yourselves together, and break bread, and give thanksgiving after having confessed your transgressions, that your sacrifice may be pure" (14:1). *Sacrifice* here has been used as the translation for the word *thusia*, with which we are quite familiar and which we meet twice more in the verses immediately following (14:2–3). Careful as always not to go beyond the explicit teaching of the texts, scholars who have closely studied this book warn us not to jump to the conclusion that what we have here is a sacrificial meal. They think that what is primarily meant here is spiritual sacrifices. They concede, however, that the closeness of the breaking of bread and sacrifice in the text has exercised a certain influence on the liturgical and ministerial ideas of later theology—and evidently not without reason.

5. If we sum up the contribution of the *Didache* for our purposes, we see how the link between ministers and liturgical celebration, and between ministers and the priestly function, is clearly defined in it. The overseers are still not called *hiereis*, but the prophets whose place they take, along with the deacons, are assimilated to the *archiereis*. And the same honor is due to the resident ministers as to the traveling ones. This is all the more important to keep in mind since

the *Didache*, as mentioned, is a document whose antiquity is comparable to that of Paul's great epistles, and at the very least to that of the Gospels and Acts.

To conclude our investigation into the bond between ministers and the celebration of the liturgy, I have to mention three authors: Clement, Ignatius, and Justin. The latter two will be examined in greater detail; however, since I have already spoken of Clement's important role in the rise of the priestly *vocabulary*, that will not keep us long here. On the priestly *function* exercised in the Eucharist, there is only one clear passage: "Indeed it will be no small sin for us if we oust men who have irreproachably and piously offered the sacrifices proper to the episcopate" (*1 Clement* 44). The expression *prospherein dora* ("to offer gifts") was used for the offering of Old Testament sacrifices, and it is picked up by the Letter to the Hebrews (5:1; 8:3–4). In *1 Clement*, the gifts signify both the material gifts that accompanied the eucharistic sacrifices that were destined for the poor and the eucharistic elements themselves. If the subject is eucharistic worship as a whole, the gifts also include the community's sacrifice of praise (35 and 52; see Heb 13:15–16). The allusion is rather precise, but it is only an allusion. Things will be clearer in Ignatius.

The Legitimate Eucharist according to Ignatius of Antioch

For the topic with which we are concerned, there are two essential passages in the letters of Ignatius. Our first comes from *Philadelphians* 4: "Take heed to have but one Eucharist. For there is one flesh of our Lord Jesus Christ, and one cup to [show forth] the unity of his blood; one altar, as there is one bishop [overseer], along with the presbyters and the deacons, my fellow servants." The text marks a clear progression from those that I have quoted up to now: *Eucharist* here has the exact same meaning that we give it now (whereas, before this, the word was closer to "thanksgiving"), and it is closely bound up with the three-step hierarchy. As for Ignatius's counsel to have one Eucharist, it is meant in opposition to the Eucharists of heretical sects, which we find mentioned in our second passage, his following letter, written to the *Smyrnaeans*:

> Let no man do anything connected with the Church without the bishop. Let that be deemed a proper Eucharist, which is [administered] either by the bishop, or by one to whom he has entrusted it. Wherever the bishop shall appear, there let the multitude [of the people] also be; even as, wherever Christ Jesus is, there is the Catholic Church. It is not lawful without the bishop either to baptize or to celebrate a love-feast; but whatever he shall approve of, that is also pleasing to God. (*Smyrnaeans* 8.1–2)

There are number of things worth noticing in these texts: Not just the Eucharist but baptism (and the love-feast, which immediately precedes the Eucharist) depend on the bishop's authority. Still, he does not exercise this role all by himself: he is surrounded by a presbyterium (the word occurs frequently in Ignatius), and he can delegate one of its members to celebrate in his absence. This is the origin of what will later be the curates of a parish. This case being made for the bishop's authority and for the uniqueness of the Eucharist plainly reveals that not everyone took it for granted, and that Ignatius had to confront some opponents: perhaps dissident groups or people nostalgic for the preceding, less centralized period?...

We only ask the question and do not have to linger over it. It is enough to observe that this image of the Church is very much the same one we will encounter in what follows. But even if we had to postdate it by fifty years or so, that would not change anything. Nevertheless, we also have to acknowledge that not all parts of the Church were in agreement on all matters. Developments took place a bit differently in the West, and what was true in Asia Minor in Ignatius's day was not yet the case in Rome, as Justin will inform us.

The Celebration of the Eucharist according to St. Justin

Justin of Nablus (ca. 100–ca. 165), that is, Justin Martyr, is well known for his *Dialogue with Trypho,* which is a fine example of the first Christian polemics against Judaism, represented here by the rabbi Trypho; he is also known for his two *Apologies,* addressed to the emperor Antoninus Pius and his adopted son Marcus Aurelius in favor of the Christians (dated 150–55). The most interesting passage for us is found in the *First Apology* (65–67), where Justin describes the ceremony of baptism, which is immediately followed by the Eucharist. Here is part of that passage:

> 65. [3] There is then brought to the president of the brethren bread and a cup of wine mixed with water; and he taking them, gives praise and glory to the Father of the universe, through the name of the Son and of the Holy Ghost, and offers thanks at considerable length for our being counted worthy to receive these things at His hands. And when he has concluded the prayers and thanksgivings, all the people present express their assent by saying Amen. [4] This word Amen answers in the Hebrew language to *genoito* [so be it]. [5] And when the president has given thanks, and all the people have expressed their assent, those who are called by us deacons give to each of those present to partake of the bread and wine mixed with water over which the thanksgiving was pronounced, and to those who are absent they carry away a portion.
>
> 66. [1] And this food is called among us *Eucharistia* [the Eucharist], of which no one is allowed to partake but the man who believes that the things which we teach are true, and who has been washed with the washing that is for the remission of sins, and unto regeneration, and who is so living as Christ has enjoined. [2] For not as common bread and common drink do we receive these; but in like manner as Jesus Christ our

Saviour, having been made flesh by the Word of God, had both flesh and blood for our salvation, so likewise have we been taught that the food which is blessed by the prayer of His word, and from which our blood and flesh by transmutation are nourished, is the flesh and blood of that Jesus who was made flesh. [3] For the apostles, in the memoirs composed by them, which are called Gospels, have thus delivered unto us what was enjoined upon them; that Jesus took bread, and when He had given thanks, said, "This do ye in remembrance of Me, this is My body;" and that, after the same manner, having taken the cup and given thanks, He said, "This is My blood."

The *First Apology* 65–67 can be read in its entirety at the end of the book (text 5 in the Appendix), but we can already notice some things about it:

1. Justin uses the term *president* ("the one who presides," *ho proestos*): the expression occurs five times in these pages. He does not seem to be familiar with the word *episkopos* (or if he knows it, he does not use it), but he is quite familiar with *diakonos*, and there is the same connection between *proestos* and *diakonos* as that noted earlier between *episkopos* and *diakonos*. These were probably the same persons with different titles.

   We recall that St. Paul uses the related term *proïstamenos* to designate those responsible for Thessalonica (1 Thess 5:12): "Respect those who labor among you, and *have charge of you* in the Lord and admonish you." This verse offers the first evidence (from early in the year 51) of the existence of leaders in the communities founded by the apostles. We also find this term in Roman 12:8: "Let the one who leads (*proïstamenos*), [do so] with zeal" (ESV), as well as in 1 Timothy 3:4. By contrast, a little further on in 1 Timothy (5:17), we find *proestotes*: "Let the elders who rule well be considered worthy of double honor." By using this word *president*, Justin is displaying a certain archaism, since it matches up with our oldest texts.

2. These texts are precious for yet another reason—for what they tell us about the Eucharist. Minus the word itself, we are quite close to the doctrine of changed substance that much later would be called transubstantiation; but this is not the place to discuss that.

3. Specialists debate whether Justin considers the Eucharist a sacrifice. Many elements point in this direction, but what *is* certain is that Justin does not separate the celebration of the Eucharist from the offering of spiritual sacrifices. The celebration is completed with the sharing and the help given to all those in need. For some scholars, Justin is actually identifying the Eucharist with the spiritual sacrifice (*logiké thusia*) that the prophets called for. "The Eucharist represents the long-awaited spiritual sacrifice (the *logiké thusia*), because the *Logos* himself is the victim" (J. Quasten).

4. It is equally important to emphasize the echo of Jesus' words at the Last Supper: "Do this in memory of me." Clearly the celebration described in Justin is wholly situated under the sign of obedience to Christ's order. So when the "presidents" of these Eucharists receive the title of "priests," that will quite simply be through an awareness of the fact that they are celebrating the memorial of Christ's sacrifice, and that in a secondary, derivative fashion they are thereby perpetuating the presence of Christ to his Church.

It is not in the least surprising that it required some time to grasp this. It would take considerably more time for theologians to realize all the implications of the Church's practice in the first two centuries. It is enough to have shown the homogeneity of the development that, starting with the apostles, finds its culmination in Ignatius and Justin. Compared with this fundamental continuity, the vicissitudes experienced by the history of the theology of priesthood and the differences in its evolution in the East and the West have only a secondary importance.

So we can halt our brief investigation into the link between the Eucharist and the ministers. The texts are discreet, but they nonetheless provide unequivocal evidence. I will limit myself to two provisional conclusions: (1) Even in this ancient period, we do not see the celebration of the Eucharist being carried out by the entire, undifferentiated liturgical assembly: Christian ministers are specially assigned to it. When these ministers acquire the title of *hiereus* or *sacerdos* toward the end of the second century or the beginning of the third, it turns out to be a perfectly coherent development. (2) It is likewise of the highest importance to note the bond that also exists between the eucharistic celebration and the spiritual sacrifice of the baptized. This is, in fact, the last line of argument that we have to explore.

THE SERVICE OF AUTHORITY AND ITS PRIESTLY DIMENSION

Following the lines of our investigation, after the prophetic and priestly functions, we come to the *royal* function. Nothing prevents us from using this word, but we have to remember that Christ did not accept it without immediately adding that his kingdom was not of this world. We can deduce from this that the authority exercised in this kingdom is unlike the authority exercised in any civil government whatsoever—be it royal or republican. The authority that pertains to the ministers in the ecclesial communion is a complex and, in some borderline cases, an ambiguous reality. I am going to try to describe its different aspects; but first the possible ambiguity must be cleared.

Conditions for Exercising Authority in the Church

The New Testament has at least four reasons that forbid us to compare the authority of the Church to that of any government:

1. Christ formally commanded a different kind of authority: "Let the greatest among you become as the youngest, and the leader as one who serves" (Luke 22:24–27); with such notable parallels as the washing of the feet (John 13:4ff.). If there are among my readers any future or already-ordained priests looking for a viable spirituality, there is no need to look any further than this.
2. There is the use of the words *serve* and *service* to designate the responsibility of Church government: It is the diaconate, in the absolute sense (Acts 1:17; 21:17; 1 Tim 1:12; Rom 11:13), and even the diaconate of the apostolate (Acts 1:25). This is too well known to need any extra references.
3. An argument perhaps still more powerful than the use of these words is the actual attitude of Peter and Paul—after Christ, the two absolute models of the Christian minister. It has been shown that Paul habitually applied to himself the prophecies of the Suffering Servant in Isaiah in a deliberate imitation of the life and sufferings of Christ. The same applies to Peter, who is also presented with the same features. Under these circumstances we can better grasp how Peter could recommend to the elders/presbyters not to "lord it over those in your charge, but be examples to the flock" (1 Pet 5:3). When we consider that this epistle of Peter dates from the year 64, this could mean that clericalism had very quickly become a fixture in the Church.
4. The word *exousia* ("power") is rarely used to designate the authority of Christ's ministers. When it *is* employed, it is in the context of the authority received from Christ: to cast out demons, for example (Matt 10:1 and parallels); to give the Holy Spirit through the laying on of hands (Acts 8:18–20); to build up and not tear down the community (2 Cor 10:8; 13:10)—but *not* to give a juridical definition of authority.

One can hardly doubt that the notorious weakness of many past features of canon law lies in the wish to see the Church as a "perfect society" (that is, modeled on a state). Canonists conceived the theory of authority in the ecclesial body in imitation of authority in the civil body. One could not imagine a more complete misunderstanding, because the Church cannot be a society like the others.

The Goals and Forms of Exercising This Authority

It is not enough to denounce the errors of interpretation that have been made. The fact remains that authority in the Church is still a grand and beautiful thing, because it is finalized by maintaining its unity of community, its cohesion, and its concern to guide the community toward its goal. People do not pay enough attention to this, but it is anchored in the exercise of the prophetic and priestly function. The authority of the ministers is practiced in the first place by the service of the Word, because that is how they guarantee the rightness of the faith, the first bond of unity in the community. As for the service of the sacraments, its first aim is the growth of Christ's ecclesial body in love until it reaches the fullness of its development. The two services are not, incidentally, separate, but are mutually related—this must never be forgotten. Yet we need to add that this authority must carry out other acts that likewise respond to the same service of community, but in a different way.

In short, these acts can be regrouped around what is suggested by the two names *poimen* and *episkopos*. As we know, the *episkopos* was defined very early on as a *poimen*. What I am about to say must not be taken too rigidly, but perhaps we can play with the etymology and say that, in virtue of his office as *episkopos* (overseer), the person placed in authority is to guard that the rightness of the order of charity is maintained and, hence, is to "inspect" and to punish when necessary. Meanwhile, in his role as *poimen,* the person in charge will also tend to the poor and needy—that is, in the language of the Gospel, will also rescue the lost sheep, heal the wounded, and so forth. Both these aspects are well attested to in the New Testament:

"As for those who persist in sin, rebuke them" (1 Tim 5:20). If we take the exercise of authority in its "episcopal" dimension, we see the apostles and elders of Jerusalem passing laws during the Council of Jerusalem: "It has seemed good to the Holy Spirit and to us..." (Acts 15:28). This is at least the beginning of the legislative power that was later recognized as belonging to the bishops. Similarly, we see Paul suggest, prescribe, and order certain behaviors: "I give this command, not I but the Lord...I and not the Lord" (1 Cor 7:10, 12). We likewise see him judging and sanctioning certain behaviors contrary to the law of the community, as with the punishment of the incestuous man in Corinth (1 Cor 5). In the latter case, we have a veritable expulsion from the community, what will later be called an excommunication. But Paul was not the only one to act this way. We find the basis for this severity in Matthew 18:16–18: If the brotherly correction that must be tried first does not work, the guilty party is removed from the community.

> [Jesus says:] "But if you are not listened to, take one or two others along with you....If the member refuses to listen to them, tell it to the church [the *ekklesia*]; and if the offender refuses to listen even to the church, let such a one be to you as a Gentile and a tax collector. Truly I tell you, whatever you bind on earth will be bound in heaven, and whatever you loose on earth will be loosed in heaven." (also see Matt 26:19 and John 20:23)

The language is very strong, and it clearly informs us of the presence of a judicial power, at least in its germinal stage, that the authority is recognized as possessing. In the same sense we recall the punishment of Ananias and Sapphira, who are literally condemned to death by St. Peter (Acts 5:1–11). We also have to remember the orders in 1 Timothy 5:17–25, where a certain number of rules are dictated about the conduct that members of the community have to exhibit. The abuses that have occurred in the history of the Church show that this aspect of authority has often been badly exercised, but we cannot deny its existence in the

New Testament. Still, it has to be repeated that these interventions are not an end in themselves. They are definitively aimed at the growth of charity, at the service of community. It is here that the exercise of authority has to find its supreme regulating principle.

The "koinonia' for the poor among the saints..." (Rom 15:26). The service of authority is exercised yet again in a more directly pastoral manner. We have already encountered this in the form of the "table service" (Acts 6:1–6: the function of the Seven); however, this is already present from the beginning of Acts (4:34–37). The sharing of goods and distribution of resources rests with the supervising authority, which brings with it administrative tasks. Thus, in his lists of charisms, Paul does not forget to mention that of "helpers" (1 Cor 12:28). This same concern for the needy is also found in Acts 11:28–30: the disciples from Antioch come to the aid of those in Jerusalem, who are suffering from famine. It is quite remarkable that the help sent is addressed to the "elders" (presbyters), and that it is entrusted to Barnabas and Paul. The ministers are thus deeply involved in this affair, and it is quite probable that they took the initiative in it.

The most interesting case in which we see this dimension of authority is surely the grand collection organized by St. Paul to help the Mother Church of Jerusalem. We already know that he uses the word *koinonia* and its derivatives to speak about the collection (2 Cor 9:13; Rom 15:26). It has a theological meaning for him because it concretely translates the unity of the Church of Christ despite its dispersion across the whole Mediterranean Basin (see 1 Cor 16:1).

In these two cases, whether he is punishing or assisting, the Apostle—and after him, the ministers he installs—is thus acting in the service of communion. Now, and it is here that we connect again with our main focus, this service is itself considered a priestly work.

Service of the Community Is Itself a Priestly Work

Dominique Barthélémy, during a week-long interdisciplinary conference that we led jointly, shared with me all the unpublished documentation that he had collected on this subject, but I shall limit myself here to what is strictly necessary for our purposes. The idea could be summed up thus: The service of the community that the ministers are charged with performing is itself akin to a priestly work. The words chosen to express this are themselves specifically priestly and cultic. Here are several examples:

The Altar of God: Widows, Poor People, Orphans. Let us go back once again to Clement of Rome as a point of departure: "Priests and Levites (*hiereis kai levitai*) are the ministers of the altar of God (*thusiasterio tou theou*)." This altar is quite materially that of the Temple in Jerusalem. But we find in a letter to the Philippians from Polycarp, bishop of Smyrna (ca. 155–60), a passage concerning widows in which he justifies all the orders he gives them by reminding them "that they are the altar of God" (*thusiasterion theou*) and that God will closely examine (*momoskopeisthai*) all things, because none of the secrets of our heart escape him. Now it happens that *momoskopeisthai* is a rare term that comes from *First Clement* (41) and that refers to the examination of victims before a sacrifice. Hence, it is a cultic term. This image of widows as the "altar of God" very quickly became a commonplace. We find it again in Tertullian's letter *To his wife*: a "clean altar of God" (*ara Dei munda*, 1.7.4), but especially in the *Syriac Didascalia*, where it is used a number of times. A widow must know that "she is the altar of God." Hence, she must not run from house to house, "because the altar of God is fixed in one place," that is, the Temple (*Didascalia* 15). But the title is not uniquely reserved for widows. In the same chapter, the bishop told to watch over the widows is this altar as well: "Thou and the widows who are such…you are the holy altar of God, (even of) Jesus Christ."[10] The title is further extended to the orphans, to the elderly, to the sick, to those raising children—all of whom must be acknowledged as the altar of God. If they have received gifts, it is not without reciprocity, for they pray assiduously for those who give to them, paying them back by prayer (17).

The Service of the Altar of God. One might wonder why all these people, like the widows, are also "altars of God." That is easy to understand now: Living from the offerings of the faithful, they are like the altar on which the offerings are placed and from which the sacrifice ascends that is pure and agreeable to God. It is here that we rediscover the ministerial service:

> Do you the bishops and the deacons be constant there-fore in the ministry of the altar of Christ—we mean the widows and the orphans—so that with all care and with all diligence you make it your endeavor to search out [examine attentively!] the things that are given, (and to learn) of what manner is the conversation [behav-ior] of him or of her, who gives for nourishment—we say again—of the altar. For when widows are nourished from (the fruits of) righteous labor, they offer a holy and acceptable ministry before Almighty God through His beloved Son and His holy Spirit. (*Didascalia* 18)

We are not used to this picturesque language, but it makes sense. The counterproof is provided by the next part of the text, which asserts that the bishops are guilty if they accept alms from those who are reprehensible.

> Wherefore, O bishops, fly and avoid such ministra-tions, for it is written: *There shall not go up upon the altar of the Lord (that which cometh) of the price of a dog, or of the hire of a harlot* [Deut 23:18; the "dog" is a male prosti-tute]. For if a widow pray for fornicators and blasphe-mers through your blindness and be not heard, not receiving their requests, you will perforce bring blas-phemy upon the word through your evil management, as though God were not good and ready to give. Take good heed therefore that you minister not to the altar of God out of the ministrations of transgression. (18)

Here again, despite the unusual examples used, we readily grasp the role assigned to the bishop: he must inspect the gifts, that is, carry out his *episkopē* so that the widows are offering a pure sacri-fice. So the "administration" here is not just a material affair, but rather the right life for each of the members and mutual help and understanding in the community.

121

The Diaconate of the Lord according to Hermas. The evidence from the *Didascalia* is relatively late (first half of the third century), but we have an exactly comparable example from a hundred years or so earlier in the *Shepherd of Hermas* (ca. 140). The author develops a similar message of "social justice," and for this purpose he uses language that is every bit as liturgical: "If you observe fasting as I have communicated to you, your sacrifice will be acceptable to God…and the service thus performed is noble, and sacred, and acceptable to the Lord" (Similitude 5.3.7–8). Elsewhere, at the end of another allegory (the elm and the vine), the author concludes, "And this is a great work…because he [the rich man] understands the object of his wealth, and has given to the poor of the gifts of the Lord, and rightly discharged his service to him." Although R. Jolly "secularizes" this last phrase as "fittingly performed his task," there is no doubt that the context here is one of "spiritual sacrifices," and it is highly significant that one of the conditions of their acceptability comes from the role of the ministers who are assigned the job of making the community the place of *agapē*, the sanctuary where the pure and spotless sacrifice is offered.

The Scriptural Foundations. This colorful phrase is plainly very close to the word *scripture* itself, and we can rightly bring together this teaching about the altar of the Lord with that of St. Paul on the community as the Temple of the Lord: "You are the house that God builds." The Apostle is the architect of this house, and everyone must continue building on the cornerstone of Christ Jesus. The thought is completed by the well-known passage, "Do you not know that you are God's temple and that God's Spirit dwells in you? If anyone destroys God's temple (*naos tou theou*), God will destroy that person. For God's temple is holy, and you are that temple" (1 Cor 3:16–17). The notes in our Bibles stress that this language implies the idea of the presence in believers of the Glory of God, which is far greater than that found in the Temple of Jerusalem. This image returns in various passages, such as 1 Corinthians 6:19 and 2 Corinthians 6:16. And in Ephesians 2:20–22: "[You are] built upon the foundation of the apostles and prophets [the mediating role of the ministers], with Christ Jesus himself as the cornerstone. In him the whole structure is joined together and grows into a holy temple [*naon haghion*] in the Lord." It is hardly necessary to recall that this is also the language of 1 Peter 2:4–10. The royal priesthood is intimately bound up with the theme of the spiritual house (*oikos pneumatikos*), which all Christians must enter as living stones (1 Pet 2:5).

The Overseer in the Service of Pure and Spotless Religion. The consequences of these ideas hardly need to be pointed out. The whole community and each of its members are the Temple of the Lord. Within this community, the widows, the children, and the various needy persons are themselves the altar of the Lord. Those who watch over the worship offered on that altar and in that Temple are those who exercise the *episcopē* ("surveillance") by the careful examination of the victims offered, among other things the alms, but also the spiritual sacrifices. That way, worship is offered that is pleasing to God. St. James ably sums up this vision of things: "Religion that is pure and undefiled before God, the Father, is this: to care for orphans and widows in their distress, and to keep oneself unstained by the world" (Jas 1:27). We get a still better grasp of this verse if we recall what Christ himself says about it (Matt 25:35–36): "I was hungry and you gave me food." In other words, the *episcopē*, that office of "government" acknowledged in the ministers, is finalized by the need to render unto God a spiritual worship worthy of that name.

I will say shortly that the priestly ministry is directed to the spiritual priesthood. I will simply be expressing in more technical terms the profound truth that we have just uncovered in these texts. Reading them shows us how mistaken it is to try to define the Christian priesthood merely by the celebration of the strictly "sacramental" rites: Christian worship is a much broader reality than that.

A SUMMARY FOR REFLECTION

At the end of our survey of the ministries in the earliest Christian literature, it remains to try to synthesize our principal results to propose at least a rough summary for reflection about them.

We started out from the absence of priestly language in the New Testament to designate the ministers. Along the way, we found at least three reasons for that silence:

1. the concern to avoid confusion with the Jewish priests and with those of the pagan religions;
2. the other side of the preceding reason: the awareness of the complexity and the novelty of Christian ministry, which forbids its being reduced to a simple function of the "sacrificer";
3. finally, and above all, the clear perception of the uniqueness of Christ's priesthood and sacrifice, which does not allow us to think that in Christianity there are other priests besides him.

If Christ's faithful are participants in his royal priesthood, it is solely to the extent that they are his members, his mystical continuation, and even in some sense himself: in Christ, we are all so many other Christs. This fundamental truth remains at the heart of our faith, today as yesterday—yet, nevertheless, the title of priest has been extended to the ministers.

The reasons for extending the title are many, although some of them are insufficient. In saying this, one thinks of the role some have wanted to attribute to nostalgia in the restoration of the priestly vocabulary. This role could, to some small degree, be evoked for the addressees of the Letter to the Hebrews (that is, the Jewish priests who might have considered apostasy out of regret for the magnificent Temple ceremonies and to whom the author of the letter describes the splendors of the celestial liturgy); however, the author himself does not slip into this fault and in no way attributes the title of priest to the ministers. Is this reason more valid for *First Clement*? It is hard to believe it.

The author of Hebrews stays within the limits of a healthy typology, drawing a parallel between the ministers of the two Covenants, but without likening those of the New to those of the Old. What happens with Clement is a bit like what happens with

Paul, who himself sets up a similar comparison in 1 Corinthians 9:13–14: "Those who are employed in the temple service get their food from the temple," and one can certainly not suspect any nostalgia here for the Old Covenant.

Nevertheless, the relation to the Old Testament seems to have played a decisive role. Once the uniqueness of the priesthood and sacrifice of Christ had been recognized, once the novelty and specificity of the Christian ministry had been admitted, it was henceforth possible to pick up the Old Testament categories again and, at the same time, to bypass the narrowing of the priestly function as it was exercised in the Jewish milieu at the time of Christ, to find the link between the three messianic functions, and to emphasize the figurative and typological value of the Old Testament ministries. So it was a perfectly legitimate and homogeneous development. But it was heavy with risk, which can be seen already in the New Testament, apropos of other things: for example, the danger of Judaizing, and the temptation to go back and conform the Christian priest into a Levite. Liturgical typology did not always avoid that danger, nor did clerical behavior (tithes for the clergy, forgetting the service of the Word, and the incapacity to perform it, which very quickly became constants in the Western Middle Ages). But that is another story.

To avoid this danger, it is not enough to change the language. One has to be on guard here. It has already been said that we talk about "priesthood." To designate a Christian "ministry," we are using a synecdoche (= simultaneous understanding), that is, a rhetorical figure that consists in evoking one of the features of a reality in order to suggest the whole: "steel" for a sword, "head" for cattle. Poetic language summons up these metaphors. The problem arises in theological reasoning and Christian behavior to the extent that one risks actually taking the part for the whole.

How to express ourselves, then? We will soon see what Vatican II teaches on this subject, and it is very enlightening, but possibilities can already be proposed here. We can talk about the "pastoral" ministry, of which the "priestly" ministry is a part. This option is well founded in Scripture and Tradition, and we can easily see how this covers the three ministerial functions. We can also simply talk about the priestly ministry, while taking care not to forget that this ministry extends beyond the sacramental aspect and also embraces the service of the Word and of authority, as we have just seen.

We will come back to these names apropos of Vatican II, but two further points have to be added: (1) When we speak of pastoral or priestly ministry, we have to understand the names of the ministry in general. We are not yet speaking of the *presbyteral* ministry. The *hiereus,* the priest whom we have been discussing up until now, is the bishop, and that is one more reason not to use the term *priest* without further specification. (2) Whatever term we do keep, we have to give up the idea of a ministry uniquely defined by the eucharistic sacrifice that a minister could celebrate solely out of personal piety. That happens, it still exists, and it is not impossible to justify theologically—but it represents an anomaly. The Christian minister is not defined uniquely in relation to the eucharistic body, but also, by this very fact, to its mystical Body, of which he is put in charge at his own level of responsibility.

In the perspective of this book, which is dedicated to the Church as the wholly priestly people, the best way to situate the priestly ministry within this people is, therefore, to emphasize that its service consists in making the royal or spiritual priesthood grow in such a way that, to speak like St. Augustine, the entire holy City of God may become a spiritual sacrifice agreeable to God through Jesus Christ. I will return to this, but we can already meditate on the following scheme, which gathers together the essentials.[11]

ROYAL PRIESTHOOD AND PRIESTLY MINISTRY
IN THE ECCLESIAL BODY OF THE ONLY PRIEST
A unique and eternal
hiereus
accomplishing once and for all
by his death and resurrection the
hierosyne
thus communicating

the sanctification of the spirit

to a People who have been won
and who therefore constitute a
hieraeuma haghion
offering throughout its life
thusias pneumatikas
acceptable to God through
Jesus Christ,

a *diakonia* or function of
justification and reconciliation
of spirit,

to ministers, within the priestly
people and the world. They are
hierourgountes
so that the offering of the
(profane) nations may be
acceptable to God because it
is sanctified in the Holy Spirit.
In other words, the *hierosyne*
(priesthood) accomplished
once and for all by the only
hiereus, who endures eternally;
they actualize it in time as
instruments, through

proclaiming the great deeds of
Him who has called them out
of darkness into his light, and
who will share with him in
eternity the title of:

preaching and ritual, so as to
constitute the *hierateuma* or
holy people, and to keep him
in their consciousness and
their witness as a people of:

hiereis

127

IV

ROYAL PRIESTHOOD AND PRIESTLY MINISTRY ACCORDING TO VATICAN II

In this fourth chapter, we are going to return to the royal priesthood of Christians, which was the book's point of departure. But this will be in a climate not quite the same as that of the early days of Christianity and on a level of elaboration that must lead us more deeply into the understanding of that reality. It would have been enlightening to pursue, at least with broad brushstrokes, the evolutionary history that has led up to the present-day situation. I shall attempt that historical sketch for the priestly ministry, but we know enough about it to situate the royal priesthood in this change of climate. The most evident sign of this new situation with respect to the first Christian centuries is that, whenever the royal priesthood is mentioned, it is now accompanied by a mention of the priestly ministry. Whereas in the New Testament we were dealing with fragmentary and rare statements, by contrast the Church's present-day teaching proposes a structured doctrine that benefits from all of Tradition, which has passed down to us these first statements.

Make no mistake: This Tradition is not the result of an accumulation of traditions and minor customs, liturgical or otherwise. Rather, we are talking about the transmission and content of the faith received from the apostles, of the *paradosis* that St. Paul speaks of at the most solemn moments of his teaching (1 Cor 11:23–27; 15:3–9). This Tradition is not simply historical; it is also dogmatic. It is not a question of human explanation, but instead of theological faith. It is the light that will guide our reflection. That is why the best service that I can provide my readers will be to facilitate their access to the texts in which the Church has condensed her teaching.

There are two great texts that we need to know here. The first, in chronological order and dogmatic importance, is Vatican II's Dogmatic Constitution on the Church (*Lumen Gentium*). The second is the Decree on the Ministry and Life of Presbyters (as I said earlier, *not* the "Ministry and Life of *Priests*," as it is usually translated). In Latin *Presbyterorum Ordinis,* this document is clarified in the light of the first one, but itself brings greater detail to some important points. The passages that interest us can be found at the end of this book (text 6 in the Appendix), but a word of warning before we approach them. Particularly dense as they are, these Council documents call for more than a simple reading. They have to be commented on word by word. So, if at times my explanations seem to digress or to make for slow going, it is only to get a better grip on the texts. They will always be the harbor to which we must keep returning.

COMMON PRIESTHOOD AND MINISTERIAL PRIESTHOOD

Reading from *Lumen Gentium* 10

Since it will be useful to have it in front of us, here is the conciliar text:

> Christ the Lord, High Priest taken from among men [cf. Heb 5:1–5], made the new people "a kingdom and priests to God the Father" [cf. Rev 1:6; 5:9–10]. The baptized, by regeneration and the anointing of the Holy Spirit, are consecrated as a spiritual house and a holy priesthood, in order that through all those works which are those of the Christian man they may offer spiritual sacrifices and proclaim the power of Him who has called them out of darkness into His marvelous light [cf. 1 Pet 2:4–10]. Therefore all the disciples of Christ, persevering in prayer and praising God [Acts 2:42–47],

should present themselves as a living sacrifice, holy and pleasing to God [cf. Rom 12:1]. Everywhere on earth they must bear witness to Christ and give an answer to those who seek an account of that hope of eternal life which is in them [cf. 1 Pet 3:15].

Readers will notice that this paragraph of the text is very close to its scriptural foundations. We find in it the main texts that I analyzed at length in the chapter on the royal priesthood. Thus, there is no need to belabor this point, but we can note at least the following:

The excerpt speaks of a "holy" priesthood and not a "common" priesthood, as it will in the next paragraph. This shows that the point of view changes from one paragraph to the other. No doubt the reality is the same, because the subject is the baptized, but that reality is viewed under the aspect where it is directly a life of grace. Outside of baptism, which gives this life of grace, the excerpt makes no mention of all the other sacraments, but of "all those works which are those of a Christian," "spiritual sacrifices," "prayer," "the offering of persons," and so forth. We have to keep this focus in mind, because it will prove useful later on.

We must also note the "global" perspective of the excerpt, that is, it does not only speak of priesthood, but also of witness— in other words, of the prophetic aspect. This is in perfect agreement with the scriptural texts, but it also conveniently reminds us that this priesthood of the holy life finds one normal expression in Christian witness. When other texts tell us that all Christians must proclaim Christ by virtue of the grace of their baptism and confirmation, and that there is no need of a supplementary mandate from the hierarchy for that, this is in complete fidelity to the teaching of this first paragraph of *Lumen Gentium* 10. The second paragraph of section 10 touches on this same reality from a different perspective:

Though they differ from one another in essence and not only in degree, the common priesthood of the faithful and the ministerial or hierarchical priesthood are nonetheless interrelated: each of them in its own

special way is a participation in the one priesthood of
Christ. The ministerial priest, by the sacred power he
enjoys, teaches and rules the priestly people; acting in
the person of Christ, he makes present the eucharistic
sacrifice, and offers it to God in the name of all the
people. But the faithful, in virtue of their royal priesthood, join in the offering of the Eucharist. They likewise
exercise that priesthood by receiving the sacraments, by
prayer and thanksgiving, by the witness of a holy life, and
by self-denial and active charity.

With this second paragraph, we first meet the expression
"common priesthood of the faithful." That will also be the last
time, because it is not mentioned again in the Dogmatic
Constitution on the Church. As we see, it is immediately followed
by a mention of the "ministerial or hierarchical priesthood." The
development includes two well-marked phases. First, it distinguishes between the common priesthood and the ministerial
priesthood. It completes the description of both by listing each
one's principal acts. It is then a matter of carefully marking the
relation and the distinction between these two priestly titles. But
before coming to this second phase of these things (relation and
distinction), we first have to try to understand what the expression *common priesthood* covers.

There are two points to be noted here: (1) This common
priesthood is also called royal. Without question the subject is the
same reality, but the other word, *royal*, from 1 Peter is used to
describe it, which is a clear invitation not to neglect this aspect.
(2) The excerpt picks up everything said in the first excerpt
about the life of grace (prayer, witness, abnegation, and so forth);
however, the sacraments are also mentioned under two forms, by
the offering of the Eucharist and by the reception of the other
sacraments. This last feature will be fully developed in the following section of *Lumen Gentium* 11, but we can already observe
that the sacraments and the life of grace normally go together,
and that the expression "common priesthood" applies to these
two aspects of the life of the baptized: their participation in
Christian worship and that holy life that normally flows from it.

A PRIESTLY PEOPLE

Reading from *Lumen Gentium* 11

It would take too long to quote this text in its entirety; but it can be found at the end of the book (text 6 in the Appendix). Here I will limit myself to highlighting what can fill out our first approach to the common priesthood:

1. The first phrase of this section deserves special attention. We will readily see in it a perfect summing up of the whole purpose of this book. It speaks of a priestly community (*basileion hierateuma*), and it stresses the organic structure of this community. This is the key word when the ecclesial body is at stake: not everyone has the same function in it (see 1 Cor 12). We encounter the same idea a little further on apropos of the Eucharist: "All take part in this liturgical service, *not indeed in the same way, but each in the way that is proper to himself.*"

2. The sacraments are listed with a minimum of description for each of them, according to a classic order: first, the three sacraments of initiation—baptism, confirmation, Eucharist; then the sacrament of forgiveness, which allows the Christian to recover baptismal grace; followed by the anointing of the sick, which is to the health of the body a little like what forgiveness is to the health of the soul; finally, the two sacraments that can be called "social," holy orders, totally concentrated on "feeding the Church in Christ's name," and marriage, which sanctifies the encounter between two human beings and allows both the Church and society to perpetuate themselves. Toward the end of the second paragraph, immediately after marriage, a new mention of baptism sheds some important light on its role: Through it the "new citizens of human society" become the children of God, capable of perpetuating the "People of God." The mention of the "domestic" Church in speaking of the family emphasizes that this is the true base community, in which

relations between the Church and the world are best realized. These few words are enough for a first approach to section 11 of *Lumen Gentium,* but anyone who wants to get a deeper view will have to complete it with section 34, which speaks of the participation of laypeople in the common priesthood and worship. At this point we still have a few questions to raise about the common priesthood.

Who Participates in the Common Priesthood?

If we ask who are the members of the common priesthood—that is, which persons participate in this common priestly quality—the answer is, doubtless, not just the "simple faithful" (as sometimes used to be said in a slightly condescending tone), but all the baptized, laypeople and ministers included. We can be sure of this for various reasons: (1) The Council has spelled it out: everything taught in chapter 2 of *Lumen Gentium* concerns all the faithful, except where it is expressly stated to the contrary, for example, in the case of ordained ministers. (2) The very expression "the common priesthood of the faithful" signifies that this quality is theirs in common and extends to all the baptized. When one wishes to distinguish between the baptized, one speaks of ministers and laypeople; and possibly of religious, but not in the same sense. (3) The sacrament of holy orders also comes up in this section, at which point it says that the ministers are *also* invested with the sacrament of holy orders, a sacrament added on to the common priestly quality without removing it and without dissolving into it. (4) Finally, later in *Lumen Gentium* (at 34), there will be a special new mention of this royal priesthood apropos of laypeople, not simply to repeat what is said here, but to specify the particular way in which they participate in the common priesthood.

Accuracy of the Expression "Common Priesthood"?

These specifics as to the extent of the common priestly quality leave untouched another question that it is hard not to ask: Is the term *common* priesthood the most accurate for designating this reality? It is enlightening to know that the theologians who prepared the Council text hesitated on this point. In a first draft, the preparatory commission wrote "universal [*universale*] priesthood." The word, in fact, is a fitting way to designate what belongs to everyone; however, it was then noticed that the word can also mean "that which includes everything" ("which contains everything in itself," *quod universa complectitur*). So *common* was preferred to avoid this ambiguity. We have to recognize that it hardly would have been better to speak about a "certain" priesthood, as one amendment proposed; that would have been too vague. Some suggested "spiritual priesthood," which would have been most suitable, since this priesthood offers spiritual victims. But the commission observed that the hierarchical priesthood is "spiritual" too, since it was instituted by a gift of the Holy Spirit. Certainly, but that is not enough to disqualify this adjective and, in some situations, it could have proved useful.

It was also necessary to reject another suggestion: to talk about an "inceptive" (= "that which has begun") priesthood. This language would have been terribly ambiguous, because it suggests that the sacrament of holy orders brings baptism to perfection along the same lines as the baptismal grace—and so at that moment, the recipient of holy orders would be some kind of super-Christian. But that is plainly an error, because there is nothing greater than baptism, which gives the baptized their dignity as children of God. It was precisely to avoid a similar misunderstanding that *Lumen Gentium* 10 specifies in its second paragraph that the common priesthood and the hierarchical priesthood do not differ only by a simple question of more or less, but really by their essence (*essentia et non gradu*). I shall return to this shortly.

On a personal level, I was struck to note that the Council did not use the expression "common priesthood" again in the rest of its work—where there were many occasions to do so (one need only think of the success of the word *sacrament* applied to the Church). One can see here the sign of a certain dissatisfaction with this language. Hence, when we learn that the adjective *common* was kept only for a simple stylistic reason, we may doubt that it was the best possible one. Of course, it has to be understood in the sense of "common to all"; however, in both French and

English, what is "common" is generally of inferior quality. Not only does that not "sound" very good, but it also runs the risk of leading astray persons who do not happen to know its origin. Without denying its theological correctness, I myself prefer a term closer to the language of Scripture, such as "royal priesthood of the baptized" or again "baptismal priesthood" or even "spiritual priesthood." By saying "baptized," one surely thinks of *all the baptized,* including ministers (and so is perhaps better than "the faithful," which in today's language always more or less implies the idea of a distinction between the faithful and the hierarchy, which is absent from "baptized").

The Two Domains of the Common Priesthood

Before going any further, it will be useful to gather together what the Council attributes to the common priesthood:

First, there is the capacity to participate actively in Christian worship as a "sanctifier." This is the character of baptism, which confers the qualification by which the baptized persons contribute to the Eucharist in their proper place, receive the other sacraments (without baptism, one cannot receive them validly), and even perform certain sacraments (such as marriage). As we see, since there is "receiving and giving," the participation of the baptized is not simply passive (to "receive," by the way, is an active attitude).

Second, there is the life of grace, which is obtained by means of that same worship (the first gift of grace comes to us by baptism), and which constitutes what can be called the priesthood of the holy life (whose material, as we know, is all the activity of the human person). So one can propose the following scheme:

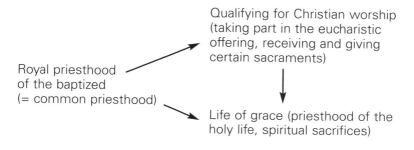

Royal priesthood of the baptized (= common priesthood)

Qualifying for Christian worship (taking part in the eucharistic offering, receiving and giving certain sacraments)

Life of grace (priesthood of the holy life, spiritual sacrifices)

As clear as they may be, the features highlighted in this diagram call for a few complementary remarks. In the idea of the common priesthood, two aspects are normally bound together, but they can be accidentally separated. It is easy to understand. One might have momentarily lost grace without, for all that, having lost the character of baptism, since that is indelible. It is not the normal Christian state of affairs, but it is true that one can be in a state of sin and still remain capable of receiving a sacrament, if not *fruitfully*, at least *validly* (holy orders or marriage, for example). In this situation, one obviously does not receive the grace that the sacrament provides, but the *first effect* of the sacrament remains: again, for example, the marriage between two baptized persons, one of whom is in a state of sin, remains a true marriage. The same applies to the sacrament of holy orders. The sacrament will not obtain its full fruit of grace until the sinner is reconciled with the Church and with God, but the possibility of participating in Christian worship through the character of baptism or of exercising the ministry by the sacrament of holy orders remains, even if one is deprived of this grace.

The regrettable side of realizing this possible separation should not mask the fact that it implies a positive reality: that is, inversely, the life of grace can exist without the sacrament being visibly received. That proves to be true for all the unbaptized just persons of whom the Council speaks (*Lumen Gentium* 16). This was the case of Noah, Daniel, and Job, as well as of the uncircumcised pagan saints (Ezek 14:14, 20; 28:3) who did not belong to the chosen people. In our time, this is still the case—our theological hope makes us desire that it is frequently the case—for all just people who may be outside the visible limits of the Church of Christ, whatever their adherence, or nonadherence, to this or that religion. There is no common priesthood here, since there is no character of baptism; however, one cannot think of refusing such people the priesthood of the holy life. That makes no sense. In fact, it is clear that, if they are just, it would be by the help of grace. This grace is the grace of Christ and the Holy Spirit, for there is no other kind. This grace brings with it all the qualities of Christic grace (Christ does not do things by half). This grace, therefore, is also priestly, royal, and prophetic; it is not, however, *sacramental*, since it has not

136

been obtained by way of the sacraments, and it is quite clear that this is a considerable deficiency. But it can be called *ecclesial*, in the sense that Christ the Head is inseparable from his ecclesial body, and all the just are members of it, whether consciously or not. Thus, by ways that God alone knows, the intercession of the baptized saints also comes into play for them; and neither is the mediation of the Church, the universal sacrament of salvation, made void. All this does not become perfectly intelligible except in the light of a good theology of the Church, but we know enough about it for this to be understandable.

RELATIONS BETWEEN THE ROYAL PRIESTHOOD AND THE MINISTERIAL PRIESTHOOD

According to the text of the Council, "though they differ from one another *in essence and not only in degree*, the common priesthood of the faithful and the ministerial or hierarchical priesthood are nonetheless interrelated: each of them in its own special way is a participation in the one priesthood of Christ." This translation is a bit ambiguous (but so are all of them). Thus, our progress in understanding this text will once again have to be accompanied by a particular attention to the manner of translating it.

Essentia et non gradu tantum

It is hard to translate this differently from the way it has been done, but we must not give *tantum* a value that it does not have. If one says the two priesthoods differ *not only in degree*, one is suggesting that they *also* differ in degree. But there is nothing of that here. The difference between them is not a simple one of more or less, as if they were situated along the same ascending line:

This scheme absolutely does not fit. It is true that, in a certain sense, the ministerial priesthood presupposes the royal priesthood. If the character of baptism is lacking, you cannot receive the sacrament of holy orders. But the same thing is true for confirmation and the other sacraments: Baptism is the basic enablement that allows us to receive the other sacraments, but there is no intention here of talking about a difference of degree with respect to them. Something else is at stake. The same thing holds for the ministerial priesthood. Between it and the royal priesthood, there is an essential difference: The two realities are diverse and not just different. In other words, they are only similar *by analogy.* The Conciliar Commission that prepared the text said this very clearly apropos of an amendment aimed at specifying that the universal priesthood is called a priesthood "in an improper fashion" (*sacerdotium universale esse improprium*). The Council replied that it *is* properly a priesthood, but in an analogous fashion (*pro parte consideratur ut proprium sed analogicum*). The difficulty came up a second time during the discussion on the Decree on the Ministry and Life of Presbyters when a bishop was astonished by the fact that anyone would talk about the *metaphoric* priesthood of the faithful before speaking about that of the priests (n. 2). The commission replied that *Lumen Gentium* had used that adjective by design (*consulto*). Precisely because of the order adopted by the Dogmatic Constitution on the Church (chapter 2 concerning all the faithful is placed before chapter 3 on the ministry), it was necessary to talk about the mystical Body in its entirety before speaking of the hierarchical priesthood, which is in the service of the priestly People of God. Thus, there is only a simple analogy between our two priesthoods. Now, according to the law of analogy, this means we are dealing with two things that are similar in a certain light. Incidentally, the rest of the text explains what these differences consist in.[1]

Similarities and Dissimilarities

The fundamental similarity lies in the fact that both forms of priesthood come from the unique priesthood of Christ. The fundamental dissimilarity is that the royal priesthood is a reality from the order of the life of grace, while the ministerial priesthood is a charism in the service of the life of grace. I have had to repeat this often enough; however, one cannot insist upon it too much because the only correct exegesis of this text depends upon it. *Essentia* does not mean an essential superiority of the ministerial priesthood, but rather the opposite. It is only by a true inversion of values that certain theologians used to be able to think otherwise. We have here the two great features that characterize this analogical similarity, but the comparison can be pursued still further.

In fact, when we ask how the royal priesthood and the ministerial priesthood are similar and how they differ, one has to respond by constantly and almost simultaneously "correcting" the similarity with the difference:

1. They are similar because they both offer sacrifices, but they are different because one offers spiritual sacrifices, whereas the other is, above all, qualified to offer ritual sacrifice, even if the ritual sacrifice—that is, the Eucharist—is also the spiritual sacrifice par excellence. Some writers have thought to distinguish the two into an internal sacrifice and an external sacrifice, but that distinction is hardly more adequate.

2. They are also similar because they are both consecrated for the offering of the Eucharist, but they are different because their consecrations qualify them for different roles: for the members of the royal priesthood, to offer in their own name and thus to concur with the offering of all; for the ministers, to offer in the name of the whole assembly. In fact, the ministry also has the capacity to act in the name of Christ to make the Body of Christ sacramentally present. Furthermore, a member of the royal priesthood only represents him- or herself in the celebration of worship; he or she acts there as one member among others in the body. As a person, the minister also acts in his own name, being himself one of the baptized, but in his quality of minister, he fulfills the

role of Christ the Head with regard to the other members of the body.

One suggestion not followed by the Council even proposed to call the ministerial priesthood "representative," because the minister represents God before the faithful, and he represents the faithful before God. If that language had been accepted, the text would have had to add that this "representative" role is no more than derivative, secondary, instrumental, and entirely dependent on Christ, but I shall have to come back to this in greater detail. For the moment, it must be repeated that you cannot place the ministerial priesthood along a line of ascending derivation, which begins at Christ and ends at the ministerial priesthood, but rather under a bracket that makes both priesthoods derive from Christ the Head, in keeping with the two senses given the word *head* in the texts of St. Paul: vital principle (as the source of grace) and principle of authority (as the source of the ministry):

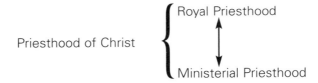

Ad invicem ordinantur

This other formula also creates a problem. If we translate it as "coordinated to one another," we readily see how the ministerial priesthood is related to the royal priesthood: It is at its service. We will rediscover other expressions of this truth in a number of texts that we have yet to read. The problem is that, even if we see clearly that one is related to the other (the ministerial priesthood to the priesthood of grace), we do not see how the latter is related to the former (the priesthood of grace to the ministerial priesthood). This problem is insurmountable so long as one fails to translate the phrase exactly. It has to be understood as "they are *mutually* related" (hence the arrow pointed both ways in the schema above). This is the very same expression with which the Conciliar

Commission had introduced its first text, which it explained thus: In the service of the priestly people, the ministerial priesthood forms it and leads it. It "celebrates" the eucharistic sacrifice, and so forth, while the faithful concur in this offering and exercise their priesthood in the entire domain of their Christian life.

We have already met this distinction, and we will encounter it again; but since we are dealing with questions of translation, let me just note that the word *celebrate* is not exact either. We have in Latin *conficit* (literally, "to accomplish"). This old liturgical word is almost the equivalent of our *consecrate*. This is not just splitting hairs; it makes us understand better the difference between the roles. In reality, all the participants (priest and faithful) "celebrate" or, better, "concelebrate," but each in his or her own way. All "concur" in offering the Eucharist, but only the priest "consecrates." Our text says it well (*Lumen Gentium* 11): "All take part in this liturgical service, not indeed all in the same way, but each in that way which is proper to himself."

To round out what must be mentioned in this realm of mutual relations between the two priesthoods, it has to be further added that it is most often by the action of the priestly ministry that the common priesthood is granted. The ministers of baptism are generally priests or deacons (but not only priests or deacons, as we have always known), and the whole of the sacramental body is destined to make the priesthood of the holy life grow in each baptized person.

But after all that I have said, it clearly does not follow that there is a subordinate relation of the royal priesthood to the ministerial priesthood. It is purely—and grandly!—a matter of the visible manifestation of the baptized person's being inserted into the body of the Church, which quite obviously precedes each of her children coming to the life of Christ. In the name of the Church, the priest inserts himself into the order of the efficient causality of salvation whose instrument and servant he is. The relation of definitive dependence always sends us back to Christ, the source of all grace and all ministry, who can give even the unbaptized just person this participation in his grace without the mediation of the ministerial priesthood. In this latter case, let us remember: We are speaking only of the priesthood of the holy life, which the common priesthood also carries out, but adding to it the power to participate in Christian worship that derives from the character of baptism.

IN PERSONA CHRISTI—IN PERSONA ECCLESIAE

A final point remains to be examined on the subject of ministerial priesthood in the commented-on second paragraph from *Lumen Gentium* 10: "The ministerial priest, by the sacred power he enjoys, teaches and rules the priestly people; acting in the person of Christ [*in persona Christi*], he makes present the eucharistic sacrifice and offers it to God in the name of all the people." This expression is not easy to translate into either French or English. Recalling its various uses will allow us better to grasp its meaning; and we will complete this operation by examining a formula with a similar meaning: "*in persona ecclesiae.*"

Uses of the Formula *"in persona [in nomine] Christi"*

These words are chosen again in a slightly different and more complete form in the Dogmatic Constitution on the Church (*Lumen Gentium*). In speaking of the sacrament of the episcopacy, the Council declares:

> By means of the imposition of hands and the words of consecration, the grace of the Holy Spirit is so conferred, and the *sacred character* [n. 11 speaks of *sacred power*, but it is aimed at the same thing] so impressed, that bishops in an eminent and visible way *sustain the roles* of Christ Himself as Teacher, Shepherd, and High Priest, and that they act in His Person [*in ejus Persona = in persona Christi*]. (21, italics added)

The formula that completes "*in persona Christi*" here is thus "*Christi partes sustinere*" (literally: "play the parts of Christ"). The perspective is broader here than the preceding one (*Lumen Gentium* 10): not only in celebrating the Eucharist, but also in teaching and governing, the bishop acts in the name of Christ.

The same expression is used yet another time in *Lumen Gentium* 28 on the subject of priests: "They exercise their sacred function especially in the Eucharistic worship or the celebration of the Mass by which acting in the person of Christ and proclaiming His Mystery they unite the prayers of the faithful with the sacrifice of their Head and renew and apply…the only sacrifice of the New Testament." The perspective is once again eucharistic, but there is an *above all* (*maxime*: the Constitution emphasizes "specially," *speciatim*), which indicates that ministry of the presbyters is not limited to that.

The formula is picked up again elsewhere (*Presbyterorum Ordinis* 2): "By the anointing of the Holy Spirit, priests are signed with a special character and conformed to Christ the priest in such a way that they can act in the person of the Christ the Head [*ita ut in persona Christi Capitis agere valeant*]." The perspective here is again a broader one, because this passage deals with the totality of the three messianic functions.

We rediscover *in persona Christi* in a fifth context, which is not directly that of the consecration, but more broadly that of the eucharistic celebration. In the Constitution on the Liturgy 33, the priest (*sacerdos*) presides over the assembly *in persona Christi*, and in this capacity he addresses prayers to God the Father in the name of all the people (*nomine totius plebis*). This last expression (*in nomine plebis*) has an equivalent that we will encounter again: *in nomine ecclesiae*, which is also pregnant with meaning and which has the advantage of drawing our attention to another formula that is likewise rather frequently used: The faithful have the duty of welcoming the teaching of the bishops, because it is given "in the name of Christ" (*in nomine Christi, Lumen Gentium* 25). Further, in *Lumen Gentium* 27, the power of government is also exercised by the bishops *in nomine Christi*, and in *Presbyterorum Ordinis* 2, the priestly function is exercised *in nomine Christi*.

The Theological Antecedents of This Formula

These two expressions are practically equivalent. They mean that in the acts performed by the priest *in persona* or *in nomine Christi*, faith sees the acts of Christ. St. Augustine already said this

143

in a celebrated and highly explicit formula: "Peter baptizes, it is Christ who baptizes.…Judas baptizes, it is Christ who baptizes" (*Homilies on St. John* 6.7). St. Thomas picks up this statement almost verbatim: "It is clear that it is Christ himself who accomplishes the sacraments: it is he who baptizes, it is he who forgives sins," and so on (*Summa Contra Gentiles* 4.76). In Thomas as in Augustine, this truth applies to all the sacraments, but Thomas brings it into play especially apropos of the Eucharist (*Summa Theologica* IIIa q. 78 and q. 82). One passage sums up the essentials by placing all of the priesthood itself under the sign of this expression:

> Christ is the source of all priesthood: the priesthood of the ancient law was a foreshadowing of him; the priesthood of the new law acts in his person [*in persona ipsius*], as the Second Epistle to the Corinthians says [2:10]: "What I have forgiven, if I have forgiven anything, has been for your sake in the person of Christ [*in persona Christi*]." (*Summa Theologica* IIIa q. 22, a. 4)

After Augustine and Thomas, Pope Pius XII borrowed these expressions for his own purpose, while also insisting on the identity and permanence of the sovereign Priest of whom today's ministry is only the representative:

> The priest is the same Jesus Christ, whose sacred Person his minister represents. Now the minister, by reason of the sacerdotal character which he has received, is made like to the High Priest and possesses the power of performing actions in virtue of Christ's very person. Wherefore in his priestly activity he in a certain manner "lends his tongue, and gives his hand" to Christ [as St. John Chrysostom said]. (*Mediator Dei* 69)

If this text primarily aims at the celebration of the Eucharist, the expression was also used by Pius XII for the pastoral assignment in general: "Each [bishop] as a true Shepherd feeds the flock entrusted to him and rules it in the name of Christ" (*Mystici Corporis* 42).

The Implications of This Formula

By speaking in this way, therefore, Vatican II is only picking up a constant teaching of the Church. From the theological point of view, we can see that all these texts regularly express two ideas, whether explicitly or implicitly. First, the minister is in some fashion likened to Christ by the character received with the sacrament of holy orders. This is the teaching of Thomas, picked up again by Pius XII and Vatican II (*Lumen Gentium* 10 and *Presbyterorum Ordinis* 2). Second, this character confers a special ability (a sacred power) to act in the order of Christian worship in the name of Christ and his ecclesial body, and this character makes the priest capable of being used by Christ as his instrument at the moment of the eucharistic consecration. Incidentally, it is striking that at this moment the person of the priest is effaced, so to speak, and he lends his voice to Christ, who repeats through him: "This is my body." St. Thomas sums up: "These words, pronounced *in persona Christi* and on his orders, obtain their effect thanks to an instrumental force [*virtus instrumentalis*], which comes from Christ" (*Summa Theologica* IIIa q. 78, a. 4). Christ is thus the principal agent, and the minister is only the instrumental agent. He certainly does something, as all instruments do: He pronounces the words and breaks the bread. But the terminal effect transcends him and comes only from the principal agent. In the strong sense, the sacramental action is an act of Christ.

In the eyes of the Catholic faith, this is incontestable; but in good theology, the explanation still is not sufficient. It has to be added that these two truths recur on the level of all the baptized. On the one hand, baptism conforms believers to Christ and gives them a participation in his priesthood (*Lumen Gentium* 10); on the other, baptism also enables believers to act in the order of Christian worship (*Lumen Gentium* 11), not only to receive the sacraments, but also to concur with the offering of the Eucharist and to give some sacraments: baptism and marriage.

Who could say that the baptized person who confers baptism is *not* acting *in persona Christi*? That would go against the principle of Augustine that lies at the foundation of this argu-

145

ment: "It is Judas who baptizes, it is Christ who baptizes." It even has to be added that non-Christians could themselves be ministers of Christ if at some point they were to baptize someone. The resemblance between these two formulas cannot be missed: "In the name of the Father and of the Son and of the Holy Spirit" is even more complete than "in the name of Christ." So we can conclude that the formula *in persona Christi* unquestionably expresses the profound truth of things, but it has been used too restrictedly. The consecration of the Eucharist lent itself admirably to it, but in reality it applies to all the ministers of all the sacraments. In the case of a member of the "simple faithful" or an unbeliever who baptizes, it is just as much Christ who gives the terminal effect of baptism (character and grace) that lies beyond the reach of any created agent. So the specificity of the ministerial priesthood cannot be grasped only on this level.

The Specificity of the Ministerial Priesthood

The specificity of the role of the ministerial priesthood can be described by four major characteristics:

1. The character of holy orders makes its recipient the only minister of certain sacraments. It is the bishop (or the priest in dependence on the bishop) who consecrates (*conficit*) the Eucharist, and it is he who transmits the ministerial function by the sacrament of holy orders. He is the habitual minister of confirmation and of the sacrament of reconciliation. (Although the situation may be less clear for confirmation, there can be no disputing the fact that the celebration of the Eucharist, the transmission of the ministry, and the celebration of the sacrament of reconciliation have, from the very start, definitely derived from the ministers.)
2. The character of holy orders enables the ministers to represent Christ in a permanent fashion among the members of the ecclesial body and to represent the whole of the body in its prayer when it faces the Father. These are the two aspects of the mediation of Christ

146

that we have often encountered in the course of our research. Christ is the living instrument of grace that the Father grants us. The ministers participate in this "descending" mediation through time and space (it is one of the clearest things that our study has allowed us to verify). But Christ is also the one who recapitulates in himself the whole of his body and represents it in an attitude of thanksgiving and intercession vis-à-vis God. This second ("ascending") aspect is equally assumed by the minister. The liturgy recalls this in each celebration, in each public prayer, when the prayer is formulated by a single person in the name of the assembly, and all answer "Amen" to signify the agreement and profound harmony of the "entire" Christ, Head and members.

3. So we must once again move past the uniquely priestly aspect if we wish to rediscover the ministerial function in the fullness of its meaning. The texts from Vatican II tell us plainly: The formula *in persona* or *in nomine Christi* is used not only to speak of the Eucharist, but to designate the entire pastoral function: in virtue of this sacred power, "the ministerial priest *teaches and rules* the priestly people...[and] makes present [*consecrates (conficit)*] the eucharistic sacrifice" (*Lumen Gentium* 10). These are our three functions: the last two are easily recognizable, but so is the first: here, the word *teaches* designates the prophetic mission. (See the parallel text of *Lumen Gentium* 9: "Step by step [God] has taught and prepared [*instruxit*] this people, making Himself known in its history"; see also *Presbyterorum Ordinis* 2 and 4.)

4. So, we must not stop any longer at the sole formula *in persona Christi*. If we understand it in the exclusive sense of the relationship with Christ as Head, it would be too narrow. It has to be completed by another expression that we often find in its immediate vicinity: *in persona [in nomine] ecclesiae (Lumen*

Gentium 10: the priest offers the sacrifice to God "in the name of all the people *[in nomine totius populi]*").

In persona [in nomine] ecclesiae

There are a multitude of texts to cite here. To limit ourselves to the ones from Vatican II, let us recall just the Decree on the Ministry and Life of Presbyters (notably 2 and 5), and the Constitution on the Sacred Liturgy (33 and 83–85). This is simply a matter of picking up and officially consecrating an element in Tradition and particularly in St. Thomas (*Summa Theologica* IIIa q. 82, a. 6, a. 7, sol. 3; IIIa q. 64, a. 9, sol. 1).[2] Without recalling these texts as a whole, it is enough for us to know that all of them, those that speak either about *in persona Christi* or about *in persona ecclesiae*, contain three principal ideas that are constantly present, but perhaps not always evident at first glance. So they have to be put in relief in order for us to grasp the scope of these formulas.

The first is that the minister who acts *in persona* is not acting in his own name. He does not act by himself or in the name of his own authority. He is just the representative and, in reality, it is the One he represents who acts through him, with the qualities, the rights, and the efficaciousness that are all his own. When the minister acts *in persona Christi*, it is truly Christ who acts. In more technical terms, we rediscover here the biblical doctrine of the *schaliach* and his full powers. In addition, when the minister acts *in persona ecclesiae*, he is not acting in his own name either. It is not his sacraments that he is celebrating or his prayer that he is formulating, but that of the Church. He acts as the head of the assembly, as a representative of the body. He gives it his voice and his action, but in reality it is the entire body that is acting through him. To make a point in passing, we can see the extent to which the intrusion of the subjectivity of the minister here has something incongruous and improper about it. As the instrument of a reality that transcends him, he is not to impose his own person but to efface himself in the action he accomplishes or before the message that he announces. His personality or his saintliness are not irrelevant, but he must never forget that he is only a servant.

The second idea should help in our better understanding

the first one. The two formulas—*in persona Christ* and *in persona ecclesiae*—are not juxtaposed on the same level. There is between them an organic unity, and thus action *in persona ecclesiae* has to be understood as an integral part of the action *in persona Christi*. This is easily explained if we consider what St. Augustine calls "the total Christ," Head and Body. In *in persona Christi* action, strictly speaking, the minister represents Christ as Head and Lord of the Body. In *in persona ecclesiae* action, he represents the Church as the Body of Christ. But he does not do this by a democratic sort of delegation (in the sense that the members of Parliament represent the people who elected them), but rather because he has received a sacrament that enables him to fill this role of Christ as Head. It is because he represents the Head that he also represents the Body, from which it is inseparable.

Properly understood, the third truth present in all these texts gathers together the first two. The Church alone is the integral subject of the liturgical celebration. This must be understood of the Church in its entirety, after the manner of Augustine. The total Christ is not just the hierarchy and not just the faithful. This total Church only becomes visible on the local level. That is why, as the Constitution on the Sacred Liturgy says in a passage recalled at the beginning of this book, the regularly constituted eucharistic assembly, having at its head the minister who represents Christ as Head, and as such recapitulating the members of the Body by whom he is surrounded, is a privileged manifestation of the Church (41). In this integral entity, all do not have the same role, but all concelebrate equally, and all really exercise their priesthood: the ministers on their level of authority, and the faithful on their level of members, who are component parts of what the head does in the name of the Body.[3]

The Presence of Christ in the Priestly People

By way of a provisional conclusion, I would like to meditate on a page from the Constitution on the Sacred Liturgy. It does not have the expression *in persona Christi* or *in persona ecclesiae*, but it does sum up many of the things that I have said, especially on the priestly activity exercised by the entire Mystical Body. When it comes to speak of the continuation by the Church of the work of salvation begun by Christ, the Council writes as follows:

> To accomplish so great a work, Christ is always present in His Church, especially in her liturgical celebrations. He is present in the sacrifice of the Mass, not only in the person of His minister, "the same now offering, through the ministry of priests, who formerly offered himself on the cross," but especially under the Eucharistic species. By His power He is present in the sacraments, so that when a man baptizes it is really Christ Himself who baptizes. He is present in His word, since it is He Himself who speaks when the holy scriptures are read in the Church. He is present, lastly, when the Church prays and sings, for He promised: "Where two or three are gathered together in my name, there am I in the midst of them" (Matt 18:20).
>
> Christ indeed always associates the Church with Himself in this great work wherein God is perfectly glorified and men are sanctified. The Church is His beloved Bride who calls to her Lord, and through Him offers worship to the Eternal Father.
>
> Rightly, then, the liturgy is considered as an exercise of the priestly office of Jesus Christ. In the liturgy the sanctification of man is signified by signs perceptible to the senses, and is effected in a way which corresponds with each of these signs; in the liturgy the whole public worship is performed by the Mystical Body of Jesus Christ, that is, by the Head and His members.
>
> From this it follows that every liturgical celebration, because it is an action of Christ the priest and of His Body which is the Church, is a sacred action surpassing all others; no other action of the Church can equal its efficacy by the same title and to the same degree. (*Sacrosanctum Concilium* 7)

Such a rich text calls for a commentary that would be out of place here, but we can note in it at least two things. The first is the great diversity of the modes of Christ's presence: first, in the person of the minister who consecrates the Eucharist; second, under the eucharistic species themselves; third, in the person of those who baptize; fourth, in his Word when it is proclaimed; fifth, when the Church prays and chants the psalms. This presence is not realized in the same way in each of these cases. As with the priesthood, we are dealing with an analogical concept. This gives a bit of a jolt to simplistic ideas (as if there were no other presence of Christ in his Church except the "real" presence in the Eucharist); but that is no reason for wasting the great richness of what is taught here.

Without refusing this wealth—and here is my second remark—the theologian must nevertheless make necessary distinctions especially concerning the ministers. Christ is not present to the same degree in sacramental and nonsacramental actions. In sacramental actions in the strict sense (consecrating, baptizing, forgiving sins), the minister is an instrumental cause. Christ acts through him, and it is the virtue of the Holy Spirit that produces the effect of the sacrament: the principal cause is Christ, who alone is the adequate agent of the gift of grace. In nonsacramental actions (proclamation of the Word, preaching, or government), the minister is no longer an instrument in the strict sense. He is indeed a principal although secondary cause, and his discourse is a human word entirely explainable, on a certain level, by the qualities of the man who pronounces it; thus, his theological training, his oratorical talent, and the more-or-less serious preparation of his sermon have a real importance in the transmission of the message. This message only becomes the Word of God to the extent that it is received by faith. But it is not the Word of God simply because of the person who is pronouncing it (unless he uses the very words of Scripture). Only the prophets could call their message "the Word of God." That obviously does not apply to the homilies of our pastors, even when delivered by the pope himself. This distinction has some practical implications, but we cannot dwell on them.

If readers now wish to gather together the results of our investigation, they will find an attempt to visualize these concepts on page 152.

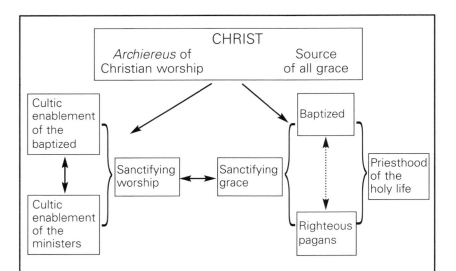

This diagram synthesizes only what concerns the priestly aspect. The figure would have been much more complex, if it had been necessary to integrate the two other messianic privileges into it.

1. At the source of everything, we have Christ, who is indissolubly the high priest who institutes the new worship in the Spirit and who is the source of all grace.
2. At the center, the domain of worship and the domain of grace are presented on the left and right side, because they are situated on two different levels (as a means and an end). But the arrow going both ways joining them together symbolizes their normal inseparability.
3. On the left, we find what strictly concerns worship. The *royal* or *common priesthood*, and the priestly ministry or ministerial priesthood, are not used here, because they normally make up grace in their concrete definition (the diagram has its limits). The bidirectional arrow recalls their mutual relations (*ad invicem ordinantur*).
4. On the right, we find what strictly concerns grace (priestly, because Christic, grace). All the faithful live from it, but so do the just pagans; this is the priesthood of the holy life and of spiritual sacrifices. The arrow symbolizes the intercession of the baptized saints, but its path is dotted because we do not know anything about the modalities according to which its influence is exercised.

THE EVOLUTION OF THE THEOLOGY OF MINISTRY (A BRIEF HISTORICAL SUMMARY)

The Bishop at the Head of the Church and of the Presbyterium

From the beginning or toward the middle of the second century, we have seen that the ecclesial ministry was centered around the bishop and supported by the deacons. Presiding over the Eucharist was normally reserved to him. The only legitimate Eucharist was one that was celebrated by him. He did not yet have the title of *hiereus*, but he did exercise its functions, as we learned from Ignatius of Antioch.

We are less familiar with the situation in the West at this same epoch, but thanks to Justin we are not completely in the dark; in any case, from the beginning of the third century, Hippolytus of Rome informs us of something exactly like what was happening in Antioch a century earlier. The bishop of Rome was likewise surrounded by his presbytery and seconded by deacons. His principal functions were to celebrate the Eucharist, baptize (as already noted in Tertullian), reconcile penitents, and order the ministries. The title of *hiereus* was given to him without hesitation.

The same is true of Cyprian and Origen, in whose writings the title of priest (*hiereus* or *sacerdos*) was already extended to the presbyters. But Cyprian and Origen also see the presbytery and the bishop as constituting an undivided, though differentiated, reality. In the East as in the West, at this period the situation could be summed up in two points: First, the bishop "recapitulates" the Church, to borrow Cyprian's language. "The Church is the people united with its bishop….[Because] the bishop is in the Church and the Church in the bishop, if someone is not with the bishop, he is not with the Church" (*Letters* 66.8.3). This is a true leitmotif in both Ignatius and Cyprian, and it can only be understood properly along the dogmatic lines already worked out. The bishop is the representative of Christ as Head, and the body is unthinkable without its head. Second, the episcopal ministry itself has a collegial character; that is, it is possessed *in common* by all those who participate in it. Once again Cyprian is very clear here: "The episcopate is one, each part of which is held by each one for the whole (*episcopates unus est, cuius a singulus in solidum pars tenetur*)" (*On the Unity of the Church* 5A:3).

Difficult to translate, the expression *in solidum* ("in an undivided state") has given rise to countless learned exegeses. Its clearest sense is that the whole episcopate belongs to all and to each of the bishops: "Beyond the affirmation of the uniqueness of the position and of solidarity on the universal level, *in solidum* suggests a paradoxical identity between the whole and the part."[4] Putting it more simply, in the words of Victor Hugo speaking of a mother's love: "Each has its part of it, and all have the whole of it." This is perhaps the most beautiful expression of episcopal collegiality, and Cyprian explains the reason for it very well: "Even though we are many pastors, the flock that we feed is one" (*Letters* 68.4.2). Only the bishops are many; the episcopate itself is only one, because the flock is only one.

Hippolytus was already making this point apropos of the consecration of a new bishop by emphasizing that the bishops are the only ones to lay their hands on him (*The Apostolic Tradition* 2). The Council of Nicaea (canon 4) prescribes that all the bishops of a province must be consulted and agree on the choice of a new bishop. If all of them cannot participate in the consecration, all must at least be there for the laying on of hands and they must be provided with the written agreement of the absent bishops.

The Collegial Character of the Presbyterate

The same thing goes for the presbytery. It is by its very origins a collegial institution. The presbyters were members of a council (of elders), and they are always mentioned in the plural. The singular *presbyterium* precisely designates this collective character. In an important passage (and I shall be getting back to this), Hippolytus clearly notes how the deacon is different from the presbyter: "The deacon is not ordained to the priesthood.... He is not part of the council of the clergy....This why only the bishops make a deacon. Upon the elder, the other elders place their hands because of a common spirit and a regular duty" (*The Apostolic Tradition* 8).

The manifest sacramental sign of the collegial unity of the ministry was the eucharistic concelebration. What still strikes certain people as a dangerous innovation was for a long time the only way—and has become so again, thanks to Vatican II—of celebrating the Eucharist. Communities would do the impossible to maintain that single celebration in a single church for each town, at the risk of compromising the welfare of the faithful. Thus, Milan and Carthage at the end of the fourth century had only one Eucharist on Sunday for the entire city. The basilica of Milan could hold only 5,000 people, whereas the city had 35,000 Christians. At Carthage, with 150,000 Christians, the biggest church held only 10,000 persons. That simple celebration was highly symbolic: a single flock under a single pastor, gathered around a single altar.

Obviously, this could not go on. As the countryside was gradually evangelized, another solution was sought. Thus, the number of bishops was increased to satisfy the needs of smaller population centers. Persons adequate for such a high number of bishoprics could not always be found, so the custom developed of sending priests to celebrate the liturgy in distant places. In the beginning, they would return to the bishops after each mission. Later they ended up staying in the remote villages, which is how we got the number of curates (associate pastors) we have today. Nevertheless, a certain number of liturgical practices were destined to emphasize this collegial unity. In Rome, there was the practice of *fermentum*: This portion of bread mixed with wine (as is still done today) came from the bishop's celebration and symbolized unity with the first pastor of the diocese. In Gaul, several sixth-century councils insistently remembered the order that obliged priests in charge of outlying churches to return to the city for major feasts in order to celebrate there with their bishop. But at that moment—exactly in the same period—another history was beginning, and this dispersion would give rise to individualism among the clergy. The collegial unity of the ministry very soon dropped out of sight, and the East and the West began to diverge in their conception of the bishop's role.

155

Evolution of the Doctrine in the East

At the cost of an outrageously oversimplified summary, I shall only say a word or two here about the evolution that took place in the Eastern Church. Under the influence of various great bishops, the theology and practice of the Church accentuated the differences between presbyters and bishops. This history, beginning with St. Epiphanius (315–403) and continued by St. John Chrysostom (347–407) and Theodore of Mopsuestia (350–428), culminated in Pseudo-Dionysius (around 500). The first three men saw in Timothy, St. Paul's disciple, the very type of the bishop, incontestably superior to the presbyters-overseers whom he put in place. They stressed the fact that the titles, which were originally interchangeable, had only a relative importance. What counted was that certain functions, above all the laying on of hands, were reserved to certain persons like Timothy, and that this functional difference was the source of the bishop's superiority. Theodore went further and saw the same difference between bishop and presbyter as that between apostles and presbyters-overseers. An excellent exegete, Theodore was certainly the one who came closest to the truth.

Pseudo-Dionysius also bases the distinction between bishop and presbyter on the apostolic writings, but he moves beyond that and finds the roots of this same distinction in the very nature of the ministerial functions. He considers the bishop the source, the principle, and the fullness of the entire ministry, in which all the others participate and from which they receive their powers. Thus, in his very hierarchical view (a simple application of Pseudo-Dionysius's general theory of the universe, which sees everything organized into successive hierarchies), the key to the distinction between bishop and presbyter is the relationship of plenary possession of the sacrament of holy orders to a limited and dependent participation. This relationship is used to stress that the presbyter is only such by the laying on of hands by the bishop, that he cannot anoint except with oil consecrated by the bishop, and that he cannot even celebrate the Eucharist except with vessels consecrated by the bishops (*Ecclesiastical Hierarchy* 5.5). This notion of the "fullness" of the ministry is fairly close to that of "sovereign priesthood" already encountered in Hippolytus. Contrary to the latter, however, Pseudo-Dionysius and the authors just mentioned seem to have completely lost sight of the collegial character of the ministry.

Evolution of the Doctrine in the West

If we trace this trajectory, we must deplore the fact that the West went through the same process of forgetting about the collegial unity of the ministry. Nevertheless, with regard to the difference between presbyter and bishop, the evolution took place in a different, not to say contrary, manner. Here three authors are at the launching point of an error that would make itself felt all the way up to the eve of Vatican II.

The first author, long identified as St. Ambrose, was actually an anonymous writer now called Ambrosiaster, who left us a collection of biblical commentaries composed under Pope Damasus (366–84). The second was St. Jerome (342–420), the great exegete best known for translating the Bible into Latin from the Hebrew and Greek. But he was also the author of numerous biblical commentaries; on the specific point with which we are concerned, he seems to have been familiar with Ambrosiaster. The third was anonymous too, the author of a little book entitled *The Seven Orders of the Church (De septem ordinibus ecclesiae)*, which was composed at the beginning of the fifth century and widely disseminated because it was handed down to posterity under the name of St. Jerome.

Without going into the details that eventually cause their personal positions to diverge from one another, these three authors agree that, where priesthood is concerned, there is no essential difference between the presbyter and the bishop. The bishop is actually superior to the presbyters from the standpoint of authority (jurisdiction), and they all must submit to him. But since this is no more than a purely human arrangement required by the concern to avoid schisms, the episcopate is not a sacrament. Still, by a happy inconsistency, our three authors recognize that only the bishop has the power to confer the Holy Spirit by the laying on of hands. It remains to be seen why.

Bolstered by the authority of Ambrose and Jerome, this point of view prevailed throughout the entire Western tradition. Thus, when Peter Lombard, in the twelfth century, synthesized the theology of his epoch, he too concluded that the episcopate was not a sacrament (IV *Sentences*, distinction 24, chapter xiv–xvii). Since the *Sentences* very quickly became the required textbook for all theologians, teachers as well as students (and remained so for roughly three centuries), all those who came after him in teaching the subject borrowed Lombard's view for their own purposes.

The same thing happened with Thomas Aquinas in his youth, which is why we cannot wholly follow him on this point. If one is tempted to refer to the section in the *Summa Theologica* entitled *Holy Orders*,[5] it is important to know that, although this work comes at the end of the *Summa*, it quite simply picks up Thomas's commentary on Lombard's *Sentences* and hence dates from the beginning of his career (between 1252 and 1256). As everyone knows, Thomas died without finishing the *Summa*. His disciples thought they were doing the right thing by completing it with the help of his earliest writings (what is called the *Supplement*, questions 34–40). In the present case, it was a mistake because Thomas's thought had evolved on this point. While he was commenting on the Epistles of St. Paul, he discovered and used the works of Pseudo-Dionysius and, thanks to the former, he immediately understood that Pseudo-Dionysius's teaching on the subject represented the Church's oldest tradition. Thus, in a number of Thomas's works written after 1260, we note that he recognized the episcopate as a sacrament distinct from the presbyterate, and so with a definite episcopal grace. Nevertheless, these are only fragments on the way to revision and not the new synthesis we would like to have had from him.

The Council of Trent

We cannot dwell on the teaching of the Council of Trent as much as we should, but in truth its importance today is more historical than doctrinal. In fact, the Second Vatican Council picked up the essentials of Trent's teaching, but it placed them in a vaster context, which was itself made possible by the renewal of exegetical, patristic, and liturgical studies (as I shall say in a moment). The fact remains, however, that the Council of Trent was practically the only Council before Vatican II that looked into this question, and so it cannot be ignored. But before proceeding, we have to remember that its teaching was very narrowly conditioned by its contemporary context, both historical and theological: first, the situation just described, in which people had lost sight of the true difference between the episcopate and the presbyterate, as well as of the collegial character of the ministry; and second, the situation created by the Reformers (Luther, Bucer, Melanchthon, and Calvin), according to whom the whole priesthood was reduced to preaching the Gospel. For them, the Mass had no sacrificial character, meaning that there was no need of ordained priests to celebrate it.

These two facts sum up very imperfectly the complexity of the situation at that time, but they have the merit of helping us understand why the Council of Trent insisted on some points and not on others. The complete text can be found in the well-known compendium of Denziger, *Enchiridion Symbolorum et Definitionum* 1763–78; but for us, if we state positively and in singular propositions what the Council formulated negatively (as condemnations) and in much more detailed language, Trent's teaching can be summed up under the following eight points:

1. The priesthood cannot simply be reduced to preaching the Word of God.
2. It is empirically defined in connection with sacrifice, because sacrifice and priesthood are tightly interconnected by a divine ordering under both the New law and the Old.
3. Priesthood implies a permanent power (its character): a man who is ordained a priest cannot "turn back" into a layman.
4. This power is that of consecrating and offering the Eucharist, and of forgiving and retaining sins.
5. This power is transferred through a sacrament instituted by the Lord and not by a simply human rite.

6. The hierarchy was instituted by a divine command and is essential to the Church. It is composed of bishops, priests, and ministers. (The Council expressed itself with deliberate prudence here, so as not to prejudge the number and quality of these ministers.)
7. The bishops are superior to the priests through their power of transmitting the sacraments of holy orders and confirmation (where necessary by delegation), as well as through the authority received from the apostles.
8. The ordination of bishops and other ministers does not depend on the consent of the people or the civil authorities, but on the sacrament that they receive.

Vatican II did not deny any of these points, but if you compare its teaching with that of Trent, you can see in a striking fashion how much it broadened Trent's perspective. Nevertheless, it must be emphasized that Trent does not deny the things that it does not say—for example, the bond with the community, the prophetic function, the whole of the pastoral assignment, the collegial character of the episcopate. On the contrary, it is possible to rediscover a number of these preoccupations (except for collegiality) in the Acts of the Council of Trent. Still, it is a fact that the following generations, which did not have access to the whole of these Acts (they were not published until long afterward), inherited from the texts that were promulgated a singularly atrophied vision of the ministry.

How Did We Arrive at Vatican II?

The answer to this question might take up far too much room, but I am simply thinking about the way in which the teaching of Vatican II on the ministry was made possible. As far as one can judge from the distance of a half-century, things progressed by four converging paths:

First, there was a renewal of biblical studies that opened the way to important exegetical research. These studies have been utilized broadly enough in this book for the reader to understand all that they have brought us: proof of the fact that a true priestly vocabulary is missing from the New Testament. This has drawn attention to the breadth of the pastoral charge, which in turn has been defined by the triple messianic function; above all, both the recognition of the priestly quality of all the baptized and the distinction between the priesthood of the holy life and priestly ministry have managed to be made in a dispassionate atmosphere even though it had become dangerously distorted since the Reformation.

Second, patristic studies have also made their contribution, the most notable of which is undoubtedly the discovery of *The Apostolic Tradition* of Hippolytus of Rome, a text that was not recovered and identified until the beginning of the twentieth century. Hippolytus's work, along with that of St. Ignatius of Antioch and the slightly later ones, such as those of Cyprian of Carthage and of Origen, has allowed us to get an idea of the Church's hierarchical structure at the moment of its flowering, which was still fairly close to the time of its origins. One can say without fear of going astray that this epoch (as I have shown on various occasions) was truly a golden age for the theology of ministry.

Third, the liturgists who enjoyed a remarkable efflorescence in the fifty years before Vatican II have likewise done their part in awakening this awareness. The attentive study of the ordination prayers, the comparison of present-day prayers with the ancient ones, the editing and publishing of the text of ordination liturgies from the later period (the High Middle Ages), and so forth—all this has made it possible to realize at what point Catholics lost sight of certain essential features of the theology of ministries (notably the sacrament of the episcopate and collegiality, which are bound up in the sacrament of holy orders itself).

Finally, the situation was already so advanced under Pope Pius XII (1939–58) that he was able to promulgate the encyclical *Mediator Dei* (1947), in which he spoke at length about the priesthood of the faithful. The same year (November 30, 1947), he published the apostolic constitution *Sacramentum Ordinis,* in which he corrected certain erroneous positions and specified that the matter of the sacrament of holy orders was definitely the laying on of hands and not the various gestures that followed (vesting with the stole and chasuble, anointing with oil, handing over the paten and chalice), as the theology of the Middle Ages had imagined, for lack of sufficient information from the past. Without going as far as affirming that the episcopate is a sacrament, Pius XII clearly distinguished between the "second-rank" responsibility of the presbyters and the bishops' full powers of the priesthood.

These are only the broad outlines of an exciting story that culminated on the eve of the Council; however, they are enough to show us that the "novelty" of the Council, which has been accused of doing so much harm, was in reality no more than a return to the sources. If there was any "novelty," then it was with respect to a situation of entirely relative "antiquity" that was based on many dubious elements.

LUMEN GENTIUM'S IMPACT ON THE MINISTRY

The teaching of Vatican II on the ministry is found in two main places: first, in *Lumen Gentium*, or the Dogmatic Constitution on the Church, at 3.18–29, which lays out the essentials concerning the ministry in all its fullness, along with—as is only right —a particular stress on the episcopacy, but one that equally situates the presbyterate and the diaconate in their relation to this first realization; second, in the decree *Presbyterorum Ordinis*, which spells out and develops the way these first considerations apply in the case of the presbyteral ministry.

It is obvious that *Lumen Gentium* is the key document here, for two reasons. It is a dogmatic constitution, whereas the decree is only a particular application of it, and must be read in the light of it. Second, because the teaching on the ministry is located, as it should be, within the overall doctrine of the Church. The decree did not have to repeat this, but it is clear that it presupposes this ecclesiological doctrine. Still, the decree amplifies and completes the constitution with a detailed exposition not only of the presbyteral ministry, but also of the life of the presbyters. Yes, it stresses the permanent underlying realities, but it also brings in new contributions that are far from negligible.

The Episcopal Ministry

A detailed commentary on chapter 3 of *Lumen Gentium* might take up several large books, but my intentions are more modest. I shall simply try to emphasize its major structures and overall purpose. This is announced very early on when the Council declares that it wishes to address the hierarchical ministry that frames the Church in a double perspective, christological and ecclesiological: "For the nurturing and constant growth of the People of God, Christ the Lord instituted in His Church a variety of ministries, which work for the good of the whole body" (18). The christological reference is clear: the establishing by Christ of these various ministries. The ecclesiological reference is no less clear: the goal for which they have been instituted is to feed the People of God. There is no difficulty in recognizing the double reference to Christ as Head and to his ecclesial body announced at the very beginning of this work and already encountered several times since then. The major outlines of the exposition are plainly stressed. We next hear about the institution of the ministry in the person of the apostles and its perpetuation in the ministers they appointed (19–20). After recalling what I have said above concerning these two subjects, the reader will be able to appropriate this teaching more easily and to look at it with fresh eyes.

The teaching of the Council continues with an exposition of holy orders in its plenary form, the episcopate (21). My brief introduction ought to help the reader understand the spectacular nature of the return to the sources that Vatican II carries out here. This can be seen in at least the following points: The laying on of hands is what transmits the gift of the Spirit. A long time ago, theologians had forgotten that, or, rather, they did not know it to begin with. Also, the consecration of the bishop does not confer the responsibility just to sanctify, but also to teach and to govern. This, then, is the triple modality of the messianic mission of Christ and the Church. Finally, the bishops play the role of Christ himself—master, shepherd, and pontiff—and act in his name as his representatives. As I said, these two formulas of "playing the part of Christ" and "acting in his name" (*ipsius partes sustineant* and *in eius persona agant*) are almost pleonastic. They translate into Latin the fullness of the institution of the *schaliach.* It is quite remarkable that they are used for the three messianic functions and not just for the priestly function.

The next section of *Lumen Gentium* concerns the collegiality of the episcopate. Ever since St. Cyprian we have known what this means. The responsibility of feeding the single flock can only be a single one and possessed in an undivided state, despite the many holders of the office. Vatican II's reference to it is accompanied by specific facts from the history of the Church, notably the development of papal primacy. Collegiality is thus envisaged by the reference to the head of the college, the pope, who himself is a part of it and without whom the college could not exist (22), then in its consequences for the relations of the members of the college among themselves (23). This emphasis on the collegial character of the ministry is also a great "novelty" that came about by going back to the sources, since it had completely faded out of sight in our Latin tradition. It cannot be said that, in the postconciliar practice of the Church, collegiality has been put into play with much boldness, but the Council's doctrinal affirmation is nonetheless on the record.

After the announcement of the major doctrinal structures, the Council moves on to the ministry of the bishops. The basic christological reference is once again strongly accented, but so is the gift of the Holy Spirit, given to the bishop at the moment of his consecration to help him accomplish his triple messianic task. As for the reference to the community, it is present again in the form of *diakonia* or "ministry," which is the principal characteristic of his responsibility (24). Then there is a detailed list of the areas covered by the doctrinal function of the bishops. This prophetic aspect of the ministry comes first because, according to the generic order, the Word usually precedes the sacraments. It is here that Vatican II announces the various forms taken by the teaching of the Church: the ordinary magisterium, if it is a matter of daily teaching by way of preaching and the different methods of transmitting the faith from generation to generation; and the extraordinary magisterium, if it is a matter of the teaching of a Council (which, in fact, rarely happens), or of an *ex cathedra* definition by the pope, who enjoys doctrinal infallibility under certain conditions (25).

From its very first lines, the exposition of the strictly priestly aspect of the episcopate stresses the Eucharist that the bishop "offers or causes to be offered" (26). It must be underlined that this passage contains the strongest possible statement in favor of what is called "eucharistic ecclesiology." It presents the grace of the Eucharist as the unity of the Mystical Body, which was already St. Thomas's teaching. In keeping with what the Fourth Gospel says—"[Jesus died] to gather into one the children of God who are scattered abroad" (John 11:52)—Thomas teaches that the sacrament of the Eucharist, which makes present the sacrifice of the cross, produces a double effect: on the one hand, the grace of personal intimacy with Christ (people all too often stop there); on the other hand, the grace of ecclesial unity in brotherly and sisterly charity (*Summa Theologica* IIIa q. 80, a. 4, and q. 73, a. 3). The result is that, where the Word is proclaimed and the Supper of the Lord celebrated, the community gathered around the bishop visibly manifests the Church Universal (26:1). In line with this, the bishop is then described as the one who has the responsibility to offer to God the worship of the Christian religion. He is the one who sees to it that everything takes place in an orderly fashion, and who carries out the canonical dispositions with a view to that, in keeping with what Ignatius of Antioch said about the only "legitimate" Eucharist (26).

The last paragraph of this section goes into everything that relates to the bishop in the domain of his priestly mission, and it is remarkable that once again first place is given to the preaching of the Gospel, a sign that this proclamation is again a sacramental act. Then come the sacraments—in the first rank, baptism, which confers a share in the royal priesthood of Christ. This is the first time that we find the royal priesthood in this context; it will not be the last. As for confirmation, we are told that the bishops are its "originating" ministers. This qualification is a manner of recalling that this prerogative was long exclusively reserved to the bishops; however, there was also a wish to keep in mind the fact that more and more frequently they delegate this to simple presbyters. Finally, it is the bishops who ordain the ministers ("dispenser of the sacred orders") and govern the penitential discipline (26). Readers who have followed me this far will probably not have learned a great deal. The essential points have been made but without many highlights. The decree that will come later will be much richer in those.

The service of the authority, the "royal" function, which belongs to the bishop within the People of God, quite logically comes at the end of the list of episcopal prerogatives (27). As one sees from reading it, this is dominated by the intent to affirm the makeup of the role of bishops vis-à-vis that of the pope (as section 22 was dominated by the concern to clearly mark out the primacy of the pope in the episcopal college). No surprise here. Although the Church is before all else an organism of grace, it is also a society of men and women where the relationships of power sometimes involve conflicts and so have to be institutionally regulated. In this case, we are dealing with a legacy of Vatican I, where the definition of papal primacy and infallibility in a very tension-filled context seemed to eclipse somewhat the proper role of the bishops. While I do not intend to dwell on that aspect of the situation, this emphatic note cannot totally be ignored. On the other hand, we rediscover the straight line of my survey by stressing the goal of the bishop's sacred power: He uses it (and never uses it except) to "edify the flock in truth and holiness" (27). The words *truth and holiness* are a deliberate echo of the prophetic responsibility and the priestly mission. This amounts to saying that the service of authority is best exercised by accomplishing the first two tasks. The ministry of authority has its specific actions, but they are ultimately subordinate to the proclamation of the Gospel and the celebration of saving worship.

The Presbyteral Ministry

After having described the nature and diverse forms through which the episcopal ministry is carried out, the Council then sets out to deal at some length with the presbyteral ministry, which is a participation in it. Before going any further, let me specify that if most of the time I use the word *presbyter*, this is neither out of affectation nor a vain attempt to add an archaic touch, but simply out of fidelity to the original text of the

Council. Most of the translations now circulating use the word *priests* when the Latin says *presbyteri*, but when the Council means "priest," it says *sacerdos*. So I am following this usage as well, and it is no longer necessary to explain why. Section 28 indicates the different divisions of the text, which heighten its intelligibility: (1) introduction, (2) reference to Christ, (3) relation to the bishop, (4) relations of the presbyters among one another, (5) service to the Christian people, and (6) moral exhortation.

Despite its brevity, the introduction is particularly substantial. It puts into operation a schema with which we are quite familiar and recreates the profusion of references that Clement of Rome already described:

> Christ, whom the Father has sanctified and sent into this world (John 10:36), has through His apostles made their successors, the bishops, partakers of His consecration and His mission. They have legitimately handed on to different individuals in the Church various degrees of participation in this ministry. Thus the divinely established ecclesiastical ministry is exercised on different levels by those who from antiquity have been called bishops, priests and deacons. (28)

The commission that edited this Council-approved text took care to point out in a note that it was perfectly aware of the difficulties presented by the texts that we have read above, and it refers to the study by Father Benoit on the origins of the episcopacy that I have made use of; so we were on the right path (in the Notes, see chapter III, n. 2).

There is, however, a point on which I have not yet spoken and which is strongly emphasized here by a repetition. The Council says that Christ, "sanctified and sent" by the Father, has himself made the apostles partakers "in his consecration and mission." The word *consecrated* is used to translate the Latin *sanctificavit*, which one might think ought to be translated as *sanctified*. In reality, *sanctificavit* is only there to render the Latin of the Vulgate (John 10:36). This in turn renders the Greek *heghiasen*, which is in fact translated in all Bibles as "consecrated," and this meaning has to be kept.

I belabor this detail because it places us at the source of much confusion concerning the effect of the sacrament of holy orders and priestly spirituality. If we say *sanctify*, we are likening the effect of the sacrament of holy orders to that of baptism, and then we understand that it transmits a new sanctifying grace, which perfects that of baptism and thus makes the priest a super-Christian. Actually, nothing of the sort happens. The sacrament of holy orders, whether in the form of the episcopate or that of the presbyterate confers a function, that of the minister of Christ and the Church at a certain level. It also gives a grace, but it is primarily destined to enable the person to fulfill his function of minister. The person granted this grace is certainly going to reap an increase of holiness from the exercise of his function, if he worthily fulfills it, but that is not the main purpose of the sacrament.[6] I shall have to return to this, but it was important to point out now that the word *consecration* orients us in this direction: consecration is setting someone apart for a mission. In the different texts that I have just cited, as in the one from St. John, we have to pay attention to the order of the words *consecrated and sent*. It is, so to speak, a constant refrain in the Bible: I have chosen you *so that* they may know me.

The relation of the presbyters to Christ is mentioned at the same time as their relation to the bishop. Thus we find this double reference intertwined in the text:

> Priests, although they do not possess the highest degree of the priesthood, and although they are dependent on the bishops in the exercise of their power, nevertheless they are united with the bishops in sacerdotal dignity. By the power of the sacrament of Orders, in the image of Christ the eternal high Priest (Heb 5:10; 7:24; 9:11–28), they are consecrated to preach the Gospel and shepherd the faithful and to celebrate divine worship, so that they are true priests of the New Testament. (28:2)

These very dense sentences contain several extremely important statements that can be summed up as follows in the order of their announcement:

1. The presbyters do not occupy "the highest degree of the priesthood." This expression from Pope Innocent I (402–17), a contemporary of the mature Augustine, recalls the expression, already mentioned, of Hippolytus of Rome (*primatus sacerdotii*). The text prefers to put things this way rather than borrow the expressions of the Roman Pontifical, which speaks of "second-order" or "second-rank" ministers and runs the risk of being judged disparaging.

2. They are "dependent on the bishops in the exercise of their powers." We have to note the word *their* (*sua*), because the commission stresses that this was not just the power of jurisdiction (*potestas regendi*). In fact, our text recalls for the presbyters everything that has already been said for the bishops.

3. This dependence does not prevent the presbyters from being "united with the bishops in the sacerdotal dignity. By the power of the sacrament of orders, in the image of Christ the eternal high Priest, they are consecrated to *preach* the Gospel and *shepherd* the faithful and to *celebrate* divine worship, so that they are *true priests* of the New Testament." We must note the *veri sacerdotes*: The commission did use the term *priests*, and it went to the trouble of justifying this in a long footnote. If you can read this footnote, you will see that it picks up and summarizes the texts that I myself have used and to which we need not return; however, one passage deserves some attention:

> The function of the rectors of the community (presbyters) appears bound up with their cultic (priestly) function....Thus, in the priesthood of the New Testament one can observe the union between the power of holy orders, that is, of sanctification, and the power of government, which both admit a certain division and gradation according to the necessities of time and place.

The commission's footnote also calls attention to the breadth of the presbyteral responsibility:

The participation of the presbyters in the priesthood of Christ is effected in the preaching of the Word, in the administration of the sacraments...and, in a general manner, in the function of shepherding the flock. This clarifies the fact that the presbytery is not just concerned with worship, but also with the pastoral government that aims to serve unity in the charity of Christ.

Hence, it is the triple function bound up with the ministry that I have spoken of, and that is one of the points in which the "novelty" of Vatican II is most manifest. In the period immediately preceding the Council, the distinction—and sometimes even the separation—was still being made between the power of holy orders and their power of jurisdiction. Bishops and priests were equal as to the first, but all the jurisdiction was thought to belong to the bishop. The same was true as regards teaching: only the bishops were the "teaching Church"; the priests belonged to the "Church being taught." The Council obliges us to rectify this perception; we must say that the participation of the presbyter in the sacrament of holy orders confers on him, *at his level of authority* and, to be sure, while depending on the bishop, the pastoral responsibility in its triple modality.

After making the above three statements, section 28 very carefully details this triple form of the single ministry. There is no further need to emphasize these three functions, but attention must be paid to two points. The first concerns the manner in which the priests are "partakers of the function of Christ, the *sole Mediator*, on their level of ministry." It is important to spell this out here—that is, *after* the statement about the triple function, but *before* the details of all that it covers. This means that if the title of mediator does regroup these three modalities, none of them all by itself exhausts the mediation of Christ. That applies in particular to the priestly aspect. Some writers have tried to define the priesthood by mediation. In fact, the idea of mediation is broader than the notion of priesthood.[7] The second point to note is the use of the formula *in persona Christi* apropos of priests, who are acting "in the name of Christ and representing him." This expression is very close to the one used for the bishops, and it exactly picks up the one used earlier in section 10. There is no need to insist on its meaning, but we have to note the commission's specificity: This is true in a special manner (*speciatim*) in the eucharistic cult—"specially," to be sure, but not uniquely; I have already pointed out the meaning of this reserve.

I will not linger just now on the end of the text of section 28, but we must not miss two other points. First, the priests are called "prudent advisors" to the bishops. That cooperation is no doubt manifested on the personal level, but this must first be understood as a collaboration between the order of presbyters and that of the bishops. The expression *ordo episcopalis* is there to recall this, as is that of the presbytery. In antiquity, people did not say, "He has been ordained a presbyter or a bishop," but rather, "He has entered the *ordo presbyterorum* or the *ordo episcoporum*." The overall assignment was too vast to be handled by isolated individuals. It was thus taken on in a body: this is the foundation of collegiality. Second, this collaboration does not take place only in the priesthood, but also in the mission. This is twice repeated in equivalent terms: "sharing in the priesthood and the mission," showing to all, and not just to Catholics, "the face of a truly sacerdotal and pastoral ministry." The context shows that mission is meant in the sense of "those who are far" from either practice or faith. This detail, which might seem of minimal interest, is in fact an echo of the discussions that were raging at the time about the definition of a priest: Was he a man of worship or a man of evangelization? The way Vatican II makes him the man of three messianic prerogatives renders this dichotomy quite pointless.

The Ministry of the Deacons

We now arrive at what the Council calls "a lower level of the hierarchy" (29). It does say "lower level" and not "first level." In the medieval perspective that prevailed up to Vatican II, the diaconate was considered the first step leading to the priesthood. But that was actually an error. The diaconate is not in itself a simple transitional stage, but a "proper and permanent rank of the hierarchy" (29). The history of the Church's liturgy teaches us that one could be ordained a priest without having previously been a deacon, just as one could be consecrated bishop without having been either a deacon or a presbyter. As a matter of fact, at a certain point—in Rome, at least—the bishops (the popes!) were taken from among the deacons because, due to their small number (the Seven!) and their administrative function, they were considerable persons. This liturgical practice, which has the value of a doctrinal teaching in action, shows us, therefore, that the diaconate must be considered an original participation in the episcopacy, so the pattern is not diaconate→presbyterate→episcopate, but rather

We must not be misled by the apparent symmetry of this diagram, however. The diaconate does not achieve the same type of participation in the episcopate and the presbyterate. That is what the Council's formula means when it says that the laying on of hands for the deacon is "not unto the priesthood, but unto a ministry of service" (*non ad sacerdotium, sed ad ministerium*) (29). This phrase comes from various liturgical documents cited in a footnote, but it is truncated if it is left as is. The word *episcopi* has to be added here. The deacon is at the service *of the bishop*. We can be absolutely sure of this because the source of all these documents is found in Hippolytus of Rome, who is quite explicit on this subject:

> When one ordains a deacon, he is chosen according to what has been said above, with only the bishop laying on his hands in the same manner. In the ordination of a deacon, only the bishop lays on his hands, because the deacon is not ordained to the priesthood, but to the service of the bishop, to do that which he commands. For he is not part of the council of the clergy, but acts as a manager, and reports to the bishop what is necessary. He does not receive the spirit common to the elders [presbyters], which the elders share, but that which is entrusted to him under the bishop's authority. This is

why only the bishop makes a deacon. Upon the elders, the other elders place their hands because of a common spirit and similar duty. Indeed, the elder has only the authority to receive this, but he has no authority to give it. Therefore he does not ordain to the clergy. Upon the ordination of the elder [priest] he seals [lays on hands]; the bishop ordains. (*The Apostolic Tradition* 8)

So we must understand that the deacon is not ordained to the *priestly* function of the bishop, but to his *diaconal* function. Thus, as far back as we go in history we find the pair bishops-and-deacons, and already Ignatius and Justin specify that the latter were assigned to serve at the altar and, after the celebration, to bring their share to the absent ones and to come to the aid of the poor. The situation is still clearer in Hippolytus. Despite that, some authors continue to write that there is a certain participation by the deacon in the priesthood. This can be grasped insofar as the communion service is conceived as a "priestly" work along the lines of the *Syriac Didascalia* (as I recalled above); however, when discussing the deacons, Hippolytus is far from speaking of participation in the ministry in the broader sense that we have become familiar with. Talking about priesthood for the deacons only confuses things; by contrast, the sharp distinction between the diaconal aspect and the priestly aspect, borrowed from Hippolytus, might have the advantage of allowing the ordination of deaconesses, without thereby implying the access of women to the priesthood.

There is no need to dwell on the diverse functions of the deacon. They are enumerated rather clearly, and they have been taken up and amplified in the *motu proprio* of Paul VI, which specifies the conditions for restoring the permanent diaconate in the Latin Church. There is, however, one thing that may be useful to underline: In keeping with the ancient practice, when we speak of the deacon as the minister of the Word, we are not quite thinking of preaching as conceived in our day. It was simply a matter of proclaiming the Gospel at Mass and, as needed, for example, if the priest was prevented by illness from speaking, the deacon could read a homily from the Fathers. This seems important to say, because entrusting the Sunday homily to deacons nowadays risks leading to considering them miniature priests (which they are not, even if some of them might be called to the priesthood in the future). It is no less regrettable to impose this practice on all of them, because that could become a burden for some who are not prepared for this task, and the faithful might also suffer from it.

The Unity of the Sacrament of Holy Orders

After having spoken of the various forms of ministry— episcopate, presbyterate, and diaconate—a question arises: Can we still talk about a singular sacrament of holy orders, or rather, do we have to consider the episcopate, the presbyterate, and the diaconate as three sacraments? Each of the three deserves this title because each one confers its particular character and grace. This has even been decisive for recognizing the sacramentality of the episcopate, and it also seems to involve the restoration of a permanent diaconate: Each one is equipped to accomplish his function on his own proper level.[8] In truth, one could put it this way: There is only one sacrament of holy orders, and yet the episcopate, the presbyterate, and the diaconate are sacraments, because each one fits the idea on different levels. The episcopate is the fullness of this sacrament, while the presbyterate and the diaconate are participations in it.

To give an account of the way in which the unity of the sacrament of holy orders is preserved despite this diversity, St. Thomas appeals to the notion of a "potential" whole, and he explains it in terms of what he calls an "integral" whole and a "universal" whole (*Supplement* q. 37, a. 1, sol. 2). The phrases are perhaps unusual, but the ideas are easy to grasp. The *integral whole* is a quantitative whole, composed of parts, none of which is the whole itself, but only an element of the whole. Thus, a house is an integral whole: it is composed of foundations, walls, roof, and so forth; it is a quantitative sum of these elements, none of which alone is the whole that constitutes the house as an integral entity. By contrast, the *universal whole* refers to a perfection that is found complete in each and every one of the subjects that participate in that perfection. For example, let us consider the "idea" of the triangle: Whatever the various forms and kinds of triangles, each one meets the definition of triangle. In the same way, whatever the differences between individual persons, each and all participate equally in the idea of human being: a rational animal.

The sacrament of holy orders cannot be a quantitative whole, because none of its individual parts (episcopate, presbyterate, diaconate) can alone be properly called "holy orders." Nor can it be a universal whole, because the episcopate, the presbyterate, and the diaconate do not participate in it in the same way. On the other hand, we can say that the episcopate and the presbyterate are universal wholes: Each bishop or each priest possesses equally and in common with his colleagues the episcopate or the presbyterate. Thus, it is the exclusion of these two first forms that led Thomas to propose the notion of *potential whole* to characterize the sacrament of holy orders. "In this case, the perfection signified by the common term is found in each of the parts, but only realizes all its possibilities in a single one, which possesses it perfectly, while the others only possess a participation" (J. Lécuyer). The idea of "life," for example, corresponds rather well to the idea of a potential whole. We run into it at different levels: rational, sensitive, vegetative, but only human beings realize the perfection of these three levels. The animals and plants realize it to a lesser degree, but all living creatures find themselves in that same perfection that is called life, analogically possessed. The comparison is enlightening, but we can explain this unity in a more appropriate way by a verse from the Book of Numbers. When Moses takes on seventy elders, the Lord tells him: "I will take some of the Spirit [or a little of the Spirit] which is upon you and put it upon them; and they shall bear the burdens of the people with you" (11:17–25). This formula, which is still in use in the Roman Pontifical, was present as far back as Hippolytus (*The Apostolic Tradition* 7). It clearly expresses the idea of a fullness possessed at different levels, but without, strictly speaking, becoming a multitude, because we are dealing with one and the same Spirit.

THE PRESBYTERAL MINISTRY IN
PRESBYTERORUM ORDINIS

This decree is the second conciliar document that speaks of the ministry at some length. From the strictly dogmatic point of view, it adds nothing to *Lumen Gentium.* Once we know that the presbyters participate on their particular level of authority in the whole of the episcopal function, everything has been said. At the time the Council was being held, however, a vast movement of dissatisfaction developed among the clergy. The bishops had seized the lion's share, while the priests only received spiritual encouragement. Thus, the decree originated with a jolt of public opinion, and perhaps even with the *sensus fidelium*: the feeling that something important was missing from the Council's teaching on the ministry. This reaction might have remained superficial and been ignored. But no, it was well taken theologically, and the document that was finally promulgated was very rich, in both its theology and its spirituality.

We can follow its evolution simply by reading the different titles given to the successive preparatory outlines. *De Clericis* ("On the Clerics," or "On the Clergy") was a document at once moralizing and canonical, but with no dogmatic dimension. It was recast beginning in January 1964 into *De Sacerdotibus* ("On Priests"), which dealt more specifically with priests, but in a way that was still unsatisfactory. In October 1964, the document submitted for discussion by the Council Fathers shows signs of a certain broadening of content, as seen by its new title: *De Vita et Ministerio Sacerdotali* ("On the Life [of Priests] and the Priestly Ministry"). After some amendments, the text came back before the Council a month later, in November 1964. This time the perspective had decidedly changed, as witnessed by the title's abandonment of *sacerdos* in favor of *presbyter*, and by the reversal of words that made ministry the central focus: *De Ministerio et Vita Presbyterorum* ("On the Ministry and Life of Presbyters"). In 1965, the definitive title of the text adopted by the Council showed only a simple stylistic correction: *De Presbyterorum Ministerio et Vita.*

For our purposes, the matter of the decree can be condensed into these points: the nature of the presbyterate, the three messianic responsibilities, and the vocation of priests to perfection. The selection of these three points in no way means that the rest of the decree is lacking in interest. Far from it! But from the point of view of the theology of the presbyterate, it is here that we find the essentials.

The Nature of the Presbyterate (*Presbyterorum Ordinis* 2)

Since this comes toward the end of our discussion, section 2 has no further need of a long commentary (in addition, the section itself can be found in toto at the back, text 7 in the Appendix). Still, it is instructive to see how it articulates the different points of the Council's aforementioned teaching. It puts on the first level the participation by all the baptized in the priesthood of Christ. The whole Body of Christ is priestly. That will cause us no surprise, since it is the basic fact revealed in the New Testament that has guided our thinking in a permanent fashion (2). Nevertheless, in this wholly priestly body, everyone does not have the same function. The ministers are enabled by the sacrament of holy orders to perform three principle acts: offering sacrifice, forgiving sins, and publicly exercising the priestly function. The word *publicly* is deliberate, because it involves the distinction between the priestly ministry, which carries out an official function in the Church, and the royal priesthood, which is mostly lived in a private fashion. Then the Council recalls the origin of the Church's mission: Christ, the apostles, the bishops, the presbyters. This, too, is something with which we are quite familiar, but we must notice the terms used: "The office of their [the bishops'] ministry has been handed down, in a lesser degree indeed, to the priests. Established in the order of the priesthood they can be coworkers of the episcopal order." These expressions recur several times in the decree, and they are even its first words: "The order of the presbyters" (*Ordo presbyterorum*). Later the episcopal order will be discussed (2:3). Collegial unity, both of presbyters and bishops, is thus clearly recalled. Apart from what was said about it in *Lumen Gentium* (sections 22 and 23 for the bishops, 28 for the priests), we have to look right here in this decree (and 8).

The continuation of the text is a direct reference to *Lumen*

Gentium 10. It defines the function of the presbyter as a participation in the authority by which Christ builds up his body (this is the proclaiming of the Word), sanctifies it (priesthood), and governs it (royal function). The priesthood of the presbyter is conferred by a particular sacrament, which marks him with a special character that enables the person who receives it to act *in persona Christi capitis.* By now all this is familiar territory to us. The decree then picks up with a little more breadth the teaching of *Lumen Gentium* 10 on the relations between the royal priesthood and the ministerial priesthood (2 and 4). It is worth the trouble to read the successive phrases one by one. In my opinion, one could not speak more strongly and more fairly concerning the relationship of the priestly ministry to the royal priesthood and at the same time about the indispensability of the priestly ministry.

1. The quotation from Romans 15:16—"the priestly service of the gospel" (we recall *hierourgein*)—underlines the sacerdotal implications of the prophetic ministry. The fact that it was put first here corresponds to the position taken by the Council in the debates taking place at that time. Did the presbyterate have to be defined by mission or by worship? The Council's answer, based on St. Paul, was very simple. From a chronological standpoint, one could say, the mission of proclaiming the Gospel is first, but this mission is itself a kind of worship, since it aims at the nations' becoming an offering agreeable to God.

2. The next phrase must be read right along with the previous, but it brings in one extra specification: Whereas the preceding one had a more universalistic bearing ("the nations"), this one is more intra-ecclesial. All the members of the People of God must themselves become a spiritual sacrifice. In both cases, it is the spiritual worship that finalizes the ministerial function: "*so that* the nations become an offering agreeable"; "*so that* all the members of the People offer themselves as a living victim."

3. The third phrase is crucial for the issue of relations between priestly ministry and royal priesthood. *Lumen Gentium* 10 had already concerned itself with these relations, but the Council was then giving special consideration to the characters of baptism and holy orders, and the description aimed at the respective acts that both of them allow. Here, the perspective is more unified.

The indispensability of the priestly ministry is highlighted by the fact that it is only in the Eucharist that the offering of the spiritual sacrifice reaches its fulfillment. Hence, there is no rivalry, but harmonious coordination, between the two priestly titles. The instrumentality of priestly ministry is, to be sure, clearly accentuated, but in a way that emphasizes that if it were not there, the spiritual sacrifice itself would suffer an irremediable loss: "Through the ministry of the priests, the spiritual sacrifice of the faithful is made perfect in union with the sacrifice of Christ. He is the only mediator who in the name of the whole Church is offered sacramentally" (2).

This can be grasped much more easily if we recall the context of 1 Peter 2:4–10. The spiritual sacrifice is, so to speak, "mounted" between two mentions of Christ's sacrifice; and we determined that the spiritual sacrifice did not exclude the ritual sacrifice, which was itself "spiritual" (that is, offered in the Spirit). With *Presbyterorum ordinis,* now we can say specifically that, with this spiritual sacrifice being accomplished by the ministers in the name of all the baptized, the ministers have the lofty role of contributing by their ministry to the completion and perfection of the spiritual sacrifices. Without the sacrifice of the Eucharist the spiritual sacrifices themselves would be deprived of their final flowering.

This becomes even more forcefully clear when we consider what takes place wherever Christ is not known and the Eucharist is not celebrated. The spiritual sacrifices of the just pagans are certainly not without value in the eyes of God; but if they have it, that is to the degree that they are carried out, in a manner that only God knows, under the impulse of Christ's grace. Now, that grace of Christ does not fully activate all its potential except when it is sacramental. When the Eucharist is not celebrated, something is lacking to that fullness. Not to mention the fragility of this grace when it is equally deprived of the other sacraments, which are the habitual means by which the priesthood of the holy life can be fortified, increased, or recovered.

If we return to section 2 of our decree, it further details the way in which the presbyteral minister contributes, on his level, to the offering of the spiritual sacrifice by a reference to the celebrated passage from *The City of God* with which we are now quite familiar (see text 2 at the end). Two expressions should be noted:

1. "The ministry of priests is directed to this goal and is perfected in it" (*Presbyterorum Ordinis* 2). We turn the preceding phrase upside down, as it were, in a sort of reverse parallelism. The spiritual sacrifice finds its accomplishment through the ministry, but the ministry only finds its meaning in the offering of this spiritual sacrifice. It is interrelated to it, as *Lumen Gentium* 10 said.

2. The ministry draws its fecundity, its efficacy, "its force and power" from the sacrifice of Christ. Here is another way of saying that the ministry is in no sense an autonomous entity. Its fruitfulness comes to it from Christ; its meaning is granted it by the reality that it serves: the growth of the Body of Christ.

The Functions of the Presbyters
(*Presbyterorum Ordinis* 4–6)

These three sections explain the triple functions—prophetic, priestly, and royal—of the presbyters. After all that I have said, they do not teach us anything very new, so I shall limit myself to a few words on each of them.

On the prophetic mission (4), however, it must be noted that the priority of the word is not just chronological. Given that it prompts listeners to faith, there is a certain logical antecedence ("by nature") with relation to the sacraments. Even if the Eucharist is in itself worthier than the mere proclamation of the Word, "The preaching of the word is needed for the very ministering of the sacraments. They are precisely sacraments of faith, a faith which is born of and nourished by the word." This cannot be taken lightly.[9] We also have to underline the diverse forms of the ministry of the Word, which ranges from the witness of a holy life to the study of contemporary problems, passing through still other aspects. This could include the presbyters' good conduct among the pagans (witness) or their transmission of Christian teaching (catechesis or homilies), their expounding of the doctrine of the Church (teaching theology) or their studying the problems of their time (dialogue with scientists). In all these cases, it is a matter of proclaiming the Word of God and of prompting people to conversion and holiness.

As for the strictly priestly mission of the presbyters (5), one point needs to be heavily stressed: The Eucharist is presented not only as the center of the whole sacramental organism, but also as "the source and apex of all the work of preaching the gospel" (5). This should come as no surprise: It is a new echo of the preconciliar discussions on the definitions of the presbyterate as either mission or worship. Vatican II's entire effort in this domain was to break down that crude dichotomy by recalling the true dimensions of worship in spirit. Plainly, Vatican II did not fail to encourage the work of evangelization, whether within the old Christian territories that had become de-Christianized or in countries still waiting for Christ. Repeating the need for mission work, which was very much in its strategic place in *Lumen Gentium* 17 and in *Ad Gentes* (the decree on the missionary activity of the Church), is enough to prevent this misunderstanding. The exhortation to mission is not lacking in this decree either. It reminds us that "the priesthood of Christ, in which all priests really share, is necessarily intended for all peoples and all times, and it knows no limit of blood, nationality or time, since it is already mysteriously prefigured in the person of Melchizedek. Let presbyters remember, therefore, that the care of all churches must be their intimate concern" (*Presbyterorum Ordinis* 10). What the Council means here is that evangelization is not only "launched" from the celebration of eucharistic worship, whence it has its fecundity, but that it "lands" there, because it is only by the Eucharist that the full insertion of believers into the Body of Christ is achieved. This is another way of saying that the spiritual sacrifice finds its completion in the eucharistic sacrifice (see *Sacrosanctum Concilium* 10).

As for the way in which the presbyters exercise "the office of Christ, the Shepherd and Head" (6), one phrase is essential for understanding their role. It is a matter of "gather[ing] the family of God together as a brotherhood, enlivened by one spirit.

Through Christ they lead them in the Holy Spirit to God the Father." But we must also note the beginning of 6:3: "Although they have obligations toward all men, priests have a special obligation to the poor and weak entrusted to them." It is truly striking to note that we rediscover here the priestly dimension of the communion service among the widows and orphans that I spoke of with the help of the *Syriac Didascalia.* If that may have been considered then as a bit marginal for the definition of priesthood, we can now see that it was nothing of the sort, and that Vatican II plainly confirms this intention from the most distant ages of the Church.

Along with this, let me end this chapter with a remark about language. The title of king or of royal function is not used in this context to describe the presbyters' function of authority or government. A quick check will lead us to realize that the adjective *royal* is reserved to Christ and to Christians to express their dignity as children of God, rather than to their "power." When it is a question of ministers, they are said to receive their sacred power from Christ "as pastor and head" of his people. It is the pastoral function that unites the other two.

V

THE CALL TO HOLINESS IN THE PRIESTLY PEOPLE

There were many ways to end this book. The most boring would have been just to sum up its findings, but the results are clear enough to render this pointless. The most depressing would have been to list all the questions that I have not been able to deal with. All authors have to resign themselves to this: They cannot say everything in a single book. Still, there is no reason for regret. Readers who have followed me this far will be in possession of the indispensable elements and an overall view that will enable them to judge competently some detailed points that I may have omitted. It struck me as more stimulating to conclude with a prospective opening: What to do with what we have learned? There is no question of simply keeping it in a corner of our memory. We have already spoken too much about spiritual sacrifices, the priesthood of the holy life, and ministry as service for us to be satisfied with that lazy solution. But all the subjects that we have brought up ought to have repercussions in our Christian life. What would knowledge of the faith be that did not turn toward love? We will learn a great deal here if we follow the Council. "The universal call to holiness in the Church" emerged as a necessary invitation that the Council fathers had to address to the People of God (*Lumen Gentium* 5).

The call to holiness in the priestly people that I propose in the few pages remaining is consistent with this line of thinking, and at the same time it continues in a quasi-natural fashion the body of our research. After all that we have been able to read, it seems evident to me that this Christian and ecclesial holiness preached by the Council also has a priestly modality. Contrary to what we might have thought before reading this book, that aspect does not concern only bishops, priests, or future priests, but just as much the men and women who do not have that sort of vocation. A mother of a family has no fewer occasions to exercise her baptismal priesthood than does a minister of the Word and Sacrament. The former will have a new motivation to become holy, but no situation is devoid of that. This is why we cannot talk about Christian spirituality without at the same time saying that it is a priestly spirituality. We cannot, in fact, discuss this question in any compartmentalized fashion, by isolating it from the overall context in which it exists. So if we want ask about what most directly concerns the ministers, we must first recall what is addressed to everyone, laypeople and ministers alike. Clearly, we are tackling an enormous subject with as many applications as there are spiritual families in the Church. Some are drawn more by St. Benedict than by St. Ignatius, others more by St. Francis than by St. Dominic, by the holy Curé of Ars more than by St. Benedict. The Mystery is too great to approach it by only one path. This is why, leaving each person the freedom to pursue his or her personal leaning, I shall content myself with evoking a few general lines.

A PRIESTLY SPIRITUALITY

The call for holiness is the common vocation of all the baptized. That does not have to be proved; it is enough to open the Bible: "Be holy, for I am holy" (Lev 11:44–45). "You, therefore, must be perfect, as your heavenly Father is perfect" (Matt 5:48). Beyond the example of "so great a cloud of witnesses" (Heb 12:1) surrounding us, the Council has also stressed this primal truth: "In the Church *everyone*, whether belonging to the hierarchy, or being cared for by it, is called to holiness" (*Lumen Gentium* 39). "All the faithful of Christ, of whatever rank or status, are called to the fullness of the Christian life and to the perfection of charity" (*Lumen Gentium* 40). We honor enough saints who were neither priests nor bishops to know that here practice has preceded official teaching. (It seems that the Curé of Ars was deeply depressed by the fact that in his time there was not a single priest canonized for his lonely ministry.)

This holiness develops on the basis of the gift of grace received in baptism. It consists essentially in the exercise of the theological virtues, especially of charity, as well as of the evangelical virtues that the Lord so strongly emphasizes, and even in the impossible paradoxes in the Beatitudes and the Sermon on the Mount (Matt 5–7). The first model of this Christian holiness is Jesus Christ himself, who is the "source and completion": Christ who is at once the "Holy One of God" (Mark 1:24) and the "fitting…high priest, holy, blameless, undefiled" (Heb 7:26). There is no need to look elsewhere for the first principle to be observed to reach holiness: "Therefore, be imitators of God, as beloved children, and live in love, as Christ loved us and gave himself up for us, a fragrant offering and sacrifice to God" (Eph 5:1–2).

Unsurprisingly for us, these few fundamental verses offer us as self-evident the idea that the holiness common to all Christians is made up of a strictly priestly characteristic: "I appeal to you, therefore, brothers and sisters, by the mercies of God, to present your bodies as a living sacrifice, holy and acceptable to God, which is your spiritual worship" (Rom 12:1). All the Scripture texts quoted at the beginning of this book are still sufficiently fresh in our memory so that it is not necessary to repeat more than one: "Like living stones, let yourselves be built into a spiritual house, to be a holy priesthood, to offer spiritual sacrifices acceptable to God through Jesus Christ" (1 Pet 2:5–9). Tradition is no less explicit. It is not a matter of a pious reflection reserved for an elite of monks and nuns entrenched behind the protecting walls of a monastery, but rather a truth inseparable from our faith. The members of the priestly people arrive at holiness according to a strictly priestly modality, which consists in offering their persons and all their acts to God as a spiritual sacrifice, at once priests and victims, like Christ, through him and with him and in him. Before any other consideration, this holds true for all Christians in their very being as Christians, as members of the Mystical Body of Christ.

Within this common and unsurpassable vocation (there is no other, there is nothing grander), there are some particular features. There are many mansions in the Father's house. There are also many ways of going to him. And so, this unique call is

185

lived differently according to the diversity of personal vocations, situations, states, and functions of each person in the world and in the People of God. We have long known that there are stages in the spiritual life. Those practices spontaneously followed by a young adult, which will no longer be followed by very old people, are still evangelical virtues, because holiness cannot be conceived without them. Without anyone's having put this in so many words—since that seemed a private preserve—the priestly dimension of holiness is no less evangelical than humility. Like charity, it entirely penetrates the Christian's being and activity. That is why, without ceasing to be priestly, there is a conjugal or religious spirituality (with various nuances here, too); a spirituality better adapted to celibates or widows and widowers; or again, a spirituality for those people with various kinds of disabilities; and, of course, a spirituality appropriate to ministers. If I talk about the last one now, it is not by a sort of preferential treatment, but rather to recognize in them a privilege analogous to the one that all the other categories of Christians can assert.

A MINISTERIAL SPIRITUALITY

Thus, everything that I have just recalled applies equally to ministers. They too are, before anything else, baptized persons, and they share with all members of the Body the priestly quality received in their baptism. Despite being unable to go into detail about what is fitting for every major kind of calling that Christians follow (it would take a whole book for each of them), I will try to discover the way in which the common priestly holiness can be colored with a nuance proper to those who by their vocation place themselves at the service of their brothers and sisters in Christ, as ministers of the Word, the sacraments, and the authority of Christ who sends them forth. The task is delicate, because after having recalled that the priestly quality applies to all without distinction, we have to take special care not to make it once again the special domain of certain select people. For lack of a better qualifier, I propose to speak of a "ministerial" spirituality, but once again we have to highlight its leading features.

186

Vatican II's Decree on the Ministry and Life of Presbyters (*Presbyterorum Ordinis*), in sections 12 to 17, was rightly used for this task, and it will not be superfluous to cite some lines through which it introduces and sums up its purpose:

> Priests are made in the likeness of Christ the Priest by the sacrament of Orders, so that they may, in collaboration with their bishops, work for the building up and care of the Church which is the whole Body of Christ, acting as ministers of him who is the Head. Like all other Christians they have received in the sacrament of Baptism the symbol and gift of such a calling and such grace that even in human weakness they can and must seek for perfection, according to the exhortation of Christ: "Be you therefore perfect, as your Heavenly Father is perfect" (Mt 5:48). Priests are bound, however, to acquire that perfection in special fashion. They have been consecrated by God in a new manner at their ordination and made living instruments of Christ the Eternal Priest that they may be able to carry on in time his marvelous work whereby the entire family of man is again made whole by power from above. Since, therefore, every priest in his own fashion acts in place of Christ himself, he is enriched by a special grace, so that, as he serves the flock committed to him and the entire People of God, he may the better grow in the grace of him whose tasks he performs, because to the weakness of our flesh there is brought the holiness of him who for us was made a High Priest "holy, guiltless, undefiled, not reckoned among us sinners" (Heb 7:26). (12)

If one can sum up more simply this somewhat turgid prose, it essentially comes down to this: Called to holiness as are all Christians, the ministers are obliged to achieve holiness in a new and particular way. The sacrament of holy orders makes them living instruments of Christ, and they receive with the sacrament a special grace that helps them to strive for that holiness through the service of God and human beings for which they have been consecrated. These few words must be rightly understood. The Council is by no means saying that the sacrament confers an increase of holiness on the minister, but that the responsibility entrusted to him represents a new demand for holiness.

So as not to be ambiguous and to avoid misleading readers, the Council's phrase that ministers are *made living instruments* needs a serious explanation. We must distinguish between an instrumentality in the strict sense (that of sacramental acts properly so called: consecrating the Eucharist, absolving sins…) and an instrumentality in the broader sense, which does not quite deserve the name (that of nonsacramental acts, such as preaching). In fact, contrary to certain authors—well-intentioned rather than theologically precise—the priest is not a *conjoint* instrument of Christ, but only his living, *animate* instrument. Only the humanity of Christ is the conjoint instrument of the person of the Word, and that is strictly reserved to him, because it is the proper effect of the hypostatic union. If you say that the priest is the conjoint instrument, you are implicitly extending the hypostatic union to include him; and you make each of his acts the acts of the Son of God. This is a kind of "priestly pan-Christism," so to speak, and it is no more defensible than the "universal pan-Christism" of Karl Pelz, the Berlin curate (long since condemned by Pius XII). Pelz pushed to the extreme—all the way to actual identity—the mystical union of all the members of the ecclesial Body of Christ with Christ himself, going so far as to compare it to the eucharistic transubstantiation.

The living or *animate* instrument is called this to describe a person who acts under command of another (a servant with relation to his master, whose orders he executes). Thus, such a person is distinguished from an *inanimate* instrument that cannot do anything by itself (a hammer!). In both cases, the principal cause has the ultimate responsibility for the final effect. This is clear with the hammer, but *mutatis mutandis*, it is no less true for the minister of the altar. The priest consecrates the Eucharist, but it is God who transforms the bread into the Body of Christ. Everyone knows that not all the acts of a priest have the same claim to being acts of him whose minister he is: That would make Christ or God take on many limitations—to say the least.[1]

It is here that we rediscover the manner in which *consecration* and *sanctification* are interconnected in the priest, as I discussed in chapter 4, and that *Presbyterorum Ordinis* 12 picks up after *Lumen Gentium* 28. St. Thomas tells us that the first effect of the sacrament of holy orders consists in the handing over of a power (*hoc sacramentum principaliter consistit in potestate tradita: Supplementum* q. 34, a. 4; see also q. 34, a. 2, sol. 1 and 2); but he immediately adds that God gives to him who receives this power the means of putting it to work in a suitable fashion. Apart from the character, God gives the newly ordained minister the sanctifying grace that will allow him to exercise worthily the commission with which he has been entrusted (*Supplementum*, q. 35 a. 1). Here we can draw a comparison with what happens in marriage: The first effect of the sacrament is the consecration of the bond between the spouses, but grace is also given them to help them confront the demands of life as a couple and as parents. The same thing happens with the sacrament of holy orders. In itself, the grace that accompanies it is not enough to give the person who receives it a greater holiness. The grace is destined to help the person better fulfill his ministry; fidelity to that grace will permit him to acquire that increase in holiness by the very carrying out of his assignment.

This is exactly what the Council itself says: "Priests who perform their duties sincerely and indefatigably in the Spirit of Christ arrive at holiness by that very fact" (*Presbyterorum Ordinis* 13). The word *duties* here is in the plural because the rest of the paragraph shows how this pursuit of holiness is realized according to the triple form with which we are well familiar: the proclamation of the Word, the celebration of the sacraments, and the exercise of authority. The same thing was already present, but in a global fashion, in an earlier paragraph: "By the sacred actions which are theirs daily as well as in their entire ministry which they share with the bishops and their fellow priests [presbyters] they are directed to perfection in their lives" (*Presbyterorum Ordinis* 12).

In the multitude of tasks that ministers must carry out, the principle that will allow them to unify their life is to "[follow] the example of Christ the Lord in their ministry. His food was to follow the will of him who had sent him to accomplish his work"

189

(*Presbyterorum Ordinis* 14). The Council makes this still more explicit: "He [Christ] remains always the source and wellspring of the unity of their lives"; it is the imitation of Christ the Good Shepherd that they will find "in the very exercise of their pastoral charity...a bond of priestly perfection which draws their life and activity to unity and coordination" (14). Now this pastoral charity flows above all from the eucharistic sacrifice, which is the center and the root of the whole life of the presbyter; and he must try hard to interiorize what is done on the altar. Without using the word, this passage takes us back again to the spiritual sacrifice accomplished under the sign of the imitation of Christ and in union with the eucharistic sacrifice. That comes down to saying that the holiness of the ministers rediscovers in its essence the holiness of the whole priestly people. Their ministry is directed, up to and including their own person, to the growth of the priesthood of the holy life. There is no more radical fashion of stressing the superiority of the latter. To put it in precise theological language, the ministerial charism of holy orders is totally at the service of the priesthood of grace.

Can one speak of a "priestly perfection" with regard to the ministers, as we have just read in the text cited above? If we explain the term carefully, by recalling as we have done that this quality belongs primarily to all the baptized, it is no doubt possible. But there are at least three reasons against using this phrase as if it were a prerogative that was peculiar to the ministers: First of all, we would not use the phrase because of the history of the words *priest* and *sacrifice.* As we have seen, they do not strictly designate more than a part of the pastoral responsibility. If we continue to use the word *priestly* without restriction, we are not respecting the facts from Scripture and Tradition. Next, neither would we be obeying the Council, which was very sparing in its use of *sacerdos* (just check the Latin text: almost everywhere that the French and English translations say *priests*, the Latin says *presbyteri*). This is all about a point of deliberate policy, which can be seen through all the stages of editing the text up to the final one. One amendment had called for replacing *presbyteri* practically everywhere with *sacerdotes*; but the commission charged with the final redaction of the text refused to do this. As it explained, *sacerdos* is used only when it is a question of priests "and" bishops (apparently the case in the text above). Now this is obviously not what people are thinking about when they say "priestly" in our modern languages. Finally, as I have repeated, it is the whole of Christian spirituality itself that has the privilege of being priestly. The title cannot be reserved to a single category of Christians. If a name absolutely has to be given, one might consider "ministerial" or "pastoral" spirituality. In French-speaking countries, it has become usual for ordination announcements to talk about "presbyteral" ordination, but most people are still not accustomed to this language. In fact, more than fifty years after Vatican II, the change of mentality in this realm still remains to be made.

Among the teachings of the Council, there is still one more that must be highlighted: this ministerial spirituality—or however else one calls it—is not a "religious" spirituality, that is, the spirituality of a religious order. On this point, the Council has taken a perfectly clear position. In the requests formulated by the Council Fathers and accepted by the commission and the Council, there was a repeated desire "to avoid the numerical and formal typology of the evangelical counsels as is current in the religious state. Besides, the text speaks rather of evangelical 'virtues,' which must be practiced according to the particular demands of the life and ministry of presbyters, rather than of the evangelical 'counsels,' which in fact always refer to the religious state." This stance is extremely important. It does not mean that some ministers cannot also be religious who have taken the three vows, but that it is not required by the nature of the presbyterate. The holiness of the ministers does not come from the observance of a Rule, but from the exercise of their ministry.

This declaration is unquestionably in line with the teaching of the Council and everything that history teaches us. But we also know that this position is very different from the one that was prevalent even shortly before the Council. Back then, their elders liked to repeat to seminarians that they were "Christ's religious" or "(their) bishop's religious," or "the religious of the order of St. Peter." It is easy to see the practical goal of such ways of speaking, which aimed to call the members of the clergy to holiness; and it would not be honest to suggest that they did not lead to excellent results. Nonetheless, they were inaccurate, and the Council formally advised against them. It is not by remaining confined in his presbytery-hermitage and reciting the canonical hours that the priest achieves his particular way of striving for holiness, but in ministerial service (not to downplay prayer!). This is not the place to dwell on that, but we can readily understand that the spirituality of the French school discussed above is far removed from this teaching of the Council. Maritain's article cited above (see note 1) shows very clearly that the confusion between character and grace, like the merging of priestly function with the religious state, is the profound characteristic of that approach.

Focusing on this, however, raises yet another question. If the presbyter is not a religious, why impose celibacy on him? The question was obviously raised during the preparation of this text, and it is too critical not to quote verbatim the explanations of the commission, which presents the sequence of ideas in this passage of *Presbyterorum Ordinis* 16. By way of introduction, the text emphasizes that, while celibacy is certainly a great gift granted by the Lord to his Church, this perfect continence "is not demanded by the very nature of the priesthood, as is apparent from the practice of the early Church and from the traditions of the Eastern Churches." This first paragraph concludes precisely by stressing that the Council has no intention of going into this discipline of the Eastern Churches, and that it recommends that married priests persevere in their vocation. The Council lists the reasons both "pastoral" and "theological" that are the basis of the suitability of celibacy for the priesthood (the commission separates the declaration of these two reasons, but they are found mixed together in the text). As for the pastoral reasons, they are evident. Celibacy frees the priest so that he can consecrate himself entirely to his mission. But it is clear that this is not enough to justify celibacy. Many married laypeople lead lives as totally dedicated as, if not more than, those of many priests. That is why there has to be an appeal to the strictly theological reasons: first, the fact of consecrating oneself to Christ in a new and excellent manner (*eximia*, which can also be translated as "preferential"); and, second, the value of witness. This means that the ministers anticipate during their lives the eschatological state in which the whole Church will be entirely at the disposition of its Spouse, and in which there will be no marriage or giving in marriage (see Luke 20:35–36).

This is how the meaning of consecrated celibacy has traditionally been defined, but one cannot help noting that the Council here is grouping together priests with religious. If you look back over the reference by the decree itself to chapters 5 and 6 of *Lumen Gentium* (42 and 44), you will notice that the same terms are already used apropos of religious. So we have to observe that there is a practical contradiction between what was said a moment ago (the priestly state and the religious state must not be confused with one another) and what is now said to motivate the celibacy of presbyters. As far as I know, the commission did not make any other attempt to clear up this misunderstanding. This paragraph concludes with an exhortation to implore the gift of grace that is celibacy lived for the kingdom and with an invitation to prayer by all the Christian people so that God will continue to grant it to his Church.

Celibacy is not the only particular demand present in the life of ministers. The Council recommends, of course, all the evangelical virtues, but among them it makes special mention of humility and obedience (*Presbyterorum Ordinis* 15) as well as poverty (17). Why these three virtues in preference to others? It is easy to see that they are most closely linked with everything that we know otherwise about the ministerial function:

1. Humility because you cannot be proud of a function of service that must be accomplished in the humble awareness of a task that transcends those who carry it out. The presbyter cannot forget that *minister* means "servant," and that Christ, whom he wishes to imitate by his whole life, has himself given the example of service in the highest degree: "He emptied himself, taking the form of a servant " (Phil 2:7); "He who is greatest among you will be your servant" (Matt 23:11). We all remember the episode of the washing of the feet, which is renewed every Holy Thursday: "So if I, your Lord and Teacher, have

washed your feet, you also ought to wash one another's feet. For I have set you an example, that you also should do as I have done to you" (John 13:13–17). If the pope calls himself "servant of the servants of God," that is surely not without reason.

2. This function can only be carried out in obedience; here too Christ is the example, because "being found in human form…he humbled himself and became obedient to the point of death" (Phil 2:8); and he went as far as to say, "My food is to do the will of him who sent me" (John 4:34); "I always do what is pleasing to him" (John 8:29). In fact, the minister has no other mandate except to do the will of the one who sends him, not his own will. The dependency of the presbyterate on the episcopate and the very collegiality of the presbyterate prohibit working in the priesthood as lone wolves. This obedience is the opposite of the clerical individualism that has gone on for centuries and was still current quite recently, in keeping with the old adage, "The curate is king in his parish." Ultimately, such an attitude would flat out contradict the command of the risen Christ: "Go therefore and make disciples of all nations" (Matt 28:2–10). Obeying does not just express an attitude of inner submission. For a minister of Christ, obeying is also evangelizing.

3. As for poverty, it is justified by a detachment of the same kind as that of celibacy: It delivers the individual from all "disordered" material concerns, and it shows that the Lord himself is the true wealth of those who serve him. Vatican II here recalls the verse from the Book of Numbers (18:20): The tribe of Aaron, that of the priests, unlike the other tribes, had no land of its own. The Lord is the share and inheritance of the priests: "The Lord is my chosen portion and my cup" (Ps 16:5).

At the final moment of this description of the calling of the presbyters to holiness, readers may feel the need of a more synthetic wrap-up of all that they have read. The nuances and uncertainties that I have managed to formulate on one point or another should not give rise to any ambiguity. The character of the sacrament of holy orders and the grace bound up with it are altogether proper to the presbyters and make them members of the Body of Christ publicly appointed for the service of their brothers and sisters in Christ. Nevertheless, without denying that this is quite central and distinctive, we must acknowledge that it is easier to eliminate what the holiness of presbyters is not than to spell out what it is. Still, we cannot neglect another feature, stressed by the Council and often neglected, but altogether specific to them. Even if it is true that they share the essential characteristics of holiness with the whole of the priestly people, and even if the ministers, like other Christians, achieve holiness through fidelity to what the Lord expects from them in the task he has assigned them, they do this in a manner that is peculiar to them. Whereas in other professions or situations the daily activities are often quite remote from God and the Christian life (and sometimes turn the persons away from them), the responsibility of the ministers, by its very nature, is a constant reminder of the holiness to which they are called. Whether it be the celebration of the Eucharist or the other sacraments, the preparation of a homily, and, especially, of an exhortation addressed to the assembly of the faithful, a spiritual conversation, or the awakening and accompaniment of a vocation, or of prayer for the men and women entrusted to him, every single thing in the activity of a presbyter is a call to keep alive in himself faith, hope, and charity, and all the other evangelical virtues. Everything is a reminder of the holiness of his state and an invitation to practice what he works at communicating. The Roman Pontifical has expressed this in lapidary fashion for centuries: "Live what you perform" (*Imitamini quod tractatis*). There is no denying that this is an immense privilege, but also a singular demand.[2]

Appendix

SELECTED TEXTS

1. FASTIDIUS/PELAGIUS(?): ALL THE FAITHFUL RECEIVE ANOINTING AS PROPHETS, PRIESTS, AND KINGS

We do not know for sure to whom to attribute this first text. It was long believed to be written by Fastidius, a bishop in England around 415 to 425, the author of a work titled De vita Christiana, *like the one by Augustine. However, the most recent specialists unhesitatingly ascribe it to Pelagius, the celebrated adversary of Augustine, who was likewise active in the early fifth century. In any event, this short treatise begins with the words:*

No one, whether scholar or simple believer, is unaware that *Christ* means "Anointed."…Only the prophets, the priests, and the kings were anointed….All those until the coming of our Lord Jesus Christ….Since that moment those who believe in him and are purified by the sanctification of his baptism, not the small number as under the old law, but one and all receive anointing as prophets, priests, and kings. This anointing imposes duties on us. If the anointing is holy, our lives must be holy as well. It is from the sacrament of this anointing that the name of Christ and all Christians comes, that is, of those who believe in Christ. One is bearing such a name in vain, if one does not imitate Christ.

Fastidius/Pelagius? *De vita Christiana*
(Patrologia Latina L, 384–85)

197

2. ST. AUGUSTINE: THE TRUE AND PERFECT SACRIFICE

Thus, a true sacrifice is every work which is done that we may be united to God in holy fellowship, and which has a reference to that supreme good and end in which alone we can be truly blessed. And therefore even the mercy we show to men, if it is not shown for God's sake, is not a sacrifice. For, though made or offered by man, sacrifice is a divine thing, as those who called it *sacrifice* meant to indicate. Thus man himself, consecrated in the name of God, and vowed to God, is a sacrifice insofar as he dies to the world that he may live to God. For this is a part of that mercy which each man shows to himself; as it is written: "Have mercy on thy soul by pleasing God." Our body, too, is a sacrifice when we chasten it by temperance, if we do so as we ought, for God's sake, that we may not yield our members instruments of unrighteousness unto sin, but instruments of righteousness unto God. Exhorting to this sacrifice, the Apostle says, "I beseech you, therefore, brethren, by the mercy of God, that ye present your bodies a living sacrifice, holy, acceptable to God, which is your reasonable service." If, then, the body, which, being inferior, the soul uses as a servant or instrument, is a sacrifice when it is used rightly, and with reference to God, how much more does the soul itself become a sacrifice when it offers itself to God, in order that, being inflamed by the fire of his love, it may receive of his beauty and become pleasing to him, losing the shape of earthly desire, and being remoulded in the image of permanent loveliness? And this, indeed, the Apostle subjoins, saying, "And be not conformed to this world; but be ye transformed in the renewing of your mind, that ye may prove what is that good, and acceptable, and perfect will of God." Since, therefore, true sacrifices are works of mercy to ourselves or others, done with a reference to God, and since works of mercy have no other object than the relief of distress or the conferring of happiness, and since there is no happiness apart from that good of which it is said, "It is good for me to be very near to God," it follows that the whole redeemed City, that is to say, the congregation or community of the saints, is offered to God as our sacrifice through the great High Priest, who offered himself to

God in his passion for us, that we might be members of this glorious Head, according to the form of a servant. For it was this form he offered, in this he was offered; because it is according to it he is Mediator, in this he is our Priest, in this the Sacrifice. Accordingly, when the Apostle had exhorted us to present our bodies a living sacrifice, holy, acceptable to God, our reasonable service, and not to be conformed to the world, but to be transformed in the renewing of our mind, that we might prove what is that good, and acceptable, and perfect will of God, that is to say, the true sacrifice of ourselves, he says, "For I say, through the grace of God which is given unto me, to every man that is among you, not to think of himself more highly than he ought to think, but to think Christ. And this also is the sacrifice which the Church continually celebrates in the sacrament of the altar, known to the faithful, in which she teaches that she herself is offered in the offering she makes to God soberly, according as God hath dealt to every man the measure of faith. For, as we have many members in one body, and all members have not the same office, so we, being many, are one body in Christ, and every one members one of another, having gifts differing according to the grace that is given to us." This is the sacrifice of Christians: we, being many, are one body in Christ. And this is the sacrifice of Christ, which the Church continually celebrates in the sacrament of the altar, known to the faithful in which she teaches that she herself is offered in the offering she makes to God.

St. Augustine, *The City of God* 10.6

3. CLEMENT OF ROME: BISHOPS AND PRESBYTERS

42. The apostles have preached the Gospel to us from the Lord Jesus Christ; Jesus Christ [has done so] from God. Christ therefore was sent forth by God, and the apostles by Christ. Both these appointments, then, were made in an orderly way, according to the will of God. Having therefore received their orders, and being fully assured by the resurrection of our Lord Jesus Christ,

and established in the word of God, with full assurance of the Holy Ghost, they went forth proclaiming that the kingdom of God was at hand. And thus preaching through countries and cities, they appointed the firstfruits [of their labors], having first proved them by the Spirit, to be bishops and deacons of those who should afterwards believe. Nor was this any new thing, since indeed many ages before it was written concerning bishops and deacons. For thus saith the Scripture in a certain place, "I will appoint their bishops in righteousness, and their deacons in faith." […]

44. Our apostles also knew, through our Lord Jesus Christ, and there would be strife on account of the office of the episcopate. For this reason, therefore, inasmuch as they had obtained a perfect foreknowledge of this, they appointed those [ministers] already mentioned, and afterward gave instructions, that when these should fall asleep, other approved men should succeed them in their ministry. We are of opinion, therefore, that those appointed by them, or afterward by other eminent men, with the consent of the whole Church, and who have blamelessly served the flock of Christ in a humble, peaceable, and disinterested spirit, and have for a long time possessed the good opinion of all, cannot be justly dismissed from the ministry. For our sin will not be small, if we eject from the episcopate those who have blamelessly and holily fulfilled its duties. Blessed are those presbyters who, having finished their course before now, have obtained a fruitful and perfect departure [from this world]; for they have no fear lest anyone deprive them of the place now appointed them. But we see that ye have removed some men of excellent behavior from the ministry, which they fulfilled blamelessly and with honor.

Clement of Rome, *1 Clement* 42, 44

4. IGNATIUS OF ANTIOCH: THE BISHOP AND THE PRESBYTERIUM

According to Ignatius, the grand unity formed by the "saints" (*Philadelphians* 5.2) is embodied in a visible society, henceforth provided with the hierarchical organization needed for its functioning. At the apex [is] the bishop: whatever his personal qualities, whatever his merit or age, it is not the man that one respects in him. It is the representative of God, visible bishop and overseer of the Church in the place of the invisible bishop (*Magnesians* 3.1–2). If it is true that the authority of the bishop derives from the mission of the apostles (*Ephesians* 5.1; according to Matt 10:40, etc.), Ignatius, unlike Clement of Rome (*1 Clement* 42–44), insists more on the fact that the bishop is the living image of the invisible God, *typos Theou* (*Magnesian* 6; *Trallians* 3.1). The bishop is at the middle of the presbyteral college, like Jesus Christ—or like God himself—amidst the apostles….Around the bishop [are] the priests, a "precious spiritual crown" (*Magnesians* 8, 1), who surround him as the apostles surrounded Jesus Christ himself (*Magnesians* 6.1; see *Trallians* 3.1). It is with this assembly of the elders that the bishop governs and administers the Church. If the bishop takes the place of Jesus Christ, the presbyterium plays for each particular Church the role played by the apostles in the Church Universal (*Philadelphians* 4.1). But henceforth the bishop is clearly distinguished from the presbyterium. Until a short time before, the college of presbyters or overseers exercised authority collectively with one of its members presiding. This, we know, is the kind of situation described in the Acts of the Apostles, the First Epistle of St. Peter, and the Pastoral Letters. It is different in the Churches to which the letters of St. Ignatius introduce us, where the monarchical authority of a bishop has taken over from the authority of a presbyteral or episcopal college.

(P.-T. Camelot, "Introduction" to Ignatius of Antioch, Polycarp of Smyrna, Letters: The Martyrdom of Polycarp [Paris: Éditions du Cerf, coll. Sources chrétiennes, 10A, 1998], pp. 37–39. I have omitted a few lines and slightly modified the text.)

5. JUSTIN MARTYR:
THE CELEBRATION OF THE EUCHARIST

We, after we have thus washed him who has been convinced and has assented to our teaching, bring him to the place where those who are called brethren are assembled, in order that we may offer hearty prayers in common for ourselves and for the baptized [illuminated] person, and for all others in every place, that we may be counted worthy, now that we have learned the truth, by our works also to be found good citizens and keepers of the commandments, so that we may be saved with an everlasting salvation. Having ended the prayers, we salute one another with a kiss. There is then brought to the president of the brethren bread and a cup of wine mixed with water; and he taking them, gives praise and glory to the Father of the universe, through the name of the Son and of the Holy Ghost, and offers thanks at considerable length for our being counted worthy to receive these things at His hands. And when he has concluded the prayers and thanksgivings, all the people present express their assent by saying Amen. This word *Amen* answers in the Hebrew language to γένοιτο ["so be it"]. And when the president has given thanks, and all the people have expressed their assent, those who are called by us deacons give to each of those present to partake of the bread and wine mixed with water over which the thanksgiving was pronounced, and to those who are absent they carry away a portion.

And this food is called among us Εὐχαριστία ["the Eucharist"], of which no one is allowed to partake but the man who believes that the things which we teach are true, and who has been washed with the washing that is for the remission of sins, and unto regeneration, and who is so living as Christ has enjoined. For not as common bread and common drink do we receive these; but in like manner as Jesus Christ our Savior, having been made flesh by the Word of God, had both flesh and blood for our salvation, so likewise have we been taught that the food which is blessed by the prayer of His word, and from which our flesh and blood by transmutation are nourished, is the flesh and blood of that Jesus who was made flesh. For the apostles, in the memoirs composed by them, which are called Gospels, have thus delivered unto us what was enjoined upon them; that Jesus took bread, and when He had given thanks, said, "This do ye in remembrance of Me, this is My body"; and that, after the same manner, having taken the cup and given thanks, He said, "This is

My blood"; and gave it to them alone. Which the wicked devils have imitated in the mysteries of Mithras, commanding the same thing to be done. For, that bread and a cup of water are placed with certain incantations in the mystic rites of one who is being initiated, you either know or can learn.

And we afterward continually remind each other of these things. And the wealthy among us help the needy; and we always keep together; and for all things wherewith we are supplied, we bless the Maker of all through His Son Jesus Christ, and through the Holy Ghost. And on the day called Sunday, all who live in cities or in the country gather together to one place, and the memoirs of the apostles or the writings of the prophets are read, as long as time permits; then, when the reader has ceased, the president verbally instructs, and exhorts to the imitation of these good things. Then we all rise together and pray, and, as we before said, when our prayer is ended, bread and wine and water are brought, and the president in like manner offers prayers and thanksgivings, according to his ability, and the people assent, saying Amen; and there is a distribution to each, and a participation of that over which thanks have been given, and to those who are absent a portion is sent by the deacons. And they who are well to do, and willing, give what each thinks fit; and what is collected is deposited with the president, who succors the orphans and widows and those who, through sickness or any other cause, are in want, and those who are in bonds and the strangers sojourning among us, and in a word takes care of all who are in need. But Sunday is the day on which we all hold our common assembly, because it is the first day on which God, having wrought a change in the darkness and matter, made the world; and Jesus Christ our Savior on the same day rose from the dead. For He was crucified on the day before that of Saturn (Saturday); and on the day after that of Saturn, which is the day of the Sun, having appeared to His apostles and disciples, He taught them these things, which we have submitted to you also for your consideration.

Justin Martyr, *The First Apology* 65–67

6. VATICAN II: THE EXERCISE OF THE COMMON PRIESTHOOD IN THE SACRAMENTS

It is through the sacraments and the exercise of the virtues that the sacred nature and organic structure of the priestly community is brought into operation. Incorporated into the Church through baptism, the faithful are destined by the baptismal character for the worship of the Christian religion; reborn as sons [and daughters] of God they must confess before men the faith that they have received from God through the Church. They are more perfectly bound to the Church by the sacrament of Confirmation, and the Holy Spirit endows them with special strength so that they are more strictly obliged to spread and defend the faith, both by word and by deed, as true witnesses of Christ. Taking part in the Eucharistic sacrifice, which is the source and summit of the whole Christian life, they offer the Divine Victim to God, and offer themselves along with Him. Thus both by reason of the offering and through Holy Communion, all take part in this liturgical service, not indeed, all in the same way, but each in that way which is proper to himself [or herself]. Strengthened in Holy Communion by the Body of Christ, they then manifest in a concrete way that unity of the People of God which is suitably signified and wondrously brought about by this most august sacrament.

Those who approach the sacrament of Penance obtain pardon from the mercy of God for the offence committed against Him and are at the same time reconciled with the Church, which they have wounded by their sins, and which by charity, example, and prayer seeks their conversion. By the sacred anointing of the sick and the prayer of her priests, the whole Church commends the sick to the suffering and glorified Lord, asking that He may lighten their suffering and save them; she exhorts them, moreover, to contribute to the welfare of the whole People of God by associating themselves freely with the passion and death of Christ. Those of the faithful who are consecrated by Holy Orders are appointed to feed the Church in Christ's name with the word and the grace of God. Finally, Christian spouses, in virtue of the sacrament of Matrimony, whereby they signify and partake of the mystery of that unity and fruitful love which exists between Christ and His Church, and help each other to attain to holiness in their married life and in the rearing and education of their children. By reason of their state and rank in life they have their own special gift among the People of God. From the wedlock of Christians there comes the family, in which new citizens of human society are born, who by the grace of the Holy Spirit received in baptism are made children of God, thus perpetuating the People of God through the centuries. The family is, so to speak, the domestic Church. In it parents should, by their word and example, be the first preachers of the faith to their children; they should encourage them in the vocation that is proper to each of them, fostering with special care a vocation to a sacred state.

Fortified by so many and such powerful means of salvation, all the faithful, whatever their condition or state, are called by the Lord, each in his own way, to that perfect holiness whereby the Father Himself is perfect.

Lumen Gentium 11

7. VATICAN II: THE NATURE OF THE PRESBYTERATE

The Lord Jesus, "whom the Father has sent into the world" (John 10:36), has made his whole Mystical Body a sharer in the anointing of the Spirit with which he himself is anointed. In him all the faithful are made a holy and royal priesthood; they offer spiritual sacrifices to God through Jesus Christ, and they proclaim the perfections of him who has called them out of darkness into his marvelous light. Therefore, there is no member who does not have a part in the mission of the whole Body; but each one ought to hallow Jesus in his [or her] heart, and in the spirit of prophecy bear witness to Jesus.

The same Lord, however, has established ministers among his faithful to unite them together in one body in which "not all the members have the same function" (Rom 12:4). These ministers in the society of the faithful are able by the sacred power of orders to offer sacrifice and to forgive sins, and they perform their priestly office publicly...in the name of Christ. Therefore, having sent the apostles just as he himself has been sent by the Father, Christ, through the apostles themselves, made their successors, the bishops, sharers in his consecration and mission. The office of their ministry has been handed down, in a lesser degree indeed, to the priests. Established in the order of the priesthood they can be coworkers of the episcopal order for the proper fulfillment of the apostolic mission entrusted to priests by Christ.

The office of priests, since it is connected with the episcopal order, also, in its own degree, shares the authority by which Christ builds up, sanctifies, and rules his Body. Wherefore the priesthood, while indeed it presupposes the sacraments of Christian initiation, is conferred by that special sacrament; through it, by the anointing of the Holy Spirit, priests are signed with a special character and are conformed to Christ the Priest in such a way that they can act in the person of Christ the Head.

In the measure in which they participate in the office of the apostles, God gives priests a special grace to be ministers of Christ among the people. They perform the sacred duty of preaching the Gospel, so that the offering of the people can be made acceptable and sanctified by the Holy Spirit. Through the apostolic proclamation of the Gospel, the People of God are called together and assembled. All belonging to this people, since they have been sanctified by the Holy Spirit, can offer themselves as "a sacrifice, living, holy, pleasing to God" (Rom 12:1). Through the ministry of the priests, the spiritual sacrifice of the faithful is made perfect in union with the sacrifice of Christ. He is the only mediator who in the name of the whole Church is offered sacramentally in the Eucharist and in an unbloody manner until the Lord himself comes. The ministry of priests is directed to this goal and is perfected in it. Their ministry, which begins with the evangelical proclamation, derives its power and force from the sacrifice of Christ. Its aim is that "the entire commonwealth of the redeemed and the society of the saints be offered to God through the High Priest who offered himself also for us in his passion that we might be the body of so great a Head."

The purpose, therefore, which priests pursue in their ministry and by their life is to procure the glory of God the Father in Christ. That glory consists in this—that men working freely and with a grateful spirit receive the work of God made perfect in Christ and then manifest it in their whole lives. Hence, priests, while engaging in prayer and adoration, or preaching the word, or offering the Eucharistic Sacrifice and administering the other sacraments, or performing other works of the ministry for men, devote all this energy to the increase of the glory of God and to man's progress in the divine life. All of this, since it comes from the Pasch of Christ, will be crowned by the glorious coming of the same Lord, when he hands over the Kingdom to God the Father.

Presbyterorum Ordinis 2

NOTES

FOREWORD

1. See http://www.vatican.va/archive/hist_councils/ii_vati can_council/documents/vat-ii_const_19641121_lumen-gen tium_en.html.

2. Avery Dulles, *The Priestly Life: A Theological Reflection* (New York / Mahwah, NJ: Paulist Press, 1997), 11.

CHAPTER II

1. It will not be extrapolating too far from our New Testament research to refer to a study I once did on this theme: "Imiter Dieu comme des enfants bien-aimés: La conformité à Dieu et au Christ dans l'oeuvre de saint Thomas," *Recherches thomasiennes* (Paris: Vrin, 2000), 225–35. I later found out that St. Thomas himself refers to the text of First Peter no fewer than twenty-three times.

2. P. Dabin, *Le Sacerdoce royal des fidèles dans la tradition anci-enne et moderne* (Brussels-Paris, collection "Museum Lessianum" 1950), 47. This survey of the priestly, royal, and prophetic quali-ties of the People of God from its origins to our time, as shown through the fathers of the Church, the theologians, and the liturgy deserves to be reissued. It remains highly valuable and has lost none of its relevance.

3. "Second Discourse on Psalm 26," 2, in *St. Augustine on the Psalms*, vol. 1, trans. Dame Scholastica Hebgin and Dame Felicitas Corrigan, Ancient Christian Writers, vol. 29 (New York / Ramsey, NJ: Paulist Press, 1960), 261–62.

4. *On the Epistle to the Hebrews* 1, 9, n. 64–65, trans. Fabian R. Larcher, OP. Father Larcher's translation is available at http://dhspriory.org/thomas/SSHebrews.htm (accessed November 16, 2012).

5. For more specifics on this discussion, I cannot recommend strongly enough the minutely detailed exegesis provided by G. Emery in "Le sacerdoce spirituel des fidèles chez saint Thomas d'Aquin," in *Revue thomiste* 99 (1999): 211–43; esp. 218–22.

CHAPTER III

1. A summary of their work can be found in the collection Sources chrétiennes, 167, pp. 78–86.

2. P. Benoit, "Les origins apostoliques de l'Épiscopat selon le Nouveau Testament," in H. Bouëssé and A. Mandouze, *L'Évêque dans l'Église du Christ* (Paris, 1963), 13–57. This article remains essential despite its date. Lacking it, one might see "Les Origines del'Épiscopat dans le Nouveau Testament," in the collection by the same author, *Exégèse et théologie*, vol. 2 (Paris: Éditions du Cerf, 1961), 232–46.

3. If one does not have direct access to it, one can refer to the Greek version published in French under the title *Les Constitutions apostoliques* (Paris: Éditions du Cerf, coll. Sources chrétiennes, 320, 329, 336, 1985–87). With regard to the hierarchy in general and the bishop in particular, see book II 26, 1–35, 4 in n. 320, pp. 235–60.

4. Origen, *Homilies on Joshua*, trans. Barbara J. Bruce, ed. Cynthia White, FOTC (Washington, DC: Catholic University of America Press, 2002), 37–38.

5. G. Bardy, who asks this question, seems to think that Origen would go this far.

6. Cf. Wiéner, *"Hiérourgein (R, 15,16),"* *Studium Paulinorum Congressus*, vol. 2 (Rome, 1963), 399–404.

7. Jean Calvin, *Commentaire sur le Nouveau Testament*, vol. 4, *Lettre aux Romains* (Geneva: Éditions Nicole, 1960), 339–40, quoted by Wiéner, *"Hiérourgein,"* p. 399, who also cites "the great Protestant commentary of Fritsche" (1839). The latter interprets

hierourgein ti as *sacerdotis modo aliquid administrare* ("to administer something after the manner of a priest").

8. J. Delorme, in *Le Ministère et les Ministères selon le Nouveau Testament* (Paris: Éditions du Seuil, 1974), 309. As far as I know, this collection offers the most complete range of materials currently available on this topic in French, even if some of the authors are more minimalist than I am when it comes to the possible priestly dimension of certain scriptural passages.

9. Geza Vermes, *The Complete Dead Sea Scrolls in English* (New York: Penguin, 1998).

10. This and subsequent excerpts are from G. Homer, trans., *The Didascalia Apostolorum. The Syriac Version Translated* (Oxford, 1929).

11. Adapted from J. Colson, *Ministre de Jesus-Christ: ou, Le sacerdoce de l'évangile; étude sur la condition sacerdotale des ministres chrétiens dans l'église primitive*, Théologie historique 4 (Paris: Beauchesne, 1966), 346.

CHAPTER IV

1. The Council's formula is the subject of a more in-depth analysis that is slightly different from mine. See B.-D. de La Soujeole, "Différence d'essence et différence de degré," *Revue thomiste* 109 (2009): 621–38, where the reader will also find ample developments that are beyond our scope.

2. For readers who would like a fuller documentation, recall the study, no longer new but still not superseded, of B. D. Marliangeas, *Clés pour une théologie du ministère. In persona Christi. In persona Ecclesiae*, Théologie historique 51 (Paris: Beauchesne, 1978).

3. Recall here the fine study, also not superseded, of Yves Congar, "L'Ecclesia ou communauté chrétienne, sujet intégral de l'action liturgique," in *La Liturgie après Vatican II. Bilans, études, prospective*, J.-P. Jossua and Y. Congar, eds. (Paris: Éditions du Cerf, coll. "*Unam Sanctam*," 66: 1967), 241–82.

4. P. Siniscaldo and P. Mattei, "Introduction," Cyprian of Carthage, *L'unité de l'église (De ecclesiae catholicae unitate)*, trans. Michel Poirier, Sources chrétiennes 500 (Paris: Cerf, 2006), 274.

5. Wikipedia: Thomas d'Aquin, *Somme théologique*, édition de la Revue des Jeunes, 68 vol., Paris, Tournai, Rome, 1925–.

6. See *Summa theologica, Supplement* q. 34, a. 4, as well as a. 2, sol. 1 and 2; q. 35, a. 1, with Lécuyer's note 19.

7. See what I have written about this in my article "Le sacerdoce du Christ dans la *Somme de théologie*," *Revue thomiste* 99 (1999): 97–100.

8. The word *character* was not used by *Lumen Gentium* apropos of the diaconate; but it is found in the Prologue to the *Motu proprio* of Paul VI, *Sacrum diaconatus ordinem* (June 18, 1967), which evokes the "indelible character and…own special grace" of the diaconate. One can also see the decree *Ad Gentes* (16) and the *Catechism of the Catholic Church* (§1570), which speaks of an "imprint" (made explicit by "character"). Still, of what I shall say further on about all "potential," I have no recollection of ever having read anything about the "order" of the deacons or diaconal "collegiality," but that would have to be checked out.

9. This question of the reciprocal priority of the proclamation of the Word and the sacrament of the Eucharist was the subject of a well-documented study by D. Logue, "Le *premier* et le *principal* du sacrament de l'ordre. Lecture de *Presbyterorum ordinis* n. 4 and n. 13," *Revue thomiste* 102 (2002): 431–53.

CHAPTER V

1. I would like to recall here an old study by Jacques Maritain that remains pertinent: "À propos de l'École française," *Revue thomiste* 71 (1971): 463–79. The reader should not be deceived by that dull-sounding title. It deals with the priestly spirituality once advocated by the French school, of which Pierre de Bérulle (1575–1629) was the initiator, and which governed the formation of practically the entire French clergy until Vatican II. Its main flaw was a dangerous tendency to confuse the *character* of holy orders with the *grace* received at the same time as the sacra-

ment, so that the priest was thought to be sanctified by that very fact. Maritain reports the stunning phrase of a historian (M. Dupuy, who seems to have been the one who "best understood" the thought of Bérulle): "You cannot define him [the priest, according to Bérulle] as a super-Christian; *because he is not just that*. But it is urgent that he be at least that" (p. 466; it is in this context that the notion of conjoint instrument comes in).

2. For those who would like to reflect further on the theme of this conclusion, I would recommend B.-D. de La Soujeole's *Prêtre du Seigneur dans son Église. Quelques requêtes actuelles de spiritualité sacerdotale*, 2nd exp. ed. (Paris: Parole et Silence, 2002). The book was written over a period of several years in collaboration with a group of bishops, priests, and laypeople whose ideas it condenses, and its success proves its usefulness. De La Soujeole considers a body of theoretical and practical questions that I obviously cannot go into here.

ONLINE RESOURCES

The following sources cited in this book can be found in their entirety on the Internet. The URLs are given below. The original printed sources for the writings of the Church Fathers are also given when these have been available. Please also see the Concise Bibliography for further resources.

VATICAN II DOCUMENTS

Lumen Gentium. http://www.vatican.va/archive/hist_councils/ii_vatican_council/documents/vat-ii_const_19641121_lumen-gentium_en.html.

Presbyterorum Ordinis. http://www.vatican.va/archive/hist_councils/ii_vatican_council/documents/vat-ii_decree_19651207_presbyterorum-ordinis_en.html.

Sacrosanctum Concilium. http://www.vatican.va/archive/hist_councils/ii_vatican_council/documents/vat-ii_const_19631204_sacrosanctum-concilium_en.html.

OTHER CHURCH DOCUMENTS

Paul VI. *Sacrum Diaconatus Ordinem.* http://www.vatican.va/holy_father/paul_vi/motu_proprio/documents/hf_p-vi_motu-proprio_19670618_sacrum-diaconatus_en.html.

Pius X. *Mediator Dei.* http://www.vatican.va/holy_father/pius_xii/encyclicals/documents/hf_p-xii_enc_20111947_mediator-dei_en.html.

————. *Mystici Corporis.* http://www.vatican.va/holy_father/pius_xii/encyclicals/documents/hf_p-xii_enc_29061943_mystici-corporis-christi_en.html.

Rite of Baptism. http://www.catholicliturgy.com/index.cfm/FuseAction/TextContents/Index/4/SubIndex/67/TextIndex/7.

CHURCH FATHERS

Augustine. *The City of God.* Trans. Marcus Dods. In Nicene and Post-Nicene Fathers, First Series, vol. 2. Edited by Philip Schaff. Buffalo, NY: Christian Literature Publishing Co., 1887. http://www.ccel.org/ccel/schaff/npnf102.titlepage.html.

Clement of Rome, *1 Clement.* Trans. Alexander Roberts and James Donaldson. Available at http://www.earlychristianwritings.com/text/1clement-roberts.html.

Didache. In Ante-Nicene Fathers, vol. 5. Edited by Alexander Roberts, James Donaldson, and A. Cleveland Coxe. Buffalo, NY: Christian Literature Publications, 1886. http://earlychristianwritings.com/text/didache-roberts.html.

Hippolytus. *The Apostolic Tradition.* http://www.bombaxo.com/hippolytus.html.

Ignatius of Antioch. *Letter of Ignatius of Antioch to the Philadelphians.* From Ante-Nicene Fathers, vol. 1. Edited by Alexander Roberts, James Donaldson, and A. Cleveland Coxe. Buffalo, NY: Christian Literature Publishing Co., 1885. Revised and edited for New Advent by Kevin Knight. http://www.newadvent.org/fathers/0108.htm.

————. *Letter of Ignatius of Antioch to the Smyrnaeans.* From Ante-Nicene Fathers, vol. 1. Edited by Alexander Roberts, James Donaldson, and A. Cleveland Coxe. Buffalo, NY: Christian Literature Publishing Co., 1885. Revised and edited for New Advent by Kevin Knight. http://www.newadvent.org/fathers/0109.htm.

Justin Martyr. *Dialogue with Trypho,* chaps. cxvi–cxvii. Edited by Alexander Roberts and James Donaldson. Available at http://www.earlychristianwritings.com/text/justinmartyr-dialoguetrypho.html.

———. *The First Apology of Justin Martyr.* Trans. Marcus Dods and George Reith. From Ante-Nicene Fathers, vol. 1. Edited by Alexander Roberts, James Donaldson, and A. Cleveland Coxe. Buffalo, NY: Christian Literature Publishing Co., 1885. Revised and edited for New Advent by Kevin Knight. http://www.newadvent.org/fathers/0126. htm.

The Shepherd of Hermas. From Ante-Nicene Fathers, vol. 2. Edited by Alexander Roberts, James Donaldson, and A. Cleveland Coxe. Buffalo, NY: Christian Literature Publishing Co., 1885. Revised and edited for New Advent by Kevin Knight. http://www.newadvent.org/fathers/0201.htm.

Tertullian. *Treatise on Baptism.* Trans. Alexander Souter. In *Tertullian's Treatises Concerning Prayer and Baptism.* London: S.P.C.K., 1919. http://www.tertullian.org/articles/souter_orat_bapt/souter_orat_bapt_04baptism.htm.

———. *Of the Prescription of the Heretics.* In Ante-Nicene Fathers, vol. 5. Edited by Alexander Roberts, James Donaldson, and A. Cleveland Coxe. Buffalo, NY: Christian Literature Publications, 1886. Revised and edited for New Advent by Kevin Knight. http://www.newadvent.org/fathers/0311. htm.

CONCISE BIBLIOGRAPHY

Books on the theology of the sacrament of holy orders came out in large numbers after Vatican II. Many of them aimed at commenting on the texts of the Council; others were dedicated to rediscovering the scriptural and patristic roots of the Council's teaching. Most of them are already old by now, but they remain indispensable because this stream has long since dried up, and some studies remain fundamental. So the best ones find their place here, whereas many of the more recent titles do not have the same interest. By contrast, very few authors have dealt with the main subject of my book. I have had to gather my material from a wide variety of studies that no one would think of including in this short list, but I will try to mention the most important items. To my great regret, I have had to leave out the ecumenical questions and those dealing with the ordination of women, which did not fit into my scheme. As for polemical writings, which have not been scarce over the past fifty years, I have chosen to ignore them. So there should be no surprise at the deliberately succinct character of this bibliography.

GENERAL WORKS

Bourgeois, Daniel. *L'Un et L'Autre Sacerdoce. Essai sur la structure sacramentale de l'Église.* Paris: Desclée de Brouwer, 1991. The subtitle is perhaps more precise than the title. There is rather little here on the baptismal priesthood, but the book does a good job of framing that priesthood's relationship with the ministry. The appendix on the definition of the layperson, pp. 177–240, is highly recommended.

Feuillet, André. *Le Sacerdoce du Christ et de ses ministres d'après la prière sacerdotale du quatrième Évangile et plusieurs données parallèles du Nouveau Testament.* Paris: Téqui, 1997.

Gallot, Jean. *Prêtre au nom du Christ.* Chabray-lès-Tours, CLD: 1985. A comprehensive work that deals with various aspects of the priestly mystery, but focuses closely on the primacy of the priesthood of grace. It has an abundant bibliography on all the subjects it addresses.

Nicolas, Marie-Joseph. *La Grâce d'être prêtre.* Paris: Desclée de Brouwer, 1966. The erudition here is less obvious than in Gallot, and it is easier to read, but very well informed on the difficulties of the subject. An experienced theologian, the author is attentive to the spiritual implications of the priesthood.

"Saint Thomas D'Aquin et le sacerdoce," Actes du Colloque organisé par l'Institut Saint-Thomas d'Aquin les 5 et 6 juin 1998 à Toulouse. *Revue thomiste* 99 (1999): 5–295. This reference work has nothing to do with the caricature long served up under the name of Thomas. On the contrary, it shows how Thomas himself was a major witness of the return to the sources that he is often described as opposing. Some of the best contributions cited below have been borrowed from this collection.

ROYAL PRIESTHOOD AND SPIRITUAL SACRIFICES

Cazelles, Henri. "Royaume de prêtres et nation consacrée (Ex. 19.6)." In C. Kanengiesser and Y. Marchasson, eds. *Humanisme et foi chrétienne.* Paris: Beauchesne, 1976. This is probably the most fully developed study of this verse of Exodus, which lies at the root of the tradition of the Septuagint and the New Testament.

Cerfaux, Lucien. "*Regale sacerdotium.*" *Revue des sciences philosophiques et théologiques* 28 (1939): 5–39. (Reprinted in *Recueil Cerfaux*, vol. II. Gembloux: Duculot, 1954.) Despite its age, this remains the classic work on the topic, and despite the Latin title, it is in French.

Dabin, Paul. *Le Sacerdoce royal des fidèles dans la tradition ancienne et moderne.* Brussels-Paris: Collection "Museum Lessianum" 48 (1950). This is a 650-page dossier on the sacerdotal, royal, and prophetic quality of the People of God, from the origins to our days, in the Fathers of the Church, the theologians, and the liturgy. It is a foundational text, and it remains a mine of precious information.

Emery, Gilles. "Sacerdoce spirituel des fidèles chez saint Thomas d'Aquin." *Revue thomiste* 99 (1999): 211–43. This extremely rich study is the best on the subject.

Feuillet, André. "Les 'sacrifices spirituels' du sacerdoce royal des baptisés (1 Pet. 2.5), leur preparation dans l'Ancien Testament." *Nouvelle revue théologique* 96 (1974): 704–22. This is an excellent study, strongly recommended as a complement to this book.

Feuillet, André. "Les chrétiens prêtres et rois d'après L'Apocalypse." *Revue thomiste* 75 (1975): 40–66. This builds on the previous article.

Hennaux, Jean-Marie. "Le rapport intrinsèque du sacerdoce ministériel et du sacerdoce commun des fidèles. Pour une symbolique du sacerdoce." *Nouvelle revue théologique* 131 (2009): 211–24. This is a short article inspired by Hans Urs von Balthasar.

Lafont, Ghislain. "Le sacrifice de la Cité de Dieu." *Recherches de science religieuse* 53 (1965): 177–219. This is a very welcome commentary on the celebrated text by St. Augustine, *The City of God* X, 6 on the true nature of sacrifice, transcribed in this book as text 2 in the Appendix.

Lamirande, É. "La signification de 'christianus' dans la théologie de saint Augustin and la tradition ancienne." *Revue des études augustiniennes* 9 (1963): 221–34. This study is valuable for showing how Augustine links the triple messianic quality to the baptismal anointing.

Philibert, P. J. *Le sacerdoce des baptisés. Clé d'une Église vivante.* Paris: Éditions du Cerf, 2007. This is an echo of some American thinking.

Tillard, Jean-Marie. "Sacerdoce." *Dictionnaire de spiritualité*, vol. XIV, col. 1–37, 1988. A complete treatment based on Scripture and Tradition, this forcefully stresses the communitarian nature of the priesthood of the faithful.

PRIESTLY MINISTRY

Scriptural Foundations

Benoit, Pierre. "Les origines apostoliques de l'épiscopat selon le Nouveau Testament." In H. Bouëssé and A. Mandouze, *L'Évêque dans l'Église du Christ*. Paris: Desclée de Brouwer, 1963, 13–57. This study had the privilege of being used in the preparation of *Lumen Gentium* 28.

Brown, Raymond E. "Episkopē and Episkopos: The New Testament Evidence." *Theological Studies* 4 (1980): 332–38. This is shorter than Benoit's article, but it follows the same direction. It presents a vigorous summary of the question of apostolic succession.

Delorme, Jean, ed. *Le Ministère et les Ministères selon le Nouveau Testament*. Paris: Éditions du Seuil, 1974. This collection offers the most complete file of materials currently available in French. Each N.T. text is provided with an exegesis and an essay in theological synthesis.

Gourgues, Michel. "Les pouvoirs en voie d'institutionalisation dans les épîtres pastorals." *Revue théologique de Louvain* 41 (2010): 465–98. This is a study based on the vocabulary of 1 Timothy and Titus, which situates the two Pastoral Epistles between the Pauline corpus and Ignatius of Antioch. It allows us to consider them as open to "future developments in a theology of apostolic succession."

Grelot, Pierre. "La structure ministérielle de l'Église d'après saint Paul." *Istina* 16 (1971): 193–230. This is a response to Hans Küng, who criticized the preceding article.

Hauser, Hermann. *L'Église à l'âge apostolique. Structure et évolution des ministères*. Paris: Éditions du Cerf, coll. "Lectio divina" 184, 1966. Critical in tone, but ultimately quite positive on the homogeneous evolution that led from the New Testament to the hierarchical model found in the second century.

Lemaire, André. *Les Ministères aux origines de l'Église*. Paris: Éditions du Cerf, coll. "Lectio divina" 68, 1971. Complete and readily accessible study of the various ministries in the New Testament and the first Christian writings. Nothing, however, on the priestly aspect in the strict sense.

Rolland, Philippe. *Les Ambassadeurs du Christ. Ministère pastoral et Nouveau Testament*. Paris: Éditions du Cerf, coll. "Lire la Bible" 92, 1991. An excellent little book, with documentation that is well focused without being overwhelming. It also proposes a welcome spirituality of ministry.

Patristic Works

Colson, Jean. *Ministre de Jésus-Christ ou le Sacerdoce de l'Évangile. Étude sur la condition sacerdotale des ministres chrétiens dans l'Église primitive*. Paris: Beauchesne, coll. "Théologie historique" 4, 1966. This book corresponds rather closely to my own approach. It contains many texts from the New Testament period and afterward that I was not able to cite.

Études sur Le Sacrament de l'Ordre. Paris: Éditions du Cerf, coll. "Lex orandi" 22, 1957. A representative collection on the subject of the liturgical, patristic, and exegetical renewal that led to the reform of the Pontifical and to Vatican II.

Lécuyer, Joseph. *Le sacrament de l'ordination. Recherche historique et théologique*. Paris: Beauchesne, coll. "Théologie historique" 65, 1983. Austere but precise, it reviews all the texts from the first to the fifth centuries that speak about the priestly character.

Marliangeas, B.-D. *Clés pour une thélogie du ministère. In persona Christi. In persona Ecclesiae*. Paris: Beauchesne, coll. "Théologie historique" 51, 1978. Spells out the meaning of these formulas in tracing them through the history of theology.

A Few More Specifically Theological Titles

Commission Internationale de Théologie. *Le Ministère sacerdotal*. Paris: Éditions du Cerf, coll. "Cogitatio fidei" 40, 1971. A well-informed and balanced synthesis.

Frost, F. "Ministère." In *Catholicisme* [encyclopedia], vol. IX, 1980, 185–226. A historically and theologically well-informed overview.

Grelot, Pierre. "Le Ministère chrétien dans sa dimension sacerdotale." *Nouvelle revue théologique* 112 (1990): 161–82. Completes the Tillard article mentioned above.

La Soujeole, Benoît-Dominique de. "Les *tria munera Christi:* contribution de saint Thomas à la recherche contemporaine." *Revue thomiste* 99 (1999): 59–74. Thoroughly documents the operative presence in St. Thomas of the traditional data on the triform messianic anointing both among the ministers and among the faithful.

La Soujeole, Benoît-Dominique de. "Différence d'essence et différence de degré dans le sacerdoce." *Reuve thomiste* 100 (2009): 621–38.

Logue, Damien. "Le *premier* et le *principal* du sacrement de l'ordre." *Revue thomiste* 102 (2002): 431–53. Studies the well-ordered interconnection of the *tria munera Christi* in the sacrament of holy orders on the basis of the decree *Presbyterorum Ordinis,* and clearly demonstrates the fundamental unity of the various aspects of the sacrament and the previous article of B.-D. de La Soujeole.

Tillard, Jean-Marie R. "*La 'qualité sacerdotale' du ministère chrétien.*" *Nouvelle revue théologique* 95 (1973): 481–514. Enlightening research on this difficult question.

Torrell, Jean-Pierre. "*Le Sacerdoce du Christ dans la Somme de théologie.*" *Revue thomiste* 99 (1999): 431–53. Article on Question 22 of the *Tertia Pars* of the *Summa,* where the expression "Christ, the source of all priesthood" is explained.

PRIESTLY SPIRITUALITY

The majority of the books cited above offer at least a few pages on priestly spirituality (which I would prefer to call "ministerial" spirituality). But, apart from papal and episcopal exhortations as well as numerous occasional booklets published to celebrate the Year of the Priest (2009–10), I cannot think of more than a few titles worth mentioning on this topic:

La Soujeole, Benoît-Dominique de. *Prêtre du Seigneur dans son Église. Quelques requêtes actuelles de spiritualité sacerdotale*, 2nd exp. ed. Paris: Parole et Silence, 2009. Written in collaboration with a group of bishops, priests, and laypeople, this book gets my highest recommendation. It condenses a train of reflections followed though several years in the light of improved theological thinking. It strikes me as right in line with contemporary expectations.

Maritain, Jacques. "À propos de l'École française." *Revue thomiste* 71 (1971): 463–79. A critical reading of the theology of priesthood once preached by the French school of spirituality, it remains essential for anyone who wants a balanced theology when it comes to priestly spirituality.

Ratzinger, Joseph Cardinal. *Ministers of Your Joy: Scriptural Meditations on Priestly Spirituality.* Servant Publications, 1989.

Verlinde, Joseph Marie. *Prières pour le IIIe millénaire. Spiritualité sacerdotale à l'école de Jean-Paul II.* Paris: Saint-Paul, 2001. Analyzes many speeches by John Paul II on this topic.